CliffsNotes®
Grade 7
Common Core
Math Review

By Sandra Luna McCune, Ph.D.

Houghton Mifflin Harcourt
Boston • New York

About the Author

Sandra Luna McCune, Ph.D., is professor emeritus and a former Regents professor in the Department of Elementary Education at Stephen F. Austin State University, where she received the Distinguished Professor Award. She now is a full-time author and consultant and resides near Austin, Texas.

Acknowledgments

I would like to thank Grace Freedson, Greg Tubach, and Christina Stambaugh for their support and encouragement during completion of the book. I also owe a debt of gratitude to Mary Jane Sterling for her meticulous editing and invaluable suggestions.

Dedication

This book is dedicated to my grandchildren—Richard, Rose, Jude, Sophia, Josephine, and Myla Mae. They fill my life with joy!

Editorial

Executive Editor: Greg Tubach
Senior Editor: Christina Stambaugh
Copy Editor: Lynn Northrup
Technical Editors: Mary Jane Sterling and Tom Page
Proofreader: Donna Wright

CliffsNotes® Grade 7 Common Core Math Review

Copyright ©2015 by Houghton Mifflin Harcourt Publishing Company
All rights reserved.

Library of Congress Control Number: 2015931943
ISBN: 978-0-544-37333-4 (pbk)

Printed in the United States of America
DOC 10 9 8 7 6 5 4 3 2 1

For information about permission to reproduce selections from this book, write to Permissions, Houghton Mifflin Harcourt Publishing Company, 215 Park Avenue South, New York, New York 10003.

www.hmhco.com

Table of Contents

Introduction

This book is organized around the Grade 7 Common Core State Standards for Mathematics. These standards define what seventh-grade students are expected to understand and be able to do in their study of mathematics. They include content standards and mathematical practice standards.

In Grade 7, the content standards are grouped under five domains:

- Ratios and Proportional Relationships
- The Number System
- Expressions and Equations
- Geometry
- Statistics and Probability

Ratios and Proportional Relationships

Analyze Proportional Relationships and Use Them to Solve Real-World and Mathematical Problems

CCSS.Math.Content.7.RP.A.1 Compute unit rates associated with ratios of fractions, including ratios of lengths, areas and other quantities measured in like or different units. *For example, if a person walks $\frac{1}{2}$ mile in each $\frac{1}{4}$ hour, compute the unit rate as the complex fraction $\frac{\frac{1}{2}}{\frac{1}{4}}$ miles per hour, equivalently 2 miles per hour.*

CCSS.Math.Content.7.RP.A.2 Recognize and represent proportional relationships between quantities.

CCSS.Math.Content.7.RP.A.2.A Decide whether two quantities are in a proportional relationship, e.g., by testing for equivalent ratios in a table or graphing on a coordinate plane and observing whether the graph is a straight line through the origin.

CCSS.Math.Content.7.RP.A.2.B Identify the constant of proportionality (unit rate) in tables, graphs, equations, diagrams, and verbal descriptions of proportional relationships.

CCSS.Math.Content.7.RP.A.2.C Represent proportional relationships by equations. *For example, if total cost t is proportional to the number n of items purchased at a constant price p, the relationship between the total cost and the number of items can be expressed as t = pn.*

CCSS.Math.Content.7.RP.A.2.D Explain what a point (x, y) on the graph of a proportional relationship means in terms of the situation, with special attention to the points $(0, 0)$ and $(1, r)$ where r is the unit rate.

CCSS.Math.Content.7.RP.A.3 Use proportional relationships to solve multistep ratio and percent problems. Examples: simple interest, tax, markups and markdowns, gratuities and commissions, fees, percent increase and decrease, percent error.

The Number System

Apply and Extend Previous Understandings of Operations with Fractions

CCSS.Math.Content.7.NS.A.1 Apply and extend previous understandings of addition and subtraction to add and subtract rational numbers; represent addition and subtraction on a horizontal or vertical number line diagram.

- **CCSS.Math.Content.7.NS.A.1.A** Describe situations in which opposite quantities combine to make 0. *For example, a hydrogen atom has 0 charge because its two constituents are oppositely charged.*

- **CCSS.Math.Content.7.NS.A.1.B** Understand $p + q$ as the number located a distance $|q|$ from p, in the positive or negative direction depending on whether q is positive or negative. Show that a number and its opposite have a sum of 0 (are additive inverses). Interpret sums of rational numbers by describing real-world contexts.

- **CCSS.Math.Content.7.NS.A.1.C** Understand subtraction of rational numbers as adding the additive inverse, $p - q = p + (-q)$. Show that the distance between two rational numbers on the number line is the absolute value of their difference, and apply this principle in real-world contexts.

- **CCSS.Math.Content.7.NS.A.1.D** Apply properties of operations as strategies to add and subtract rational numbers.

CCSS.Math.Content.7.NS.A.2 Apply and extend previous understandings of multiplication and division and of fractions to multiply and divide rational numbers.

- **CCSS.Math.Content.7.NS.A.2.A** Understand that multiplication is extended from fractions to rational numbers by requiring that operations continue to satisfy the properties of operations, particularly the distributive property, leading to products such as $(-1)(-1) = 1$ and the rules for multiplying signed numbers. Interpret products of rational numbers by describing real-world contexts.

- **CCSS.Math.Content.7.NS.A.2.B** Understand that integers can be divided, provided that the divisor is not zero, and every quotient of integers (with nonzero divisor) is a rational number. If p and q are integers, then $-\left(\dfrac{p}{q}\right) = \dfrac{(-p)}{q} = \dfrac{p}{(-q)}$. Interpret quotients of rational numbers by describing real-world contexts.

- **CCSS.Math.Content.7.NS.A.2.C** Apply properties of operations as strategies to multiply and divide rational numbers.

- **CCSS.Math.Content.7.NS.A.2.D** Convert a rational number to a decimal using long division; know that the decimal form of a rational number terminates in 0s or eventually repeats.

CCSS.Math.Content.7.NS.A.3 Solve real-world and mathematical problems involving the four operations with rational numbers.

Expressions and Equations

Use Properties of Operations to Generate Equivalent Expressions

CCSS.Math.Content.7.EE.A.1 Apply properties of operations as strategies to add, subtract, factor, and expand linear expressions with rational coefficients.

CCSS.Math.Content.7.EE.A.2 Understand that rewriting an expression in different forms in a problem context can shed light on the problem and how the quantities in it are related. *For example, a + 0.05a = 1.05a means that "increase by 5%" is the same as "multiply by 1.05."*

Solve Real-Life and Mathematical Problems Using Numerical and Algebraic Expressions and Equations

CCSS.Math.Content.7.EE.B.3 Solve multistep real-life and mathematical problems posed with positive and negative rational numbers in any form (whole numbers, fractions, and decimals), using tools strategically. Apply properties of operations to calculate with numbers in any form; convert between forms as appropriate; and assess the reasonableness of answers using mental computation and estimation strategies. *For example: If a woman making $25 an hour gets a 10% raise, she will make an additional $\frac{1}{10}$ of her salary an hour, or $2.50, for a new salary of $27.50. If you want to place a towel bar $9\frac{3}{4}$ inches long in the center of a door that is $27\frac{1}{2}$ inches wide, you will need to place the bar about 9 inches from each edge; this estimate can be used as a check on the exact computation.*

CCSS.Math.Content.7.EE.B.4 Use variables to represent quantities in a real-world or mathematical problem, and construct simple equations and inequalities to solve problems by reasoning about the quantities.

- **CCSS.Math.Content.7.EE.B.4.A** Solve word problems leading to equations of the form $px + q = r$ and $p(x + q) = r$, where p, q, and r are specific rational numbers. Solve equations of these forms fluently. Compare an algebraic solution to an arithmetic solution, identifying the sequence of the operations used in each approach. *For example, the perimeter of a rectangle is 54 centimeters. Its length is 6 centimeters. What is its width?*

- **CCSS.Math.Content.7.EE.B.4.B** Solve word problems leading to inequalities of the form $px + q > r$ or $px + q < r$, where p, q, and r are specific rational numbers. Graph the solution set of the inequality and interpret it in the context of the problem. *For example: As a salesperson, you are paid $50 per week plus $3 per sale. This week you want your pay to be at least $100. Write an inequality for the number of sales you need to make, and describe the solutions.*

Geometry

Draw, Construct, and Describe Geometrical Figures and Describe the Relationships Between Them

CCSS.Math.Content.7.G.A.1 Solve problems involving scale drawings of geometric figures, including computing actual lengths and areas from a scale drawing and reproducing a scale drawing at a different scale.

CCSS.Math.Content.7.G.A.2 Draw (freehand, with ruler and protractor, and with technology) geometric shapes with given conditions. Focus on constructing triangles from three measures of angles or sides, noticing when the conditions determine a unique triangle, more than one triangle, or no triangle.

CCSS.Math.Content.7.G.A.3 Describe the two-dimensional figures that result from slicing three-dimensional figures, as in plane sections of right rectangular prisms and right rectangular pyramids.

Solve Real-Life and Mathematical Problems Involving Angle Measure, Area, Surface Area, and Volume

CCSS.Math.Content.7.G.B.4 Know the formulas for the area and circumference of a circle and use them to solve problems; give an informal derivation of the relationship between the circumference and area of a circle.

CCSS.Math.Content.7.G.B.5 Use facts about supplementary, complementary, vertical, and adjacent angles in a multistep problem to write and solve simple equations for an unknown angle in a figure.

CCSS.Math.Content.7.G.B.6 Solve real-world and mathematical problems involving area, volume, and surface area of two- and three-dimensional objects composed of triangles, quadrilaterals, polygons, cubes, and right prisms.

Statistics and Probability

Use Random Sampling to Draw Inferences about a Population

CCSS.Math.Content.7.SP.A.1 Understand that statistics can be used to gain information about a population by examining a sample of the population; generalizations about a population from a sample are valid only if the sample is representative of that population. Understand that random sampling tends to produce representative samples and support valid inferences.

CCSS.Math.Content.7.SP.A.2 Use data from a random sample to draw inferences about a population with an unknown characteristic of interest. Generate multiple samples (or simulated samples) of the same size to gauge the variation in estimates or predictions. *For example, estimate the mean word length in a book by randomly sampling words from the book; predict the winner of a school election based on randomly sampled survey data. Gauge how far off the estimate or prediction might be.*

Draw Informal Comparative Inferences about Two Populations

CCSS.Math.Content.7.SP.B.3 Informally assess the degree of visual overlap of two numerical data distributions with similar variabilities, measuring the difference between the centers by expressing it as a multiple of a measure of variability. *For example, the mean height of players on the basketball team is 10 centimeters greater than the mean height of players on the soccer team, about twice the variability (mean absolute deviation) on either team; on a dot plot, the separation between the two distributions of heights is noticeable.*

CCSS.Math.Content.7.SP.B.4 Use measures of center and measures of variability for numerical data from random samples to draw informal comparative inferences about two populations. *For example, decide whether the words in a chapter of a seventh-grade science book are generally longer than the words in a chapter of a fourth-grade science book.*

Investigate Chance Processes and Develop, Use, and Evaluate Probability Models

CCSS.Math.Content.7.SP.C.5 Understand that the probability of a chance event is a number between 0 and 1 that expresses the likelihood of the event occurring. Larger numbers indicate greater likelihood. A probability near 0 indicates an unlikely event, a probability around $\frac{1}{2}$ indicates an event that is neither unlikely nor likely, and a probability near 1 indicates a likely event.

CCSS.Math.Content.7.SP.C.6 Approximate the probability of a chance event by collecting data on the chance process that produces it and observing its long-run relative frequency, and predict the approximate relative frequency given the probability. *For example, when rolling a number cube 600 times, predict that a 3 or 6 would be rolled roughly 200 times, but probably not exactly 200 times.*

CCSS.Math.Content.7.SP.C.7 Develop a probability model and use it to find probabilities of events. Compare probabilities from a model to observed frequencies; if the agreement is not good, explain possible sources of the discrepancy.

CCSS.Math.Content.7.SP.C.7.A Develop a uniform probability model by assigning equal probability to all outcomes, and use the model to determine probabilities of events. *For example, if a student is selected at random from a class, find the probability that Jane will be selected and the probability that a girl will be selected.*

CCSS.Math.Content.7.SP.C.7.B Develop a probability model (which may not be uniform) by observing frequencies in data generated from a chance process. *For example, find the approximate probability that a spinning penny will land heads up or that a tossed paper cup will land open-end down. Do the outcomes for the spinning penny appear to be equally likely based on the observed frequencies?*

CCSS.Math.Content.7.SP.C.8 Find probabilities of compound events using organized lists, tables, tree diagrams, and simulation.

CCSS.Math.Content.7.SP.C.8.A Understand that, just as with simple events, the probability of a compound event is the fraction of outcomes in the sample space for which the compound event occurs.

CCSS.Math.Content.7.SP.C.8.B Represent sample spaces for compound events using methods such as organized lists, tables, and tree diagrams. For an event described in everyday language (e.g., "rolling double sixes"), identify the outcomes in the sample space that compose the event.

CCSS.Math.Content.7.SP.C.8.C Design and use a simulation to generate frequencies for compound events. *For example, use random digits as a simulation tool to approximate the answer to the question: If 40% of donors have type A blood, what is the probability that it will take at least four donors to find one with type A blood?*

Mathematical Practice

The standards for Mathematical Practice describe the ways in which students ought to engage with the mathematics content standards as they develop in mathematical proficiency and understanding.

CCSS.Math.Practice.MP.1 Make sense of problems and persevere in solving them.

CCSS.Math.Practice.MP.2 Reason abstractly and quantitatively.

CCSS.Math.Practice.MP.3 Construct viable arguments and critique the reasoning of others.

CCSS.Math.Practice.MP.4 Model with mathematics.

CCSS.Math.Practice.MP.5 Use appropriate tools strategically.

CCSS.Math.Practice.MP.6 Attend to precision.

CCSS.Math.Practice.MP.7 Look for and make use of structure.

CCSS.Math.Practice.MP.8 Look for and express regularity in repeated reasoning.

1. Ratios and Proportional Relationships

In this chapter, you will build upon your understanding of ratios, rates, and unit rates to compute unit rates associated with ratios of fractions. You will recognize and represent proportional relationships, identify the constant of proportionality, and use proportional relationships to solve mathematical and real-world problems.

Computing Unit Rates Involving Ratios of Fractions

(CCSS.Math.Content.7.RP.A.1, CCSS.Math.Content.7.RP.A.3)

In the sixth grade, you learned a **ratio** is the result of a multiplicative comparison of two quantities or measures. In the seventh grade, you will continue to work with ratios; however, the comparisons will include fractions. Here is an example.

A motor uses $3\frac{1}{4}$ gallons of gasoline every $\frac{1}{2}$ day.

(a) What is the rate of gallons per day?
(b) What is the unit rate?
(c) In words, explain what the unit rate means in the context of this problem.
(d) How many gallons of gasoline are needed for the motor to run 5 days?

(a) The **rate** is the number of gallons per day. Using fractional notation, the number of gallons per day is

$$\frac{3\frac{1}{4}\text{ gallons}}{\frac{1}{2}\text{ day}} = \frac{\frac{13}{4}}{\frac{1}{2}} \cdot \frac{\text{gallons}}{\text{day}} = \frac{\frac{13}{4}}{\frac{1}{2}}\text{ gallons per day. The fraction }\frac{\frac{13}{4}}{\frac{1}{2}}\text{ is a complex fraction.}$$

A **complex fraction** is a fraction in which the numerator or denominator is a fraction or both are fractions (and all denominators are nonzero).

One way to simplify a complex fraction is to perform the indicated division.

$$\frac{\frac{13}{4}}{\frac{1}{2}} = \frac{13}{4} \div \frac{1}{2} = \frac{13}{4} \times \frac{2}{1} = \frac{13}{2\cancel{4}} \times \frac{\cancel{2}^{1}}{1} = \frac{13}{2} = 6\frac{1}{2} = 6.5$$

Another way to simplify a complex fraction is to multiply both the numerator and denominator by their least common denominator.

$$\frac{\frac{13}{4}}{\frac{1}{2}} = \frac{\left(\frac{13}{4}\right)\cdot\frac{4}{1}}{\left(\frac{1}{2}\right)\cdot\frac{4}{1}} = \frac{\left(\frac{13}{1\cancel{4}}\right)\cdot\frac{\cancel{4}^{1}}{1}}{\left(\frac{1}{1\cancel{2}}\right)\cdot\frac{\cancel{4}^{2}}{1}} = \frac{\frac{13}{1}}{\frac{2}{1}} = \frac{13}{2} = 6\frac{1}{2} = 6.5$$

Either way, the rate is 6.5 gallons per day.

(b) The **unit rate** is the numerical portion of the rate.

The unit rate is 6.5. *Tip:* The unit rate is the value of the ratio of gallons to days.

(c) For every 6.5 gallons of gasoline, the motor will run 1 day.

(d) $\dfrac{6.5 \text{ gallons}}{1 \text{ day}} \times 5 \text{ days}$

$= \dfrac{6.5 \text{ gallons}}{1 \text{ day}} \times \dfrac{5 \text{ days}}{1} = 32.5 \text{ gallons}$

So, 32.5 gallons of gasoline are needed for the motor to run 5 days.

☞ Try These

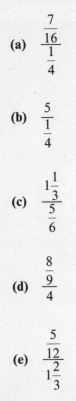

1. Perform the indicated division to simplify the complex fraction.

   (a) $\dfrac{\frac{7}{16}}{\frac{1}{4}}$

   (b) $\dfrac{5}{\frac{1}{4}}$

   (c) $\dfrac{1\frac{1}{3}}{\frac{5}{6}}$

   (d) $\dfrac{\frac{8}{9}}{4}$

   (e) $\dfrac{\frac{5}{12}}{1\frac{2}{3}}$

2. Multiply by the least common denominator to simplify the complex fraction.

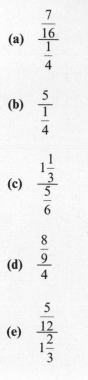

(a) $\dfrac{\frac{7}{16}}{\frac{1}{4}}$

(b) $\dfrac{5}{\frac{1}{4}}$

(c) $\dfrac{1\frac{1}{3}}{\frac{5}{6}}$

(d) $\dfrac{\frac{8}{9}}{4}$

(e) $\dfrac{\frac{5}{12}}{1\frac{2}{3}}$

3. Henao walked $1\frac{3}{4}$ miles in $\frac{1}{2}$ hour.

   (a) What is Henao's rate of miles per hour?
   (b) What is the unit rate?
   (c) In words, explain what the unit rate means in the context of this problem.
   (d) At this rate, how many miles can Henao walk in 3 hours?

4. Nadine typed 140 words in 2 minutes 20 seconds.

   (a) What is Nadine's rate of words per minute?
   (b) What is the unit rate?
   (c) In words, explain what the unit rate means in the context of this problem.
   (d) At this rate, how many words can Nadine type in 5 minutes?

5. A recipe requires $\frac{2}{3}$ cup of milk for $1\frac{1}{2}$ cups of flour.

   (a) What is the ratio of milk to flour?
   (b) What is the unit rate?
   (c) In words, explain what the unit rate means in the context of this problem.
   (d) How many cups of milk are needed for $4\frac{1}{2}$ cups of flour?

Solutions

1. (a) $\dfrac{\frac{7}{16}}{\frac{1}{4}} = \dfrac{7}{16} \div \dfrac{1}{4} = \dfrac{7}{16} \times \dfrac{4}{1} = \dfrac{7}{\cancel{16}_4} \times \dfrac{\cancel{4}^1}{1} = \dfrac{7}{4} = 1\dfrac{3}{4} = 1.75$

(b) $\dfrac{\frac{5}{1}}{\frac{1}{4}} = \dfrac{5}{1} \div \dfrac{1}{4} = \dfrac{5}{1} \times \dfrac{4}{1} = \dfrac{20}{1} = 20$

(c) $\dfrac{1\frac{1}{3}}{\frac{5}{6}} = 1\dfrac{1}{3} \div \dfrac{5}{6} = \dfrac{4}{3} \times \dfrac{6}{5} = \dfrac{4}{\cancel{3}_1} \times \dfrac{\cancel{6}^2}{5} = \dfrac{8}{5} = 1\dfrac{3}{5} = 1.6$

(d) $\dfrac{\frac{8}{9}}{\frac{4}{1}} = \dfrac{8}{9} \div \dfrac{4}{1} = \dfrac{8}{9} \times \dfrac{1}{4} = \dfrac{\cancel{8}^2}{9} \times \dfrac{1}{\cancel{4}_1} = \dfrac{2}{9}$

(e) $\dfrac{\frac{5}{12}}{1\frac{2}{3}} = \dfrac{5}{12} \div \dfrac{5}{3} = \dfrac{5}{12} \times \dfrac{3}{5} = \dfrac{\cancel{5}^1}{\cancel{12}_4} \times \dfrac{\cancel{3}^1}{\cancel{5}_1} = \dfrac{1}{4} = 0.25$

2. (a) $\dfrac{\frac{7}{16}}{\frac{1}{4}} = \dfrac{\left(\frac{7}{16}\right)\cdot\frac{16}{1}}{\left(\frac{1}{4}\right)\cdot\frac{16}{1}} = \dfrac{\left(\frac{7}{\cancel{16}_1}\right)\cdot\frac{\cancel{16}^1}{1}}{\left(\frac{1}{\cancel{4}_1}\right)\cdot\frac{\cancel{16}^4}{1}} = \dfrac{7}{4} = 1\dfrac{3}{4} = 1.75$

(b) $\dfrac{\frac{5}{1}}{\frac{1}{4}} = \dfrac{(5)\cdot 4}{\left(\frac{1}{4}\right)\cdot\frac{4}{1}} = \dfrac{(5)\cdot 4}{\left(\frac{1}{\cancel{4}_1}\right)\cdot\frac{\cancel{4}^1}{1}} = \dfrac{20}{\frac{1}{1}} = 20$

(c) $\dfrac{1\frac{1}{3}}{\frac{5}{6}} = \dfrac{\left(\frac{4}{3}\right)\cdot\frac{6}{1}}{\left(\frac{5}{6}\right)\cdot\frac{6}{1}} = \dfrac{\left(\frac{4}{\cancel{3}_1}\right)\cdot\frac{\cancel{6}^2}{1}}{\left(\frac{5}{\cancel{6}_1}\right)\cdot\frac{\cancel{6}^1}{1}} = \dfrac{\frac{8}{1}}{\frac{5}{1}} = \dfrac{8}{5} = 1\dfrac{3}{5} = 1.6$

(d) $\dfrac{\frac{8}{9}}{\frac{4}{1}} = \dfrac{\left(\frac{8}{9}\right)\cdot\frac{9}{1}}{(4)\cdot 9} = \dfrac{\left(\frac{8}{\cancel{9}_1}\right)\cdot\frac{\cancel{9}^1}{1}}{(4)\cdot 9} = \dfrac{\frac{8}{1}}{36} = \dfrac{8}{36} = \dfrac{8\div 4}{36\div 4} = \dfrac{2}{9}$

(e) $\dfrac{\frac{5}{12}}{1\frac{2}{3}} = \dfrac{\left(\frac{5}{12}\right)\cdot\frac{12}{1}}{\left(\frac{5}{3}\right)\cdot\frac{12}{1}} = \dfrac{\left(\frac{5}{\cancel{12}_1}\right)\cdot\frac{\cancel{12}^1}{1}}{\left(\frac{5}{\cancel{3}_1}\right)\cdot\frac{\cancel{12}^4}{1}} = \dfrac{\frac{5}{1}}{\frac{20}{1}} = \dfrac{5}{20} = \dfrac{5\div 5}{20\div 5} = \dfrac{1}{4} = 0.25$

3. **(a)** $\dfrac{1\frac{3}{4}\text{ miles}}{\frac{1}{2}\text{ hour}} = \dfrac{\left(\frac{7}{4}\right)\cdot\frac{4}{1}\text{ miles}}{\left(\frac{1}{2}\right)\cdot\frac{4}{1}\text{ hour}} = \dfrac{\left(\frac{7}{\cancel{4}_1}\right)\cdot\frac{\cancel{4}^1}{1}\text{ miles}}{\left(\frac{1}{\cancel{2}_1}\right)\cdot\frac{\cancel{4}^2}{1}\text{ hour}} = \dfrac{\frac{7}{1}\text{ miles}}{\frac{2}{1}\text{ hour}} = \dfrac{7\text{ miles}}{2\text{ hour}} = \dfrac{3.5\text{ miles}}{1\text{ hour}} = 3.5\text{ miles per hour}$

(b) The unit rate is 3.5.

(c) Every 1 hour, Henao walks 3.5 miles.

(d) $\dfrac{3.5\text{ miles}}{1\text{ hour}} \times 3\text{ hours} = \dfrac{3.5\text{ miles}}{1\text{ hour}} \times \dfrac{3\text{ hours}}{1} = \dfrac{10.5\text{ miles}}{1} = 10.5\text{ miles}$

Henao can walk 10.5 miles in 3 hours.

4. **(a)** $1\text{ s} = \dfrac{1}{60}\text{ min}$ (see Appendix A)

So, $20\text{ seconds} = \dfrac{20\text{ s}}{1} \times \dfrac{1\text{ min}}{60\text{ s}} = \dfrac{\cancel{20}^1\text{ s}}{1} \times \dfrac{1\text{ min}}{\cancel{60}_3\text{ s}} = \dfrac{1}{3}\text{ min}$

$\dfrac{140\text{ words}}{2\frac{1}{3}\text{ minutes}} = \dfrac{140}{\frac{7}{3}}\dfrac{\text{words}}{\text{minute}} = \left(140 \div \dfrac{7}{3}\right)\dfrac{\text{words}}{\text{minute}} = \left(\dfrac{140}{1} \times \dfrac{3}{7}\right)\dfrac{\text{words}}{\text{minute}}$

$= \left(\dfrac{\cancel{140}^{20}}{1} \times \dfrac{3}{\cancel{7}_1}\right)\dfrac{\text{words}}{\text{minute}} = \dfrac{60}{1}\dfrac{\text{words}}{\text{minute}} = 60\text{ words per minute}$

(b) The unit rate is 60.

(c) For every 1 minute, Nadine can type 60 words.

(d) $\dfrac{60\text{ words}}{1\text{ minute}} \times 5\text{ minutes} = \dfrac{60\text{ words}}{1\text{ minute}} \times \dfrac{5\text{ minutes}}{1} = 300\text{ words}$

Nadine can type 300 words in 5 minutes.

5. **(a)** $\dfrac{\frac{2}{3}\text{ cup}}{1\frac{1}{2}\text{ cups}} = \dfrac{\left(\frac{2}{3}\right)\cdot\frac{6}{1}\text{ cup}}{\left(\frac{3}{2}\right)\cdot\frac{6}{1}\text{ cup}} = \dfrac{\left(\frac{2}{\cancel{3}_1}\right)\cdot\frac{\cancel{6}^2}{1}}{\left(\frac{3}{\cancel{2}_1}\right)\cdot\frac{\cancel{6}^3}{1}} = \dfrac{\frac{4}{1}}{\frac{9}{1}} = \dfrac{4}{9}$

(b) The unit rate is $\dfrac{4}{9}$.

(c) For every 1 cup of flour, the recipe requires $\frac{4}{9}$ cup of milk.

(d) $\dfrac{\frac{4}{9} \text{ cup of milk}}{1 \text{ cup of flour}} \times 4\frac{1}{2} \text{ cups of flour} = \dfrac{\frac{4}{9} \text{ cup of milk}}{1 \text{ cup of flour}} \times \frac{9}{2} \text{ cups of flour} = \left(\frac{\overset{2}{\cancel{4}}}{\underset{1}{\cancel{9}}} \times \frac{\overset{1}{\cancel{9}}}{\underset{1}{\cancel{2}}} \right) \text{ cups of milk}$

$= \dfrac{2}{1} \text{ cups of milk} = 2 \text{ cups of milk}$

2 cups of milk are needed for $4\frac{1}{2}$ cups of flour.

Recognizing Proportional Relationships

(CCSS.Math.Content.7.RP.A.1, CCSS.Math.Content.7.RP.A.2.A)

A set of ratios represents a **proportional relationship** between two variable quantities if either

(a) The ratios in the set are equivalent ratios; or

(b) The ordered pairs of the graph of the ratios in the set lie on a straight line that passes through the origin.

Thus, you have two ways of determining whether a set of ratios represents a proportional relationship between two variable quantities.

Method 1: Test whether the ratios in the set are equivalent. *Tip:* Divide the values of the second variable quantity by the corresponding values of the first variable quantity. If the results are all the same, then the ratios are equivalent.

Method 2: Test whether the ordered pairs of the graph of the ratios in the set lie on a straight line that passes through the origin.

Here are examples.

The table shows corresponding values for the cost, c (in dollars), for the number, n, of used books purchased. Do n and c have a proportional relationship?

Number, n, of Books Purchased	Cost, c (in Dollars)
4	20
7	35
8	40
11	55

Method 1: Test whether the ratios in the table are equivalent.

$$\frac{20}{4} = 5; \quad \frac{35}{7} = 5; \quad \frac{40}{8} = 5; \quad \frac{55}{11} = 5$$

Because each ratio has a value of 5, the ratios in the table are equivalent. So, variables n and c have a proportional relationship.

Method 2: Test whether the ordered pairs (4, 20), (7, 35), (8, 40), and (11, 55) lie on a straight line that passes through the origin.

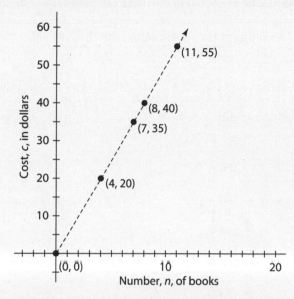

The ordered pairs do lie on a straight line that passes through the origin. So, variables n and c have a proportional relationship. ***Tip:*** The number of books must be a whole number. So, the line through the ordered pairs is dashed because not every point on the line is an ordered pair in the proportional relationship between n and c. Only those points for which n is a whole number are included.

The table shows corresponding values for the distance, d (in miles), that Kalama traveled in time, t (in hours). Do t and d have a proportional relationship?

Time, t, in Hours	Distance, d, in Miles
$\frac{3}{4}$	52.5
$1\frac{1}{2}$	105
$3\frac{1}{5}$	224
$4\frac{3}{10}$	301

Method 1: Test whether the ratios in the table are equivalent.

$$\frac{52.5}{\frac{3}{4}} = \frac{52.5}{0.75} = 52.5 \div 0.75 = 70; \quad \frac{105}{1\frac{1}{2}} = \frac{105}{1.5} = 105 \div 1.5 = 70;$$

$$\frac{224}{3\frac{1}{5}} = \frac{224}{3.2} = 224 \div 3.2 = 70; \quad \frac{301}{4\frac{3}{10}} = \frac{301}{4.3} = 301 \div 4.3 = 70$$

Tip: Converting fractions to decimals before dividing can make computations easier to do.

Each ratio has a value of 70. The ratios in the set are equivalent. So, variables t and d have a proportional relationship.

Method 2: Test whether the ordered pairs $\left(\frac{3}{4}, 52.5\right)$, $\left(1\frac{1}{2}, 105\right)$, $\left(3\frac{1}{5}, 224\right)$, and $\left(4\frac{3}{10}, 301\right)$ lie on a straight line that passes through the origin.

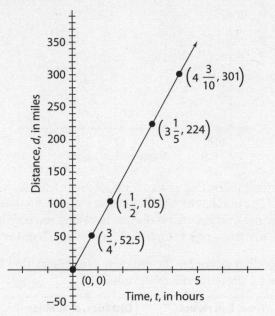

The ordered pairs lie on a straight line that passes through the origin. So, variables t and d have a proportional relationship.

The table shows corresponding values for the cost, c (in dollars), for the number, n, of toy vehicles purchased. Do n and c have a proportional relationship?

Number, n, of Toy Vehicles Purchased	Cost, c (in Dollars)
2	3.96
3	5.94
4	7.60
5	9.25

Method 1: Test whether the ratios in the table are equivalent.

$$\frac{3.96}{2} = 1.98; \quad \frac{5.94}{3} = 1.98; \quad \frac{7.60}{4} = 1.90; \quad \frac{9.25}{5} = 1.85$$

Only the first two ratios are equivalent. So, variables n and c do not have a proportional relationship.

Method 2: Test whether the ordered pairs (2, 3.96), (3, 5.94), (4, 7.60), and (5, 9.25) lie on a straight line that passes through the origin.

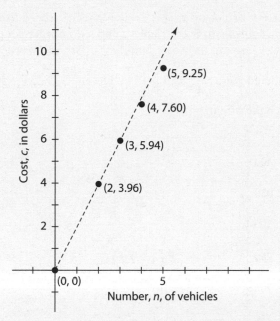

The four ordered pairs do not lie on a straight line that passes through the origin. Only two of the points, (2, 3.96) and (3, 5.94), have a proportional relationship. Points (4, 7.60) and (5, 9.25) do not lie on the line between those two points. So, variables n and c do not have a proportional relationship.

The table shows corresponding values for the distance, d (in miles), that Jordan is from home in time, t (in hours). Do t and d have a proportional relationship?

Time, t, in Hours	Distance, d, in Miles
$\dfrac{3}{4}$	82.5
$1\dfrac{1}{2}$	135
$3\dfrac{1}{5}$	254
$4\dfrac{3}{10}$	331

Method 1: Test whether the ratios in the table are equivalent.

$$\frac{82.5}{\frac{3}{4}} = \frac{82.5}{0.75} = 82.5 \div 0.75 = 110; \quad \frac{135}{1\frac{1}{2}} = \frac{135}{1.5} = 135 \div 1.5 = 90;$$

$$\frac{254}{3\frac{1}{5}} = \frac{254}{3.2} = 254 \div 3.2 = 79.375; \quad \frac{331}{4\frac{3}{10}} = \frac{331}{4.3} = 331 \div 4.3 = 76.9767\ldots$$

None of the ratios in the set are equivalent. So, variables t and d do not have a proportional relationship.

Method 2: Test whether the ordered pairs $\left(\frac{3}{4}, 82.5\right)$, $\left(1\frac{1}{2}, 135\right)$, $\left(3\frac{1}{5}, 254\right)$, and $\left(4\frac{3}{10}, 331\right)$ lie on a straight line that passes through the origin.

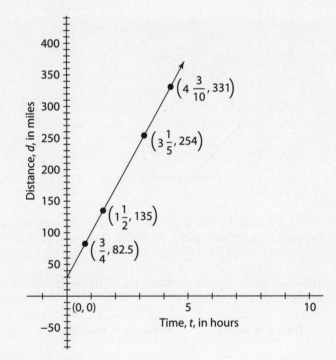

The ordered pairs do lie on a straight line, but the line does not pass through the origin. So, variables t and d do not have a proportional relationship.

☞ Try These

1. Use Method 1 to determine whether the ratios in the table represent a proportional relationship between the two variable quantities.

(a)

Number, p, of Pizzas Purchased	Cost, c (in Dollars)
1	6.99
2	13.98
4	27.96
7	48.93

(b)

Number, c, of Children	Number, m, of Minutes
1	3
2	5.2
5	12
7	14

2. Use Method 2 to determine whether the ratios in the table represent a proportional relationship between the two variable quantities.

(a)

Number, p, of Pizzas Purchased	Cost, c (In Dollars)
1	6.99
2	13.98
4	27.96
7	48.93

(b)

Number, c, of Children	Number, m, of Minutes
1	3
2	5.2
5	12
7	14

3. State whether the graph represents a proportional relationship. Explain your answer.

(a)

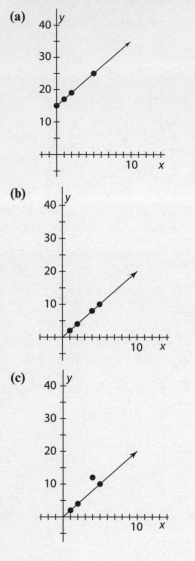

(b)

(c)

Solutions

1. (a) $\dfrac{6.99}{1} = 6.99$; $\dfrac{13.98}{2} = 13.98 \div 2 = 6.99$; $\dfrac{27.96}{4} = 27.96 \div 4 = 6.99$; $\dfrac{48.93}{7} = 48.93 \div 7 = 6.99$

Each ratio has a value of 6.99. The ratios in the set are equivalent. So, variables p and c have a proportional relationship.

(b) $\dfrac{3}{1} = 3$; $\dfrac{5.2}{2} = 2.6$; $\dfrac{12}{5} = 2.4$; $\dfrac{14}{7} = 2$

None of the ratios in the set are equivalent. So, variables c and m do not have a proportional relationship.

2. Use Method 2 to determine whether the ratios in the table represent a proportional relationship between the two variable quantities.

(a)

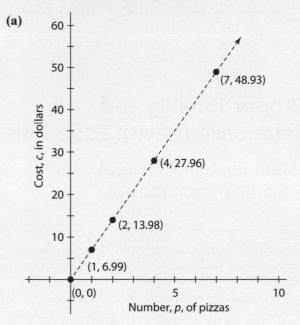

The four ordered pairs lie on a straight line that passes through the origin. So, variables p and c do have a proportional relationship.

(b)

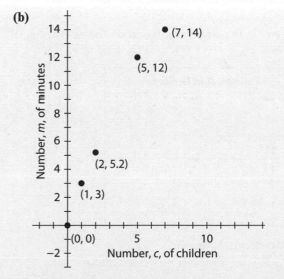

The four ordered pairs do not lie on a straight line that passes through the origin. So, variables c and m do not have a proportional relationship.

3. **(a)** The graph does not represent a proportional relationship. The graph is a straight line, but it does not pass through the origin.

   (b) The graph does represent a proportional relationship. The graph is a straight line that passes through the origin.

   (c) The graph does not represent a proportional relationship. The graph is not a straight line. One point is not aligned with the other points.

Identifying the Constant of Proportionality and Representing Proportional Relationships with Equations

(CCSS.Math.Content.7.RP.A.1, CCSS.Math.Content.7.RP.A.2.A, CCSS.Math.Content.7.RP.A.2.B, CCSS.Math.Content.7.RP.A.2.C, CCSS.Math.Content.7.RP.A.3)

When the ratio of two variable quantities is constant, their relationship is a proportional relationship. In other words, two variable quantities x and y have a proportional relationship if there is a positive number k for which $y = kx$ for every pair of corresponding values of x and y. The number k is the **constant of proportionality.** The equation $y = kx$ represents the proportional relationship between x and y.

> **Tip: In a collection of equivalent ratios, the constant of proportionality is the common unit rate.**

Here is an example.

The table shows a proportional relationship between Uzo's earnings, p, based on the number, h, of hours worked.

Number, h, of Hours Worked	Earnings, p, in Dollars
$2\frac{1}{2}$	18.75
4	30.00
5	37.50
$6\frac{1}{2}$	48.75

(a) What is the constant of proportionality (to two decimal places)?

(b) Write an equation that represents the proportional relationship between h and p.

(c) Using the equation in part (b), determine Uzo's earnings for working $3\frac{1}{2}$ hours.

(d) Using the equation in part (b), determine how many hours Uzo must work to earn $45.

(a) $\dfrac{18.75}{2\frac{1}{2}} = \dfrac{18.75}{2.5} = 18.75 \div 2.5 = 7.50;\quad \dfrac{30.00}{4} = 7.50;\quad \dfrac{37.50}{5} = 7.50;\quad \dfrac{48.75}{6\frac{1}{2}} = \dfrac{48.75}{6.5} = 48.75 \div 6.5 = 7.50$

The constant of proportionality is 7.50.

(b) The equation $p = 7.50h$ represents the proportional relationship.

(c) Substitute $h = 3\frac{1}{2}$ into the equation $p = 7.50h$ and solve for p.

$$p = 7.50h$$
$$p = 7.50\left(3\frac{1}{2}\right)$$
$$p = 7.50(3.5)$$
$$p = 26.25$$

Uzo will earn \$26.25 for working $3\frac{1}{2}$ hours.

(d) Substitute $p = 45$ into the equation $p = 7.50h$ and solve for h.

$$p = 7.50h$$
$$45 = 7.50h$$

$7.50h = 45$ (for convenience rewrite the equation with the variable on the left side)

$$\dfrac{\cancel{7.50}h}{\cancel{7.50}} = \dfrac{45}{7.50}$$
$$h = 45 \div 7.50$$
$$h = 6$$

Uzo must work 6 hours to earn \$45.

☞ Try These

1. The table shows a proportional relationship between the cost, c (in dollars), and the number, n, of used books purchased.

Number, n, of Books Purchased	Cost, c (in Dollars)
4	20
7	35
8	40
11	55

   (a)   What is the constant of proportionality?
   (b)   Write an equation that represents the proportional relationship between n and c.
   (c)   Using the equation in part (b), determine the cost for 6 books.
   (d)   Using the equation in part (b), determine how many books can be purchased for \$60.

2. The table shows a proportional relationship between the distance, d (in miles), traveled in time, t (in hours).

Time, t, in Hours	Distance, d, in Miles
$\frac{3}{4}$	52.5
$1\frac{1}{2}$	105
$3\frac{1}{5}$	224
$4\frac{3}{10}$	301

    (a)   What is the constant of proportionality?

    (b)   Write an equation that represents the proportional relationship between t and d.

    (c)   Using the equation in part (b), determine the distance traveled in 2.4 hours.

    (d)   Using the equation in part (b), determine how many hours it takes to travel 266 miles.

Solutions

1. **(a)** $\frac{20}{4} = 5$; $\frac{35}{7} = 5$; $\frac{40}{8} = 5$; $\frac{55}{11} = 5$

The constant of proportionality is 5.

(b) The equation $c = 5n$ represents the proportional relationship between n and c.

(c) Substitute $n = 6$ into the equation $c = 5n$ and solve for c.

$$c = 5n$$
$$c = 5(6)$$
$$c = 30$$

The cost for 6 books is $30.

(d) Substitute $c = 60$ into the equation $c = 5n$ and solve for n.

$$c = 5n$$
$$60 = 5n$$
$$5n = 60$$
$$\frac{\cancel{5}n}{\cancel{5}} = \frac{60}{5}$$
$$n = 60 \div 5$$
$$n = 12$$

12 books can be purchased for $60.

2. **(a)** $\dfrac{52.5}{\frac{3}{4}} = \dfrac{52.5}{0.75} = 52.5 \div 0.75 = 70;\quad \dfrac{105}{1\frac{1}{2}} = \dfrac{105}{1.5} = 105 \div 1.5 = 70;\quad \dfrac{224}{3\frac{1}{5}} = \dfrac{224}{3.2} = 224 \div 3.2 = 70;$

$\dfrac{301}{4\frac{3}{10}} = \dfrac{301}{4.3} = 301 \div 4.3 = 70$

The constant of proportionality is 70.

(b) The equation $d = 70t$ represents the proportional relationship between t and d.

(c) Substitute $t = 2.4$ into the equation $d = 70t$ and solve for d.

$$d = 70t$$
$$d = 70(2.4)$$
$$d = 168$$

The distance traveled in 2.4 hours is 168 miles.

(d) Substitute $d = 266$ into the equation $d = 70t$ and solve for t.

$$d = 70t$$
$$266 = 70t$$
$$70t = 266$$
$$\frac{70t}{70} = \frac{266}{70}$$
$$t = 266 \div 70$$
$$t = 3.8$$

It will take 3.8 hours to travel a distance of 266 miles.

Analyzing Graphs of Proportional Relationships

(CCSS.Math.Content.7.RP.A.2.B, CCSS.Math.Content.7.RP.A.2.D)

Suppose you have the graph of a proportional relationship represented by the equation $y = kx$, where k is the constant of proportionality. The following information about the graph is helpful to know.

- If (a, b) is a point (not the origin) on the graph, then $\dfrac{b}{a} = k$ (the constant of proportionality) $= r$ (the unit rate).
- The point $(0, 0)$ lies on the graph. It indicates when there is 0 amount of x, there is also 0 amount of y.
- The point $(1, r)$, where r is the unit rate, lies on the graph.
- The constant of proportionality (unit rate) is the amount of vertical increase in y for every horizontal increase of 1 unit by x.

Here is an example.

The graph of $y = kx$ shown below represents the weight, y (in pounds), of x gallons of a liquid.

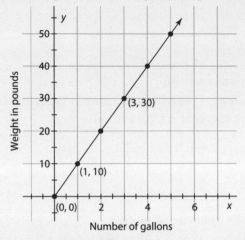

(a) What is k, the constant of proportionality?
(b) Interpret the meaning of k in terms of the situation.
(c) What does the point (3, 30) on the graph mean in terms of the situation?
(d) What does the point (0, 0) on the graph mean in terms of the situation?
(e) What does the point (1, 10) on the graph mean in terms of the situation?

(a) From the graph, the point (3, 30) yields $k = \dfrac{30}{3} = 10$ as the constant of proportionality. **Tip:** Any ordered pair, except (0, 0), on the graph will yield 10 as the constant of proportionality.
(b) The constant of proportionality (unit rate) of 10 means the equation, $y = 10x$, represents the proportional relationship, and that y increases 10 units for every 1 unit increase by x. See the illustration below.

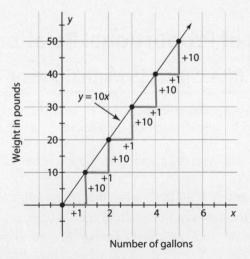

(c) The ordered pair (3, 30) means 3 gallons weighs 30 pounds.
(d) The ordered pair (0, 0) means 0 gallons weighs 0 pounds.
(e) The ordered pair (1, 10) means 1 gallon weighs 10 pounds, so the unit rate is 10.

☞Try These

1. Fill in the blank.

   (a) In a proportional relationship, the constant of proportionality equals the _____ rate.

   (b) The point $(1, r)$, where r is the unit rate, and the point _____ always lie on the graph of any proportional relationship.

   (c) For the graph of $y = kx$, the constant of proportionality is the amount of vertical increase in y for every horizontal increase of _____ unit by x.

2. The graph of $y = kx$ shown below represents the cost, y (in dollars), of x pounds of mixed nuts.

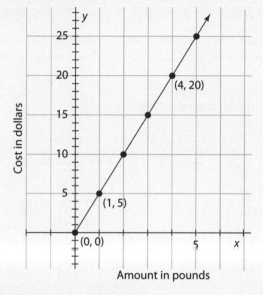

Amount in pounds

   (a) What is k, the constant of proportionality?

   (b) Interpret the meaning of k in terms of the situation.

   (c) What does the point $(4, 20)$ on the graph mean in terms of the situation?

   (d) What does the point $(0, 0)$ on the graph mean in terms of the situation?

   (e) What does the point $(1, 5)$ on the graph mean in terms of the situation?

Solutions

1. (a) unit

   (b) $(0, 0)$

   (c) 1

2. (a) From the graph, the point $(4, 20)$ yields $k = \dfrac{20}{4} = 5$ as the constant of proportionality.

   (b) The constant of proportionality (unit rate) of 5 means the equation, $y = 5x$, represents the proportional relationship and that y increases 5 units for every 1 unit increase by x.

   (c) The ordered pair $(4, 20)$ means 4 pounds cost $20.

   (d) The ordered pair $(0, 0)$ means 0 pounds cost 0 dollars.

   (e) The ordered pair $(1, 5)$ means 1 pound costs $5, so the unit rate is 5.

Using Proportional Relationships to Solve Multistep Ratio Problems

(CCSS.Math.Content.7.RP.A.2)

A **proportion** is a mathematical statement that the values of two ratios are equal. The **terms** of the proportion are the four numbers that make up the two ratios. For example, the proportion $\frac{3}{4} = \frac{9}{12}$ has terms 3, 4, 9, and 12. The **fundamental property of proportions** is $\frac{a}{b} = \frac{c}{d}$ if and only if $ad = bc$. In other words, cross products of a proportion are equal. **Cross products** are the product of the numerator of the first ratio times the denominator of the second ratio and the product of the denominator of the first ratio times the numerator of the second ratio.

Here is an illustration of obtaining the cross products for $\frac{3}{4} = \frac{9}{12}$.

$$\frac{3}{4} \bowtie \frac{9}{12} \longrightarrow 3 \times 12 = 4 \times 9 \longrightarrow 36 = 36$$

A simple way to prove that cross products of the proportion, $\frac{3}{4} = \frac{9}{12}$, should be equal is to write each fraction as an equivalent fraction that has the common denominator 4×12, which is 48.

$$\frac{3}{4} = \frac{9}{12}$$
$$\frac{3 \times 12}{4 \times 12} = \frac{9 \times 4}{12 \times 4}$$
$$\frac{3 \times 12}{48} = \frac{9 \times 4}{48}$$

The denominators are the same, so the numerators must be equal. That is, $3 \times 12 = 4 \times 9$. Thus, the cross products are equal.

When you have a proportion that has a variable in place of a missing term, you can use cross products to find the value of the variable. Look at this example.

Suppose the ratio of boys in the band to the number of the students in the band is 2 to 5. There are 18 boys in the band. How many students are in the band? Let x = the number of students in the band. The ratios 2 to 5 and 18 to x are equivalent. Write a proportion and solve for x.

$$\frac{2}{5} = \frac{18}{x}$$

Find the cross products.

$$2 \cdot x = 5 \cdot 18$$

Then solve for x.

$$2x = 90$$

$$\frac{\cancel{2}x}{\cancel{2}} = \frac{90}{2}$$

$$x = 90 \div 2$$

$$x = 45$$

There are 45 students in the band.

Here is a multistep example.

Suppose the ratio of girls to boys in a club is 4 to 5. There are 12 girls in the club. How many students are in the club?

Step 1. Determine the number of boys in the club.

Let b = the number of boys in the club. The ratios 4 to 5 and 12 to b are equivalent. Write a proportion and solve for b.

$$\frac{4}{5} = \frac{12}{b}$$

Find the cross products.

$$4 \cdot b = 5 \cdot 12$$

Then solve for b.

$$4b = 60$$

$$\frac{\cancel{4}b}{\cancel{4}} = \frac{60}{4}$$

$$b = 60 \div 4$$

$$b = 15$$

There are 15 boys in the club.

Step 2. Determine the number of students in the club.

There are 12 girls and 15 boys in the club. So, there are $12 + 15 = 27$ students in the club.

☞ Try These

1. The ratio of milk to flour in a recipe is $\frac{2}{3}$ to 4. How much milk is needed for 9 cups of flour?

2. The school colors are red and black. At the school spirit rallies, students wave either red or black bandanas. At a recent spirit rally, the ratio of students waving red bandanas to those waving black bandanas was 3 to 5. There were 120 students waving red bandanas. How many students were waving bandanas at the spirit rally?

Solutions

1. Let m = the amount (in cups) of milk needed. The ratios $\dfrac{\frac{2}{3}}{4}$ and $\dfrac{m}{9}$ are equivalent. Write a proportion and solve for m.

$$\frac{\frac{2}{3}}{4} = \frac{m}{9}$$

Find the cross products.

$$\frac{2}{3} \cdot 9 = 4 \cdot m$$

$$\frac{2}{{}_1\cancel{3}} \cdot \frac{\cancel{9}^{\,3}}{1} = 4m$$

$$\frac{6}{1} = 4m$$

$$6 = 4m$$

$$4m = 6$$

Then solve for m.

$$4m = 6$$

$$\frac{\cancel{4}m}{\cancel{4}} = \frac{6 \div 2}{4 \div 2}$$

$$m = \frac{3}{2} \text{ or } 1\frac{1}{2}$$

$1\frac{1}{2}$ cups of milk are needed for 9 cups of flour.

2. *Step 1.* Determine the number of students waving black bandanas.

    Let b = the number of students waving black bandanas. The ratios 3 to 5 and 120 to b are equivalent. Write a proportion and solve for b.

$$\frac{3}{5} = \frac{120}{b}$$

Find the cross products.

$$3 \cdot b = 5 \cdot 120$$

Then solve for b.

$$3b = 600$$
$$\frac{\cancel{3}b}{\cancel{3}} = \frac{600}{3}$$
$$b = 600 \div 3$$
$$b = 200$$

There were 200 students waving black bandanas.

Step 2. Determine the total number of students waving bandanas.

There were 120 students waving red bandanas and 200 students waving black bandanas. So, there were 120 + 200 = 320 students waving bandanas at the spirit rally.

Using Proportional Relationships to Revisit Percent Problems

(CCSS.Math.Content.7.RP.A.2)

A percent always represents a relationship between a part and a whole. The relationship between the three elements—*r,* **part,** and **whole**—can be explained in a percent statement:

The part is $r\%$ of the whole.

You can solve percent problems using a "percent proportion" that has the following form:

$$\frac{r}{100} = \frac{\text{part}}{\text{whole}}$$

The secret to solving percent problems is being able to correctly identify the three elements. Here are some helpful hints:

- The *r* has a % sign attached.
- The **whole** (or its description) immediately follows the word "of."
- The **part** is very near the word "is."

Start with *r* and the whole because they are usually easier to find. The part will be the other amount in the problem. The value of two of the elements will be given in the problem, and you will solve for the third element. After you identify the three elements, plug the two you know into the percent proportion and solve for the one you don't know.

Tip: Think *"is* over *of"* to get $\dfrac{\text{part (``is'')}}{\text{whole (``of'')}}$ correct.

Tip: As you know, the percent is the quantity with the % sign attached. It cannot be used as such in a computation. You must convert it to an equivalent decimal or fraction, first.

Finding the Part, Given the Percent and the Whole

Look at this example.

30% of 200 spectators are students. How many of the spectators are students?

Let x = the number of spectators who are students. Write a percent statement for the question.

$$x \text{ is } 30\% \text{ of } 200$$

The part is x, the percent is 30%, and the whole is 200.

List the elements for the percent proportion.

$$r = 30$$
$$\text{part} = ? = x$$
$$\text{whole} = 200$$

Plug into the percent proportion.

$$\frac{r}{100} = \frac{\text{part}}{\text{whole}}$$
$$\frac{30}{100} = \frac{x}{200}$$
$$\frac{30 \div 10}{100 \div 10} = \frac{x}{200}$$ ***Tip:*** Reducing fractions simplifies computations.
$$\frac{3}{10} = \frac{x}{200}$$

Solve the proportion.

$$\frac{3}{10} = \frac{x}{200}$$

Find the cross products.

$$3 \cdot 200 = 10 \cdot x$$

Then solve for x.

$$600 = 10x$$
$$10x = 600$$
$$\frac{\cancel{10}x}{\cancel{10}} = \frac{600}{10}$$
$$x = 600 \div 10$$
$$x = 60$$

Sixty students are spectators.

☞ Try These

1. In an auditorium of 500 students, 25% are seventh graders. How many of the students are seventh graders?

2. There are 80 vehicles in a parking lot. Fifteen percent of the vehicles are vans. How many vans are in the parking lot?

Solutions

1. Let x = the number of seventh graders in the auditorium. Write a percent statement for the question.

$$x \text{ is } 25\% \text{ of } 500$$

The part is x, the percent is 25%, and the whole is 500.

List the elements for the percent proportion.

$$r = 25$$
$$\text{part} = ? = x$$
$$\text{whole} = 500$$

Plug into the percent proportion.

$$\frac{r}{100} = \frac{\text{part}}{\text{whole}}$$
$$\frac{25}{100} = \frac{x}{500}$$
$$\frac{25 \div 25}{100 - 25} = \frac{x}{500}$$
$$\frac{1}{4} = \frac{x}{500}$$

Solve the proportion.

$$\frac{1}{4} = \frac{x}{500}$$

Find the cross products.

$$1 \cdot 500 = 4 \cdot x$$

Then solve for x.

$$500 = 4x$$
$$4x = 500$$
$$\frac{4x}{\cancel{4}} = \frac{500}{4}$$
$$x = 500 \div 4$$
$$x = 125$$

There are 125 seventh graders in the auditorium.

2. Let x = the number of vans in the parking lot. Write a percent statement for the question.

$$x \text{ is } 15\% \text{ of } 80$$

The part is x, the percent is 15%, and the whole is 80.

List the elements for the percent proportion.

$$r = 15$$
$$\text{part} = ? = x$$
$$\text{whole} = 80$$

Plug into the percent proportion.

$$\frac{r}{100} = \frac{\text{part}}{\text{whole}}$$
$$\frac{15}{100} = \frac{x}{80}$$
$$\frac{15 \div 5}{100 \div 5} = \frac{x}{80}$$
$$\frac{3}{20} = \frac{x}{80}$$

Solve the proportion.

$$\frac{3}{20} = \frac{x}{80}$$

Find the cross products.

$$3 \cdot 80 = 20 \cdot x$$

Then solve for x.

$$240 = 20x$$
$$20x = 240$$
$$\frac{20x}{20} = \frac{240}{20}$$
$$x = 240 \div 20$$
$$x = 12$$

There are 12 vans in the parking lot.

Finding the Whole, Given the Percent and the Part

Look at this example.

Forty percent of the students in the stadium are girls. There are 120 girls in the stadium. How many students are in the stadium?

Let s = the number of students in the stadium. Write a percent statement for the question.

$$120 \text{ is } 40\% \text{ of } s$$

The part is 120, the percent is 40%, and the whole is *s*.

List the elements for the percent proportion.

$$r = 40$$
$$\text{part} = 120$$
$$\text{whole} = ? = s$$

Plug into the percent proportion.

$$\frac{r}{100} = \frac{\text{part}}{\text{whole}}$$
$$\frac{40}{100} = \frac{120}{s}$$
$$\frac{40 \div 20}{100 \div 20} = \frac{120}{s}$$
$$\frac{2}{5} = \frac{120}{s}$$

Solve the proportion.

$$\frac{2}{5} = \frac{120}{s}$$

Find the cross products.

$$2 \cdot s = 5 \cdot 120$$

Then solve for *s*.

$$2s = 600$$
$$\frac{2s}{2} = \frac{600}{2}$$
$$s = 600 \div 2$$
$$s = 300$$

There are 300 students in the stadium.

☞Try These

1. Flaxseed is 15% of a mixture. The amount of flaxseed is 45 ounces. How many ounces are in the mixture?

2. Diaval has driven 75 miles. This distance is 25% of the total distance Diaval will be driving. What is the total distance?

Solutions

1. Let m = the amount (in ounces) in the mixture. Write a percent statement for the question (omitting units for convenience).

    $$45 \text{ is } 15\% \text{ of } m$$

    The part is 45, the percent is 15%, and the whole is m.

    List the elements for the percent proportion.

    $$r = 15$$
    $$\text{part} = 45$$
    $$\text{whole} = ? = m$$

    Plug into the percent proportion.

    $$\frac{r}{100} = \frac{\text{part}}{\text{whole}}$$
    $$\frac{15}{100} = \frac{45}{m}$$
    $$\frac{15 \div 5}{100 \div 5} = \frac{45}{m}$$
    $$\frac{3}{20} = \frac{45}{m}$$

    Solve the proportion.

    $$\frac{3}{20} = \frac{45}{m}$$

    Find the cross products.

    $$3 \cdot m = 20 \cdot 45$$

    Then solve for m.

    $$3m = 900$$
    $$\frac{\cancel{3}m}{\cancel{3}} = \frac{900}{3}$$
    $$m = 900 \div 3$$
    $$m = 300$$

    There are 300 ounces in the mixture.

2. Let d = the total distance in miles. Write a percent statement for the question (omitting units for convenience).

    $$75 \text{ is } 25\% \text{ of } d$$

    The part is 75, the percent is 25%, and the whole is d.

List the elements for the percent proportion.

$$r = 25$$
$$\text{part} = 75$$
$$\text{whole} = ? = d$$

Plug into the percent proportion.

$$\frac{r}{100} = \frac{\text{part}}{\text{whole}}$$
$$\frac{25}{100} = \frac{75}{d}$$
$$\frac{25 \div 25}{100 \div 25} = \frac{75}{d}$$
$$\frac{1}{4} = \frac{75}{d}$$

Solve the proportion.

$$\frac{1}{4} = \frac{75}{d}$$

Find the cross products.

$$1 \cdot d = 4 \cdot 75$$

Then solve for d.

$$d \quad 300$$

The total distance is 300 miles.

Finding the Percent, Given the Part and the Whole

Look at this example.

Four hundred dollars is what percent of $500?

Let $r\% =$ the percent. Write a percent statement for the question (omitting units for convenience).

400 is $r\%$ of 500

The part is 400, the percent is $r\%$, and the whole is 500.

List the elements for the percent proportion.

$$r = ?$$
$$\text{part} = 400$$
$$\text{whole} = 500$$

Plug into the percent proportion.

$$\frac{r}{100} = \frac{400}{500}$$

$$\frac{r}{100} = \frac{400 \div 100}{500 \div 100}$$

$$\frac{r}{100} = \frac{4}{5}$$

Solve the proportion.

$$\frac{r}{100} = \frac{4}{5}$$

Find the cross products.

$$r \cdot 5 = 100 \cdot 4$$

Then solve for r.

$$5r = 400$$

$$\frac{\cancel{5}r}{\cancel{5}} = \frac{400}{5}$$

$$r = 400 \div 5$$

$$r = 80$$

$$r\% = 80\%$$

Four hundred dollars is 80% of $500.

☞ Try These

1. A survey of 250 seventh graders showed that 105 of them had read at least one book during their summer break. What percent of the seventh graders had read at least one book during their summer break?

2. Fifty-four of 150 students in the auditorium are student athletes. What percent of the students in the auditorium are student athletes?

Solutions

1. Let $r\%$ = the percent. Write a percent statement for the question (omitting units for convenience).

$$105 \text{ is } r\% \text{ of } 250$$

The part is 105, the percent is $r\%$, and the whole is 250.

List the elements for the percent proportion.

$$r = ?$$

$$\text{part} = 105$$

$$\text{whole} = 250$$

Plug into the percent proportion.

$$\frac{r}{100} = \frac{105}{250}$$

$$\frac{r}{100} = \frac{105 \div 5}{250 \div 5}$$

$$\frac{r}{100} = \frac{21}{50}$$

Solve the proportion.

$$\frac{r}{100} = \frac{21}{50}$$

Find the cross products.

$$r \cdot 50 = 100 \cdot 21$$

Then solve for r.

$$50r = 2{,}100$$

$$\frac{50r}{50} = \frac{2{,}100}{50}$$

$$r = 2{,}100 \div 50$$

$$r = 42$$

$$r\% = 42\%$$

Forty-two percent of the seventh graders had read at least one book during their summer break.

2. Let $r\%$ = the percent. Write a percent statement for the question (omitting units for convenience).

54 is $r\%$ of 150

The part is 54, the percent is $r\%$, and the whole is 150.

List the elements for the percent proportion.

$$r = ?$$
$$\text{part} = 54$$
$$\text{whole} = 150$$

Plug into the percent proportion.

$$\frac{r}{100} = \frac{54}{150}$$

$$\frac{r}{100} = \frac{54 \div 6}{150 \div 6}$$

$$\frac{r}{100} = \frac{9}{25}$$

Solve the proportion.

$$\frac{r}{100} = \frac{9}{25}$$

Find the cross products.

$$r \cdot 25 = 100 \cdot 9$$

Then solve for r.

$$25r = 900$$
$$\frac{\cancel{25}r}{\cancel{25}} = \frac{900}{25}$$
$$r = 900 \div 25$$
$$r = 36$$
$$r\% = 36\%$$

Thirty-six percent of the students in the auditorium are student athletes.

Using Proportional Relationships to Solve Real-World Percent Problems

(CCSS.Math.Content.7.RP.A.2, CCSS.Math.Content.7.RP.A.3, CCSS.Math.Content.7.EE.A.2)

Percents are an unavoidable part of everyday living. This section presents a number of real-world problems that can be solved using proportional relationships.

Solving Discount Problems

In business, a **discount** is an amount subtracted from the **list price** of an item. The **sale price** is the list price minus the discount. The **discount rate** is a percent of the list price.

Tip: The list price might also be called the regular price or the original price.

Here is an example.

A home stereo system is on sale for 20% off its list price of $560. What is the sale price of the stereo system after the 20% discount?

The sale price of the stereo system is the list price minus 20% of the list price. The sale price = $560 – (20% of $560).

Method 1: To determine the sale price, find 20% of $560, and then subtract the amount from $560.

Step 1. Find 20% of $560.

Let $x = 20\%$ of $560.

List the elements for the percent proportion (omitting units for convenience).

$$r = 20$$
$$\text{part} = ? = x$$
$$\text{whole} = 560$$

Plug into the percent proportion.

$$\frac{r}{100} = \frac{\text{part}}{\text{whole}}$$
$$\frac{20}{100} = \frac{x}{560}$$
$$\frac{20 \div 20}{100 \div 20} = \frac{x}{560}$$
$$\frac{1}{5} = \frac{x}{560}$$

Solve the proportion.

$$\frac{1}{5} = \frac{x}{560}$$

Find the cross products.

$$1 \cdot 560 = 5 \cdot x$$

Then solve for x.

$$560 = 5x$$
$$5x = 560$$
$$\frac{\cancel{5}x}{\cancel{5}} = \frac{560}{5}$$
$$x = 560 \div 5$$
$$x = 112$$

$112 is 20% of $560.

Step 2. Subtract the amount from $560.

$$\$560 - \$112 = \$448$$

The sale price of the stereo system is $448.

Method 2: The sale price = $560 – (20% of $560).

Step 1. Determine the percent of the list price to be paid.

$$\$560 - (20\% \text{ of } \$560) =$$

$$
\begin{array}{l}
100\% \text{ of } \$560 \\
-20\% \text{ of } \$560 \\
\hline
80\% \text{ of } \$560
\end{array}
$$
  Tip: A whole is always 100% of itself.

Tip: Do Step 1 mentally. Think: *"If you save 20% of the list price, then the percent you pay of the list price is 100% – 20% = 80%."*

Step 2. Determine the sale price by finding 80% of $560.

Identify the elements (omitting units for convenience).

$$r = 80$$
$$\text{part} = ? = x$$
$$\text{whole} = 560$$

Plug into the percent proportion.

$$\frac{r}{100} = \frac{\text{part}}{\text{whole}}$$
$$\frac{80}{100} = \frac{x}{560}$$
$$\frac{80 \div 20}{100 \div 20} = \frac{x}{560}$$
$$\frac{4}{5} = \frac{x}{560}$$

Solve the proportion.

$$\frac{4}{5} = \frac{x}{560}$$

Find the cross products.

$$4 \cdot 560 = 5 \cdot x$$

Then solve for x.

$$2,240 = 5x$$
$$5x = 2,240$$
$$\frac{\cancel{5}x}{\cancel{5}} = \frac{2,240}{5}$$
$$x = 2,240 \div 5$$
$$x = 448$$

Eighty percent of $560 is $448, the sale price.

☞ Try These

1. Use mental math to answer as indicated.

   (a) If you get a 30% discount off the list price of an item, what percent of the list price is the sale price?

   (b) If you save 15% of the original price, what percent of the original price do you pay?

   (c) If you get a 25% discount on an item that has a regular price of $600, what percent of $600 will you pay for the item?

   (d) If you save 10% of $250, what percent of $250 do you pay?

2. How much money did Caleb save if he received a 3% discount on an item that cost $1,750?

3. At a 15% off sale, what is the sale price of a $350 coat?

Solutions

1. (a) 70%

   (b) 85%

   (c) 75%

   (d) 90%

2. Caleb saved 3% of $1,750.

   Let x = 3% of $1,750.

   List the elements for the percent proportion (omitting units for convenience).

   $$r = 3$$
   $$\text{part} = ? = x$$
   $$\text{whole} = 1,750$$

   Plug into the percent proportion.

   $$\frac{r}{100} = \frac{\text{part}}{\text{whole}}$$
   $$\frac{3}{100} = \frac{x}{1,750}$$

Solve the proportion.

$$\frac{3}{100} = \frac{x}{1,750}$$

Find the cross products.

$$3 \cdot 1,750 = 100 \cdot x$$

Then solve for x.

$$5,250 = 100x$$
$$100x = 5,250$$
$$\frac{\cancel{100}x}{\cancel{100}} = \frac{5,250}{100}$$
$$x = 5,250 \div 100$$
$$x = 52.50$$

Caleb saved $52.50.

3. Using **Method 2:** The sale price is 85% of $350 (because $100\% - 15\% = 85\%$).
   Let $x = 85\%$ of $350.
   List the elements for the percent proportion (omitting units for convenience).

$$r = 85$$
$$\text{part} = ? = x$$
$$\text{whole} = 350$$

Plug into the percent proportion.

$$\frac{r}{100} = \frac{\text{part}}{\text{whole}}$$
$$\frac{85}{100} = \frac{x}{350}$$
$$\frac{85 \div 5}{100 \div 5} = \frac{x}{350}$$
$$\frac{17}{20} = \frac{x}{350}$$

Solve the proportion.

$$\frac{17}{20} = \frac{x}{350}$$

Find the cross products.

$$17 \cdot 350 = 20 \cdot x$$

Then solve for x.

$$5{,}950 = 20x$$
$$20x = 5{,}950$$
$$\frac{\cancel{20}x}{\cancel{20}} = \frac{5{,}950}{20}$$
$$x = 5{,}950 \div 20$$
$$x = 297.50$$

The sale price of the coat is $297.50.

Solving Markdown and Markup Problems

A **markdown** is a reduction in the list price of an item. It is similar to a discount. The **markdown price** is the list price minus the markdown amount.

Here is an example.

An e-book reader is marked down by 25% of the list price. The list price is $140. What is the markdown price of the e-book reader?

The markdown price is the list price minus 25% of the list price. The list price is $140. So, because 100% − 25% = 75%, you can reason that the markdown price is 75% of $140.

Let $x = 75\%$ of $140

List the elements for the percent proportion (omitting units for convenience).

$$r = 75$$
$$\text{part} = ? = x$$
$$\text{whole} = 140$$

Plug into the percent proportion.

$$\frac{r}{100} = \frac{\text{part}}{\text{whole}}$$
$$\frac{75}{100} = \frac{x}{140}$$
$$\frac{75 \div 25}{100 \div 25} = \frac{x}{140}$$
$$\frac{3}{4} = \frac{x}{140}$$

Solve the proportion.

$$\frac{3}{4} = \frac{x}{140}$$

Find the cross products.

$$3 \cdot 140 = 4 \cdot x$$

Then solve for x.

$$420 = 4x$$
$$4x = 420$$
$$\frac{\cancel{4}x}{\cancel{4}} = \frac{420}{4}$$
$$x = 420 \div 4$$
$$x = 105$$

The markdown price is $105.

A **markup** is an increase in the wholesale price of an item. The **wholesale price** is the price the merchant paid for the item. The **retail price** is the wholesale price plus the markup amount.

Here is an example.

> A music player that has a wholesale price of $80 is marked up by 100% before it is offered for sale. What is the retail price of the music player?

The retail price is the wholesale price plus 100% of the wholesale price. The wholesale price is $80.

100% of $80 is $80. Therefore, the markup price is $80 + $80 = $160.

☞ Try These

1. A flat-screen television is marked down by 40% of the list price. The list price is $520. What is the markdown price of the television?

2. A watch that has a wholesale price of $60 is marked up by 50% before it is offered for sale. What is the retail price of the watch?

Solutions

1. The markdown price is the list price minus 40% of the list price. The list price is $520. So, because 100% − 40% = 60%, the markdown price is 60% of $520.

   Let x = 60% of $520.

   List the elements for the percent proportion (omitting units for convenience).

$$r = 60$$
$$\text{part} = ? = x$$
$$\text{whole} = 520$$

Plug into the percent proportion.

$$\frac{r}{100} = \frac{\text{part}}{\text{whole}}$$

$$\frac{60}{100} = \frac{x}{520}$$

$$\frac{60 \div 20}{100 \div 20} = \frac{x}{520}$$

$$\frac{3}{5} = \frac{x}{520}$$

Solve the proportion.

$$\frac{3}{5} = \frac{x}{520}$$

Find the cross products.

$$3 \cdot 520 = 5 \cdot x$$

Then solve for x.

$$1{,}560 = 5x$$
$$5x = 1{,}560$$
$$\frac{\cancel{5}x}{\cancel{5}} = \frac{1{,}560}{5}$$
$$x = 1{,}560 \div 5$$
$$x = 312$$

The markdown price is $312.

2. The retail price is the wholesale price plus 50% of the wholesale price. The wholesale price is $60. 50% of $60 $= \frac{1}{2} \times \$60 = \$30$. Therefore, the markup price is $60 + $30 = $90.

> **Tip:** Knowing the fractional equivalents of common percents (such as 50% is $\frac{1}{2}$) can simplify calculations.

Solving Sales Tax and Gratuity Problems

A **sales tax** is a fee imposed by a state or local government entity on certain sales transactions. The **sales tax rate** is a percent of the amount of the sale. The sales tax is the sales tax rate times the amount of the sale.

Here is an example.

Shauna bought a pair of shoes for $35 and a blouse for $40. Shauna's purchases are subject to a sales tax rate of 8.75%. Including tax, what did Shauna pay for the shoes and blouse? Give your answer to the nearest cent.

Method 1:

Step 1. Find the total amount of Shauna's purchases.

$$\$35 + \$40 = \$75$$

Step 2. Determine the sales tax on Shauna's purchases.

$$\text{sales tax} = 8.75\% \text{ of } \$75$$

Let $x = 8.75\%$ of $75.

List the elements for the percent proportion (omitting units for convenience).

$$r = 8.75$$
$$\text{part} = ? = x$$
$$\text{whole} = 75$$

Plug into the percent proportion.

$$\frac{r}{100} = \frac{\text{part}}{\text{whole}}$$
$$\frac{8.75}{100} = \frac{x}{75}$$

Solve the proportion.

$$\frac{8.75}{100} = \frac{x}{75}$$

Find the cross products.

$$8.75 \cdot 75 = 100 \cdot x$$

Then solve for x.

$$656.25 = 100x$$
$$100x = 656.25$$
$$\frac{100x}{100} = \frac{656.25}{100}$$
$$x = 656.25 \div 100$$
$$x = 6.5625$$

To the nearest cent, the sales tax is $6.56.

Step 3. Add the sales tax to the purchases.

$$\$75.00 + \$6.56 = \$81.56$$

Including tax, Shauna paid $81.56 for the shoes and blouse.

Method 2:

Step 1. Find the total amount of Shauna's purchases.

$$\$35 + \$40 = \$75$$

Step 2. Determine the total amount Shauna will pay: $75 plus (8.75% of $75).

$$\$75 + (8.75\% \text{ of } \$75) =$$

$$
\begin{array}{r}
100\% \text{ of } \$75 \\
+\ 8.75\% \text{ of } \$75 \\
\hline
108.75\% \text{ of } \$75
\end{array}
$$

Shauna will pay 108.75% of $75.

Tip: Shauna pays more than 100% because she is paying more than $75, the amount of her purchases.

Let x = 108.75% of $75.

List the elements for the percent proportion (omitting units for convenience).

$$r = 108.75$$
$$\text{part} = ? = x$$
$$\text{whole} = 75$$

Plug into the percent proportion.

$$\frac{r}{100} = \frac{\text{part}}{\text{whole}}$$
$$\frac{108.75}{100} = \frac{x}{75}$$

Solve the proportion.

$$\frac{108.75}{100} = \frac{x}{75}$$

Find the cross products.

$$108.75 \cdot 75 = 100 \cdot x$$

Then solve for x.

$$8{,}156.25 = 100x$$
$$100x = 8{,}156.25$$
$$\frac{\cancel{100}\,x}{\cancel{100}} = \frac{8{,}156.25}{100}$$
$$x = 8{,}156.25 \div 100$$
$$x = 81.5625$$

To the nearest cent, Shauna paid $81.56 for the shoes and blouse, including tax.

A **gratuity** is an amount of money called a **tip** that you give to a person (such as a food server) who has performed a service for you. For most situations, you do not have to give a tip if you do not want to. If you voluntarily decide to give a tip, the percentage you give is up to you, and you will not be charged sales tax on the amount you give as a tip. Also, you may choose to base your tip on either the cost before sales tax is added or on the total bill including tax.

Here is an example.

> Taio's total bill (including tax) at a restaurant is $160. Taio gives a tip that is 15% of the total bill. How much money did Taio give as a tip?

The tip is 15% of $160.

Let x = 15% of $160.

List the elements for the percent proportion (omitting units for convenience).

$$r = 15$$
$$\text{part} = ? = x$$
$$\text{whole} = 160$$

Plug into the percent proportion.

$$\frac{r}{100} = \frac{\text{part}}{\text{whole}}$$
$$\frac{15}{100} = \frac{x}{160}$$
$$\frac{15 \div 5}{100 \div 5} = \frac{x}{160}$$
$$\frac{3}{20} = \frac{x}{160}$$

Solve the proportion.

$$\frac{3}{20} = \frac{x}{160}$$

Find the cross products.

$$3 \cdot 160 = 20 \cdot x$$

Then solve for x.

$$480 = 20x$$
$$20x = 480$$
$$\frac{20x}{20} = \frac{480}{20}$$
$$x = 480 \div 20$$
$$x = 24$$

The tip is $24.

☞ Try These

1. The sales tax rate is 6%. What is the sales tax on a new car that has a list price of $35,000?

2. A restaurant meal is $295 before sales tax is added. The sales tax rate is 9.25%. What is the total bill after sales tax is added? Give your answer to the nearest cent.

3. A customer tips a taxi driver 20% of the cost of the ride. The ride cost $24.60. How much money did the customer tip the driver?

Solutions

1. sales tax = 6% of $35,000

   Let x = 6% of $35,000.

   List the elements for the percent proportion (omitting units for convenience).

   $$r = 6$$
   $$\text{part} = ? = x$$
   $$\text{whole} = 35,000$$

   Plug into the percent proportion.

   $$\frac{r}{100} = \frac{\text{part}}{\text{whole}}$$
   $$\frac{6}{100} = \frac{x}{35,000}$$
   $$\frac{6 \div 2}{100 \div 2} = \frac{x}{35,000}$$
   $$\frac{3}{50} = \frac{x}{35,000}$$

   Solve the proportion.

   $$\frac{3}{50} = \frac{x}{35,000}$$

   Find the cross products.

   $$3 \cdot 35,000 = 50 \cdot x$$

   Then solve for x.

   $$105,000 = 50x$$
   $$50x = 105,000$$
   $$\frac{50x}{50} = \frac{105,000}{50}$$
   $$x = 105,000 \div 50$$
   $$x = 2,100$$

   The sales tax is $2,100.

2. The total bill will be $295 plus 9.25% of $295, which is 109.25% of $295.

    Let x = 109.25% of $295.

    List the elements for the percent proportion (omitting units for convenience).

    $$r = 109.25$$
    $$\text{part} = ? = x$$
    $$\text{whole} = 295$$

    Plug into the percent proportion.

    $$\frac{r}{100} = \frac{\text{part}}{\text{whole}}$$
    $$\frac{109.25}{100} = \frac{x}{295}$$

    Solve the proportion.

    $$\frac{109.25}{100} = \frac{x}{295}$$

    Find the cross products.

    $$109.25 \cdot 295 = 100 \cdot x$$

    Then solve for x.

    $$32,228.75 = 100x$$
    $$100x = 32,228.75$$
    $$\frac{100x}{100} = \frac{32,228.75}{100}$$
    $$x = 32,228.75 \div 100$$
    $$x = 322.2875$$

    To the nearest cent, the total bill is $322.29, including tax.

3. The tip is 20% of $24.60.

    Let x = 20% of $24.60.

    List the elements for the percent proportion (omitting units for convenience).

    $$r = 20$$
    $$\text{part} = ? = x$$
    $$\text{whole} = 24.60$$

Plug into the percent proportion.

$$\frac{r}{100} = \frac{\text{part}}{\text{whole}}$$

$$\frac{20}{100} = \frac{x}{24.60}$$

$$\frac{20 \div 20}{100 \div 20} = \frac{x}{24.60}$$

$$\frac{1}{5} = \frac{x}{24.60}$$

Solve the proportion.

$$\frac{1}{5} = \frac{x}{24.60}$$

Find the cross products.

$$1 \cdot 24.60 = 5 \cdot x$$

Then solve for x.

$$24.60 = 5x$$

$$5x = 24.60$$

$$\frac{\cancel{5}x}{\cancel{5}} = \frac{24.60}{5}$$

$$x = 24.60 \div 5$$

$$x = 4.92$$

The tip was $4.92. (*Note:* In reality, the customer would probably round the tip up to $5.00.)

Solving Commission Problems

A **commission** is a sum of money paid to an employee for selling goods or services. The **commission rate** is a percent of the **total sales.** The commission is the commission rate times the total sales.

Here is an example.

Julie works at a department store that pays a commission rate of 6% to employees for sales. Yesterday, Julie's total sales were $540. What commission did she earn for her sales yesterday?

The commission is 6% of $540.

Let x = 6% of $540.

List the elements for the percent proportion (omitting units for convenience).

$$r = 6$$

$$\text{part} = ? = x$$

$$\text{whole} = 540$$

Plug into the percent proportion.

$$\frac{r}{100} = \frac{\text{part}}{\text{whole}}$$

$$\frac{6}{100} = \frac{x}{540}$$

$$\frac{6 \div 2}{100 \div 2} = \frac{x}{540}$$

$$\frac{3}{50} = \frac{x}{540}$$

Solve the proportion.

$$\frac{3}{50} = \frac{x}{540}$$

Find the cross products.

$$3 \cdot 540 = 50 \cdot x$$

Then solve for x.

$$1,620 = 50x$$

$$50x = 1,620$$

$$\frac{\cancel{50}x}{\cancel{50}} = \frac{1,620}{50}$$

$$x = 1,620 \div 50$$

$$x = 32.40$$

Julie's commission is $32.40.

☞ Try These

1. The commission rate is 7%. What commission is earned on sales of $322?

2. The commission rate is 9%. What commission is earned on sales of $148?

Solutions

1. The commission is 7% of $322.

    Let x = 7% of $322.

    List the elements for the percent proportion (omitting units for convenience).

    $$r = 7$$

    $$\text{part} = ? = x$$

    $$\text{whole} = 322$$

Plug into the percent proportion.

$$\frac{r}{100} = \frac{\text{part}}{\text{whole}}$$
$$\frac{7}{100} = \frac{x}{322}$$

Solve the proportion.

$$\frac{7}{100} = \frac{x}{322}$$

Find the cross products.

$$7 \cdot 322 = 100 \cdot x$$

Then solve for x.

$$2,254 = 100x$$
$$100x = 2,254$$
$$\frac{\cancel{100}x}{\cancel{100}} = \frac{2,254}{100}$$
$$x = 2,254 \div 100$$
$$x = 22.54$$

The commission is $22.54.

2. The commission is 9% of $148.

Let x = 9% of $148.

List the elements for the percent proportion (omitting units for convenience).

$$r = 9$$
$$\text{part} = ? = x$$
$$\text{whole} = 148$$

Plug into the percent proportion.

$$\frac{r}{100} = \frac{\text{part}}{\text{whole}}$$
$$\frac{9}{100} = \frac{x}{148}$$

Solve the proportion.

$$\frac{9}{100} = \frac{x}{148}$$

Find the cross products.

$$9 \cdot 148 = 100 \cdot x$$

Then solve for x.

$$1,332 = 100x$$
$$100x = 1,332$$
$$\frac{\cancel{100}x}{\cancel{100}} = \frac{1,332}{100}$$
$$x = 1,332 \div 100$$
$$x = 13.32$$

The commission is $13.32.

Solving Simple Interest Problems

Simple interest is money you earn on deposits or that you pay on a loan. The formula for simple interest is $I = PRT$, where I is the interest earned or owed, P is the amount deposited or borrowed, R is the interest rate per time period, and T is the number of time periods.

Here is an example.

What is the simple interest on $400 for 1 year at 1% per year?

$$I = ?, P = \$400, R = 1\%, \text{ and } T = 1 \text{ year}$$

Plug into the simple interest formula (omitting units for convenience).

$$I = PRT$$
$$I = (400)(1\%)(1)$$
$$I = (400)(1\%)$$

From this equation, list the elements for the percent proportion.

$$r = 1$$
$$\text{part} = ? = I$$
$$\text{whole} = 400$$

Plug into the percent proportion.

$$\frac{r}{100} = \frac{\text{part}}{\text{whole}}$$
$$\frac{1}{100} = \frac{I}{400}$$

Solve the proportion.

$$\frac{1}{100} = \frac{I}{400}$$

Find the cross products.

$$1 \cdot 400 = 100 \cdot I$$

Then solve for I.

$$400 = 100I$$
$$100I = 400$$
$$\frac{\cancel{100}I}{\cancel{100}} = \frac{400}{100}$$
$$I = 4$$

The simple interest is $4.

☞ Try These

1. Jamie borrowed $5,000 for 1 year at 12% per year. What is the simple interest owed?
2. Danila invested $3,500 for 1 year at 2.5% per year. What is the simple interest earned?

Solutions

1. $I = ?$, $P = \$5,000$, $R = 12\%$, and $T = 1$ year

   Plug into the simple interest formula (omitting units for convenience).

$$I = PRT$$
$$I = (5,000)(12\%)(1)$$
$$I = (5,000)(12\%)$$

From this equation, list the elements for the percent proportion.

$$r = 12$$
$$\text{part} = ? = I$$
$$\text{whole} = 5,000$$

Plug into the percent proportion.

$$\frac{r}{100} = \frac{\text{part}}{\text{whole}}$$
$$\frac{12}{100} = \frac{I}{5,000}$$
$$\frac{12 \div 4}{100 \div 4} = \frac{I}{5,000}$$
$$\frac{3}{25} = \frac{I}{5,000}$$

Solve the proportion.

$$\frac{3}{25} = \frac{I}{5,000}$$

Find the cross products.

$$3 \cdot 5,000 = 25 \cdot I$$

Then solve for I.

$$15,000 = 25I$$
$$25I = 15,000$$
$$\frac{25I}{25} = \frac{15,000}{25}$$
$$I = 600$$

Jamie owes $600 in simple interest.

2. $I = ?$, $P = \$3,500$, $R = 2.5\%$, and $T = 1$ year

Plug into the simple interest formula (omitting units for convenience).

$$I = PRT$$
$$I = (3,500)(2.5\%)(1)$$
$$I = (3,500)(2.5\%)$$

From this equation, list the elements for the percent proportion.

$$r = 2.5$$
$$\text{part} = ? = I$$
$$\text{whole} = 3,500$$

Plug into the percent proportion.

$$\frac{r}{100} = \frac{\text{part}}{\text{whole}}$$
$$\frac{2.5}{100} = \frac{I}{3,500}$$

Solve the proportion.

$$\frac{2.5}{100} = \frac{I}{3,500}$$

Find the cross products.

$$2.5 \cdot 3,500 = 100 \cdot I$$

Then solve for I.

$$8,750 = 100I$$
$$100I = 8,750$$
$$\frac{\cancel{100}I}{\cancel{100}} = \frac{8,750}{100}$$
$$I = 87.50$$

Danila earned \$87.50 in simple interest.

Solving Percent Change and Percent Error Problems

Percent change is the percent gain or loss in value. A percent gain in value is a **percent increase.** A percent loss in value is a **percent decrease.**

Tip: Even though a percent change can be an increase or decrease, it is <u>never</u> negative.

Calculate percent change using three steps. First, find the absolute value of the difference between the new and old values. Next, divide the difference by the old value. Then multiply the resulting decimal by 100%. Here is the formula.

$$\text{Percent Change (Increase or Decrease)} = \frac{|\text{New Value} - \text{Old Value}|}{\text{Old Value}} \times 100\%$$

Tip: Always divide by the value that (time-wise) occurred first.

Here is an example.

Pencils were reduced from \$2.50 a dozen to \$2.20 a dozen. What was the percent decrease in price?

The old price is \$2.50. The new price is \$2.20. Plug into the formula (omitting units for convenience).

$$\text{Percent Decrease} = \frac{|\text{New Value} - \text{Old Value}|}{\text{Old Value}} \times 100\%$$
$$= \frac{|2.20 - 2.50|}{2.50} \times 100\% = \frac{|-0.30|}{2.50} \times 100\% = \frac{0.30}{2.50} \times 100\% = 0.12 \times 100\% = 12\%$$

The price of the pencils decreased by 12%.

Percent error is a way of conveying the magnitude of error in a measurement (or estimate). Calculate percent error using three steps. First, find the absolute value of the difference between the actual measurement (or estimate) and the correct (or accepted) measurement. Next, divide the difference by the correct measurement. Then multiply the resulting decimal by 100%. Here is the formula.

$$\text{Percent Error} = \frac{|\text{Actual or Estimated Measurement} - \text{Correct Measurement}|}{\text{Correct Measurement}} \times 100\%$$

Tip: Percent error is <u>never</u> negative.

Here is an example.

> Using a protractor, a student measured the sum of the measures of the angles of a triangle. The student's sum was 178.2°. What is the percent error of the student's measurement?

The actual measurement is 178.2°. The correct measurement is 180°. Plug into the formula (omitting units for convenience).

$$\text{Percent Error} = \frac{|\text{Actual Measurement} - \text{Correct Measurement}|}{\text{Correct Measurement}} \times 100\%$$

$$= \frac{|178.2 - 180|}{180} \times 100\% = \frac{|-1.8|}{180} \times 100\% = \frac{1.8}{180} \times 100\% = 0.01 \times 100\% = 1\%$$

The percent error is 1%.

☞ Try These

1. The price of a bracelet increased from $410.00 to $524.80. What was the percent increase in the price of the bracelet?

2. A smart phone is marked down from $130.00 to $98.80. What is the percent decrease in the price of the phone?

3. A student estimates there are 450 students in the auditorium. There are 480 students in the auditorium. What is the student's percent error?

Solutions

1. The old price is $410.00. The new price is $524.80. Plug into the formula (omitting units for convenience).

$$\text{Percent Increase} = \frac{|\text{New Value} - \text{Old Value}|}{\text{Old Value}} \times 100\%$$

$$= \frac{|524.80 - 410.00|}{410.00} \times 100\% = \frac{|114.80|}{410.00} \times 100\% = \frac{114.80}{410.00} \times 100\% = 0.28 \times 100\% = 28\%$$

The price of the bracelet increased by 28%.

2. The old price is $130.00. The new price is $98.80. Plug into the formula (omitting units for convenience).

$$\text{Percent Decrease} = \frac{|\text{New Value} - \text{Old Value}|}{\text{Old Value}} \times 100\%$$

$$= \frac{|98.80 - 130.00|}{130.00} \times 100\% = \frac{|-31.20|}{130.00} \times 100\% = \frac{31.20}{130.00} \times 100\% = 0.24 \times 100\% = 24\%$$

The price of the phone decreased by 24%.

3. The student's estimate is 450. The correct number is 480. Plug into the formula (omitting units for convenience).

$$\text{Percent Error} = \frac{|\text{Estimate} - \text{Correct Number}|}{\text{Correct Number}} \times 100\%$$

$$= \frac{|450 - 480|}{480} \times 100\% = \frac{|-30|}{480} \times 100\% = \frac{30}{480} \times 100\% = 0.0625 \times 100\% = 6.25\%$$

The student's percent error is 6.25%.

2. The Number System

In this chapter, you will deepen your previous understanding of rational numbers. You will extend and apply your knowledge of operations with rational numbers and their properties and solve mathematical and real-world problems involving rational numbers.

Revisiting Your Previous Understanding of Rational Numbers

The **rational numbers** are all the numbers that can be written in the form $\frac{a}{b}$, where a and b are integers and b

is not zero. The rational numbers include zero and all the numbers that can be written as positive or negative fractions. They are the numbers you are familiar with from school and from your everyday experiences with numbers.

The rational numbers include whole numbers and integers.

Here are examples.

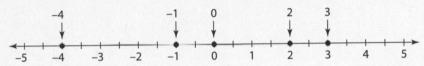

The rational numbers include positive and negative fractions.

Here are examples.

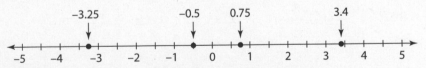

The rational numbers include positive and negative decimals.

Here are examples.

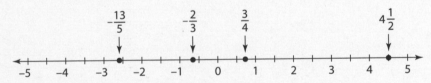

The rational numbers include positive and negative percents.

Here are examples.

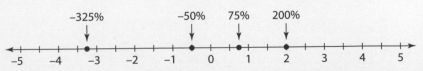

Every rational number has an opposite. If a rational number is positive, its opposite is negative. If a rational number is negative, its opposite is positive. For instance, the numbers 4 and –4 are opposites. The numbers $\frac{3}{4}$ and $-\frac{3}{4}$ are opposites. The numbers –3.25 and 3.25 are opposites. The numbers 3.4 and –3.4 are opposites. The numbers 0.5 and –0.5 are opposites. The numbers 75% and –75% are opposites. The number 0 is its own opposite. A number and its opposite are the same distance from zero on the number line.

Understanding Fractions, Decimals, and Percents as Rational Numbers

(CCSS.Math.Content.7.NS.A.2.D)

You can express rational numbers as fractions, decimals, or percents.

Writing Fractions as Equivalent Decimals

When a rational number is expressed as a fraction, $\frac{n}{d}$, it has a numerator, n, and a denominator, d. But it is important for you to realize that even though it takes two numerical components—the numerator and denominator—to make a fraction, the fraction itself is just <u>one</u> number. Specifically, it is a rational number.

For instance, $\frac{3}{4}$ is a rational number that lies between 0 and 1 on the number line, as shown here.

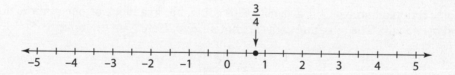

You can obtain the equivalent decimal representation of a fraction, such as $\frac{3}{4}$, by performing the indicated division. (*Tip:* Remember, $\frac{3}{4} = 3 \div 4$.) You divide the numerator by the denominator. Insert a decimal point in the numerator and zeros to the right of the decimal point to complete the division.

$$
\begin{array}{r}
0.75 \\
4\overline{)\,3.00} \\
-28 \\
\hline
20 \\
-20 \\
\hline
0
\end{array}
$$

Tip: To remember the denominator is the divisor, notice both of these words begin with the letter *d*. A visual way to remember is to imagine the fraction as a cowhand riding a horse: $\dfrac{\text{cowhand (numerator)}}{\text{horse (denominator)}}$. The bunkhouse, where the cowhand sleeps, is the long division symbol ($\overline{)}$). The horse stays outside when the cowhand goes into the bunkhouse: $\text{denominator (horse)} \overline{)\,\text{numerator (cowhand)}}^{\ \text{decimal representation}}$.

The fraction $\dfrac{3}{4}$ and the decimal 0.75 are different representations of the same rational number. They are both located at the same location on the number line.

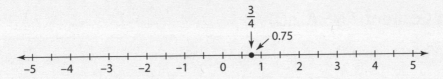

If the fraction is a negative number, perform the division without the negative sign, and then attach the negative sign to the decimal representation. For example, $-\dfrac{3}{4} = -0.75$.

It is important that you know the decimal equivalent of a rational number either **terminates** in 0s or eventually **repeats.** In the case of $\dfrac{3}{4}$, you need to insert only two zeros after the decimal point for the division to finally reach a zero remainder. Inserting additional zeros would lead to repeated 0s to the right of 0.75 (like this: 0.75000…). You say that the decimal representation of $\dfrac{3}{4}$ **terminates** in 0s.

However, for some rational numbers, the decimal keeps going, but in a block of one or more digits that repeats over and over again. The repeating digits are not all zero. Here is an example.

$$\frac{2}{3} = 3\overline{)\begin{array}{l} 0.666... \\ 2.000... \end{array}}$$
$$\begin{array}{r} -18 \\ \hline 20 \\ -18 \\ \hline 20 \\ -18 \\ \hline \vdots \end{array}$$

No matter how long you continue to add zeros and divide, the 6s in the quotient continue without end. You say that the decimal representation of $\dfrac{2}{3}$ **repeats.** You can put a bar over the repeating digit (or digits when more than one digit repeats) to indicate the repetition. Thus, $\dfrac{2}{3} = 0.\overline{6}$. Or you can stop the division at some point and write the remainder as a fraction whose denominator is the divisor. For example,

$$\frac{2}{3} = 3\overline{)\,2.00\,} = 0.66\frac{2}{3}$$

with the long division showing:
$$0.66$$
$$-18$$
$$20$$
$$-18$$
$$2$$

Either form is correct. That is, $\frac{2}{3} = 0.\overline{6} = 0.66\frac{2}{3}$.

> **Tip:** It is incorrect to write $\frac{2}{3} = 0.6$ or $\frac{2}{3} = 0.66$. Still, when decimals repeat, they are usually rounded to a specified degree of accuracy. For instance, $\frac{2}{3}$ does not equal 0.67, but $\frac{2}{3} = 0.666\ldots$ is approximately 0.67 when *rounded* to 2 decimal places.

☞ Try These

1. Fill in the blank(s).

   (a) Even though it takes two numerical components—the numerator and denominator—to make a fraction, the fraction itself is just _____ number.

   (b) You can obtain the equivalent decimal representation of a fraction by dividing the _____ by the _____.

2. Express the fraction in equivalent decimal form.

   (a) $\frac{1}{2}$

   (b) $\frac{1}{4}$

   (c) $-\frac{3}{5}$

   (d) $\frac{5}{8}$

   (e) $\frac{7}{4}$

   (f) $\frac{1}{3}$

   (g) $-\frac{7}{2}$

Solutions

1. **(a)** one

   (b) numerator; denominator

2. **(a)** 0.5

   (b) 0.25

   (c) –0.6

   (d) 0.625

   (e) 1.75

   (f) $0.\overline{3}$ or $0.33\frac{1}{3}$

   (g) –3.5

Writing Percents as Equivalent Fractions and Decimals

Percents are rational numbers. **Percent** means "per hundred." The percent sign is a short way of writing $\frac{1}{100}$ or 0.01. When you see a percent sign, you can substitute multiplying by $\frac{1}{100}$ or by 0.01 for the percent sign.

A percent is a way of writing fractions whose denominators are 100. Thus, $23\% = 23 \cdot \frac{1}{100} = \frac{23}{100}$. Think of percents as special ways to write ordinary decimals or fractions. For instance, 75% is a special way to write $\frac{3}{4}$ because $75\% = \frac{75}{100} = \frac{75 \div 25}{100 \div 25} = \frac{3}{4}$. The fraction $\frac{3}{4}$ and 75% are different representations of the same rational number. They are all found at the same location on the number line.

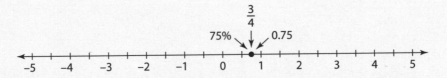

Also, 100% is just a special way to write the number 1, because $100\% = 100 \cdot \frac{1}{100} = \frac{100}{100} = 1$. If you have 100% of something, you have all of it. A percent that is less than 100% is less than 1. When you have less than 100% of something, you have less than the whole thing. A percent that is greater than 100% is greater than 1. When you have more than 100% of something, you have more than the whole thing.

You can write a percent as an equivalent fraction by writing the number in front of the percent sign as the numerator of a fraction in which the denominator is 100. The resulting fraction may then be reduced, if possible. Here are examples.

$$5\% = \frac{5}{100} = \frac{5 \div 5}{100 \div 5} = \frac{1}{20}$$

$$60\% = \frac{60}{100} = \frac{60 \div 20}{100 \div 20} = \frac{3}{5}$$

$$125\% = \frac{125}{100} = \frac{125 \div 25}{100 \div 25} = \frac{5}{4} = 1\frac{1}{4}$$

$$33\frac{1}{3}\% = \frac{33\frac{1}{3}}{100} = \frac{\frac{100}{3}}{100} = \frac{\left(\frac{100}{\cancel{3}_1}\right) \cdot \cancel{3}^1}{(100) \cdot 3} = \frac{\frac{100}{1}}{300} = \frac{100}{300} = \frac{1}{3}$$

You can write a percent as an equivalent decimal number by multiplying the number in front of the percent sign by 0.01.

Here are examples.

25% = 25(0.01) = 0.25

8% = 8(0.01) = 0.08

12.5% = 12.5(0.01) = 0.125

200% = 200(0.01) = 2

Tip: Remember, when you see a percent sign, you can substitute multiplying by $\frac{1}{100}$ or by 0.01 for the percent sign.

☞ Try These

1. Fill in the blank(s).

   (a) When you see a percent sign, you can substitute multiplying by _____ or by _____ for the percent sign.

   (b) A percent is a way of writing fractions whose denominators are _____.

   (c) If you have 100% of something, you have _____ of it.

   (d) A percent can be written as an equivalent fraction by writing the number in front of the percent sign as the numerator of a fraction in which the denominator is _____.

   (e) A percent can be written as an equivalent decimal number by multiplying the number in front of the percent sign by _____.

2. Express the percent as an equivalent fraction.

   (a) 10%

   (b) $12\frac{1}{2}\%$

   (c) 20%

   (d) 25%

   (e) 50%

   (f) 90%

   (g) 350%

3. Express the percent as an equivalent decimal.

    (a) 1%

    (b) 5%

    (c) 20%

    (d) 25%

    (e) 50%

    (f) 90%

    (g) 350%

Solutions

1. **(a)** $\dfrac{1}{100}$; 0.01

    (b) 100

    (c) all

    (d) 100

    (e) 0.01

2. **(a)** $10\% = \dfrac{10}{100} = \dfrac{1}{10}$

    (b) $12\dfrac{1}{2}\% = \dfrac{12\dfrac{1}{2}}{100} = \dfrac{\dfrac{25}{2}}{100} = \dfrac{\left(\dfrac{25}{\cancel{2}_1}\right)\cdot\cancel{2}^1}{100\cdot 2} = \dfrac{25}{200} = \dfrac{25 \div 25}{200 \div 25} = \dfrac{1}{8}$

    (c) $20\% = \dfrac{20}{100} = \dfrac{20 \div 20}{100 \div 20} = \dfrac{1}{5}$

    (d) $25\% = \dfrac{25}{100} = \dfrac{25 \div 25}{100 \div 25} = \dfrac{1}{4}$

    (e) $50\% = \dfrac{50}{100} = \dfrac{50 \div 50}{100 \div 50} = \dfrac{1}{2}$

    (f) $90\% = \dfrac{90}{100} = \dfrac{90 \div 10}{100 \div 10} = \dfrac{9}{10}$

    (g) $350\% = \dfrac{350}{100} = \dfrac{350 \div 50}{100 \div 50} = \dfrac{7}{2}$ or $3\dfrac{1}{2}$

3. **(a)** 1% = 1(0.01) = 0.01

    (b) 5% = 5(0.01) = 0.05

    (c) 20% = 20(0.01) = 0.20 = 0.2

    (d) 25% = 25(0.01) = 0.25

    (e) 50% = 50(0.01) = 0.50 = 0.5

    (f) 90% = 90(0.01) = 0.90 = 0.9

    (g) 350% = 350(0.01) = 3.50 = 3.5

Adding and Subtracting Rational Numbers

(CCSS.Math.Content.7.NS.A.1.A, CCSS.Math.Content.7.NS.A.1.B, CCSS.Math.Content.7.NS.A.1.C, CCSS.Math.Content.7.NS.A.1.D, CCSS.Math.Content.7.NS.A.3)

Rational numbers also are called **signed numbers** because these numbers may be positive, negative, or zero. From your work with numbers in earlier grades, you already know how to add and subtract positive numbers and zero. To do these operations with all signed numbers, you simply use the absolute values of the numbers and follow five simple rules.

Tip: The absolute value of a specific rational number is the value of the number with no sign attached.

Rule 1: Zero Plus a Number Is the Number.

The sum of a number and zero is the number.

Here are examples.

$$-10 + 0 = -10$$
$$0 + 25 = 25$$
$$-\frac{3}{4} + 0 = -\frac{3}{4}$$
$$0 + 0.875 = 0.875$$

Rule 2: A Number Plus Its Opposite Is Zero.

The sum of a number and its opposite is zero.

Here is an example.

$$5 + -5 = 0$$

To illustrate $5 + -5 = 0$ on the number line, start at zero, move a distance of 5 units in the positive direction, then move a distance of 5 units in the negative direction, giving a sum of 0.

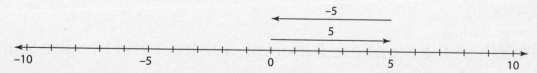

Here are additional examples.

$0 + 0 = 0$ (**Remember:** The number 0 is its own opposite.)
$$-\frac{4}{9} + \frac{4}{9} = 0$$
$$3.58 + -3.58 = 0$$

Rule 3: When the Signs Are the Same, Add and Use the Same Sign.

To add two numbers that have the same sign, add their absolute values and give the sum the same sign.

Here is a step-by-step example.

Compute: $-3 + -5$

Step 1. Check the signs.

The signs are both negative.

Step 2. Add the absolute values of the two numbers.

$3 + 5 = 8$

Step 3. Make the sum negative because both numbers are negative.

$-3 + -5 = -8$

Does this answer make sense to you? Look at the number-line diagram.

To illustrate $-3 + -5 = -8$ on the number line, start at zero, move a distance of 3 units in the negative direction, then move a distance of 5 *more* units in the negative direction, giving a sum of -8.

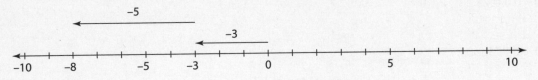

Here are additional examples.

$25 + 15 = 40$

$-\dfrac{1}{5} + -\dfrac{3}{5} = -\dfrac{4}{5}$

$\dfrac{1}{2} + \dfrac{3}{2} = \dfrac{4}{2} = 2$

$-6.135 + -9.4 = -15.535$

$8.5 + 4.5 = 13$

Rule 4: When the Signs Are Different, Subtract and Use the Sign of the Larger Magnitude.

To add two numbers that have different signs, subtract the lesser absolute value from the greater absolute value and give the sum the sign of the number with the greater absolute value.

Here is a step-by-step example.

Compute: $2 + -7$

Step 1. Check the signs.

The signs are different.

Step 2. Subtract the lesser absolute value from the greater absolute value.

$7 - 2 = 5$

Step 3. Make the sum negative because the absolute value of –7 is greater than the absolute value of 2.

$2 + -7 = -5$

To illustrate $2 + -7 = -5$ on a number line, start at zero, move a distance of 2 units in the positive direction, then move a distance of 7 units in the negative (opposite) direction, giving a sum of –5.

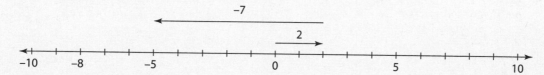

Here are additional examples.

$$-20 + 35 = 15$$
$$20 + -35 = -15$$
$$\frac{7}{8} + -\frac{3}{8} = \frac{4}{8} = \frac{1}{2}$$
$$-\frac{7}{8} + \frac{3}{8} = -\frac{4}{8} = -\frac{1}{2}$$
$$23.49 + -85.95 = -62.46$$
$$-23.49 + 85.95 = 62.46$$

As you can see, addition of signed numbers is different from the addition you've done in the past. For one thing, you don't always "add" to get the sum. In fact, if the signs are different, you subtract to find the sum. How does this make sense? Keep in mind that the numbers you worked with in arithmetic were amounts only—they had no signs. A rational number has an amount *and* a sign (except for zero). The amount is its **magnitude** or **size**. The **sign** adds a direction to the number. The number 5 is 5 units in the positive direction. The number –5 is 5 units in the negative direction. When you add signed numbers, you have to take into account both the magnitude and direction of the number.

Before going on to subtraction, it is important that you distinguish a number's negative sign from the minus sign. They look alike, but they have different purposes. A number's negative sign is part of the number to which it is attached. Its purpose is to inform you that the number is a negative number and lies to the left of zero on the number line. The minus sign has an entirely different purpose. It is used to indicate subtraction. It will always have a number on its immediate left.

Tip: "On its immediate left" means on the left of it with no number or other symbol in between.

Rule 5: To Subtract, Add the Opposite.

To subtract a number, add its opposite.

The minus sign reverses the direction of the number that follows it. Think: *"Keep, change, change,"* meaning "Keep the first number, <u>change</u> minus to plus, and <u>change</u> the sign of the second number."

Here are examples.

Tip: Recite "Keep, change, change" as you review the examples.

$$10 - 16 = 10 + {-16} = -6$$
$$16 - 10 = 16 + {-10} = 6$$
$$-5 - 20 = -5 + {-20} = -25$$
$$2 - {-6} = 2 + 6 = 8$$
$$-18 - {-4} = -18 + 4 = -14$$
$$\frac{1}{5} - \left(-\frac{4}{5}\right) = \frac{1}{5} + \frac{4}{5} = \frac{5}{5} = 1$$
$$-7.93 - 19.34 = -7.93 + {-19.34} = -27.27$$

The **distance** between any two numbers is the absolute value of their difference. Using symbols, the distance between p and q is $|p - q|$.

Tip: The absolute value bars are needed because distance is never negative.

Here are examples with number-line diagrams.

Find the distance between –8 and 5.

The distance is $|{-8} - 5| = |{-8} + {-5}| = |{-13}| = 13$.

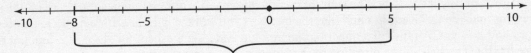

Distance between –8 and 5 is 13 units

Find the distance between 5 and –8.

The distance is $|5 - {-8}| = |5 + 8| = |13| = 13$.

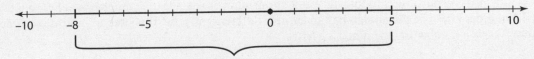

Distance between 5 and –8 is 13 units

Find the distance between –8 and –5.

The distance is |–8 – –5| = |–8 + 5| = |–3| = 3.

Distance between –8 and –5 is 3 units

Here are additional examples.

Find the distance between $\frac{3}{4}$ mile and $\frac{1}{2}$ mile.

Omitting units, $\left|\frac{3}{4} - \frac{1}{2}\right| = \left|\frac{3}{4} + -\frac{1}{2}\right| = \left|\frac{3}{4} + -\frac{2}{4}\right| = \left|\frac{1}{4}\right| = \frac{1}{4}$.

The distance is $\frac{1}{4}$ mile.

Find the vertical distance between an elevation of –908 feet and an elevation of –420 feet.

Omitting units, |–908 – –420| = |–908 + 420| = |–488| = 488. The vertical distance is 488 feet.

Here is a summary of the rules in this section.

Rule 1: Zero plus a number is the number.

Rule 2: A number plus its opposite is zero.

Rule 3: When the signs are the same, add and use the same sign.

Rule 4: When the signs are different, subtract and use the sign of the larger magnitude.

Rule 5: To subtract, add the opposite.

☞ Try These

1. Fill in the blank(s).

   (a) The sum of a number and zero is the _____.

   (b) A number plus its opposite is _____.

   (c) The sum of two positive numbers is _____, and the sum of two negative numbers is _____.

   (d) The sum of a positive and a negative number has the same sign as the number with the _____ (smaller, greater) magnitude.

   (e) To subtract a number, add its _____.

2. Compute the sum.

   (a) $-6 + -18$

   (b) $-16 + 80$

   (c) $105.64 + -235$

   (d) $\dfrac{2}{3} + -\dfrac{3}{4}$

   (e) $30.1 + 9.58$

   (f) $-10.5 + -65.82$

3. Compute the difference.

   (a) $100 - 45$

   (b) $45 - 100$

   (c) $100 - -45$

   (d) $-100 - -45$

   (e) $2\dfrac{3}{4} - 3\dfrac{1}{4}$

   (f) $-85.99 - 0.01$

4. Find the distance between the two numbers.

   (a) -102 and -500

   (b) -102 and 500

   (c) -500 and 102

   (d) $-\dfrac{1}{8}$ and $\dfrac{5}{8}$

   (e) 934.125 and 128.64

5. Model the problem using rational numbers, and then solve.

   (a) At 9:00 p.m. the thermometer reading was 8°F. By 2:00 a.m., the temperature had dropped 10 degrees. What was the thermometer reading at 2:00 a.m.?

   (b) Emily has a balance of $525 in her savings account. She withdraws $140. Assume there are no other transactions. What is her balance after the withdrawal?

   (c) Harper wrote a $50.00 check at a department store. She didn't realize that she had $0.00 in her checking account. The bank paid the $50.00 check, but charged Harper a fee of $35 for the overdraft to her account. (*Tip:* An **overdraft** occurs when the account balance goes below zero.) Harper's overdraft of $50 plus the $35 fee resulted in an account balance $–85.00. Suppose Harper deposits $200 into her checking account. What is her new balance if no other transactions occur?

   (d) Anton devised a number-line diagram to show horizontal distance relative to his home. His home corresponds to 0. A distance due east is labeled as positive, and a distance due west is labeled as negative. Suppose Anton rides his bike 9 kilometers, then goes –12 kilometers, and stops. What is Anton's location on the number-line diagram? Describe Anton's location in words.

   (e) Find the distance between $\dfrac{7}{8}$ mile and $\dfrac{1}{4}$ mile.

   (f) Find the vertical distance between an elevation of –516 feet and an elevation of –324 feet.

Solutions

1. (a) number
   (b) zero
   (c) positive; negative
   (d) greater
   (e) opposite

2. (a) $-6 + -18 = -24$
   (b) $-16 + 80 = 64$
   (c) $105.64 + -235 = 129.36$
   (d) $\dfrac{2}{3} + -\dfrac{3}{4} = \dfrac{8}{12} + -\dfrac{9}{12} = -\dfrac{1}{12}$
   (e) $30.1 + 9.58 = 39.68$
   (f) $-10.5 + -65.82 = -76.32$

3. (a) $100 - 45 = 100 + -45 = 55$
   (b) $45 - 100 = 45 + -100 = -55$
   (c) $100 - -45 = 100 + 45 = 145$
   (d) $-100 - -45 = -100 + 45 = -55$
   (e) $2\dfrac{3}{4} - 3\dfrac{1}{4} = \dfrac{11}{4} + -\dfrac{13}{4} = -\dfrac{2}{4} = -\dfrac{1}{2}$
   (f) $-85.99 - 0.01 = -85.99 + -0.01 = -86.00$

4. (a) $|-102 - -500| = |-102 + 500| = |398| = 398$
   (b) $|-102 - 500| = |-102 + -500| = |-602| = 602$
   (c) $|-500 - 102| = |-500 + -102| = |-602| = 602$
   (d) $\left|-\dfrac{1}{8} - \dfrac{5}{8}\right| = \left|-\dfrac{1}{8} + -\dfrac{5}{8}\right| = \left|-\dfrac{6}{8}\right| = \dfrac{6}{8} = \dfrac{3}{4}$
   (e) $|934.125 - 128.64| = |934.125 + -128.64| = |805.485| = 805.485$

5. (a) $8°F - 10°F = 8°F + -10°F = -2°$. The thermometer reading at 2:00 a.m. was $-2°$.
   (b) $\$525 - \$140 = \$525 + -\$140 = \$385$. Emily's balance after the withdrawal is $385.
   (c) $\$-85.00 + \$200.00 = \$115.00$. Harper's new balance is $115.
   (d) $9 \text{ km} + -12 \text{ km} = -3 \text{ km}$. Anton's location on the number-line diagram is -3 km. Anton is 3 kilometers due west of home.
   (e) Omitting units, $\left|\dfrac{7}{8} - \dfrac{1}{4}\right| = \left|\dfrac{7}{8} + -\dfrac{1}{4}\right| = \left|\dfrac{7}{8} + -\dfrac{2}{8}\right| = \left|\dfrac{5}{8}\right| = \dfrac{5}{8}$.

   The distance is $\dfrac{5}{8}$ mile.

   (f) Omitting units, $|-516 - -324| = |-516 + 324| = |-192| = 192$.

   The vertical distance is 192 feet.

Multiplying and Dividing Rational Numbers

(CCSS.Math.Content.7.NS.A.2.A, CCSS.Math.Content.7.NS.A.2.B, CCSS.Math.Content.7.NS.A.2.C, CCSS.Math.Content.7.NS.A.3)

You already know how to multiply and divide positive numbers and zero. To do these operations with all signed numbers, you simply use the absolute values of the numbers and follow five simple rules.

Rule 1: Zero Times Any Number Is Zero.

The product of 0 and any number is 0.

Here are examples.

$$(-75)(0) = 0$$

$$0 \cdot \frac{1}{3} = 0$$

$$(0)(-4.59) = 0$$

Rule 2: The Product of Two Numbers with the Same Signs Is Positive.

To multiply two numbers that have the same sign, multiply their absolute values and keep the product positive.

Here is a step-by-step example.

Compute: $(-4)(-5)$

Step 1. Check the signs.

The signs are both negative.

Step 2. Multiply the absolute values of the two numbers.

$4 \cdot 5 = 20$

Step 3. Keep the product positive.

$(-4)(-5) = 20$

Here are additional examples.

$$(-10)(-3) = 30$$

$$-\frac{1}{3} \cdot -\frac{2}{5} = \frac{2}{15}$$

$$(-23.8)(-9.1) = 216.58$$

Rule 3: The Product of Two Numbers with Different Signs Is Negative.

To multiply two numbers that have opposite signs, multiply their absolute values and make the product negative.

Here is a step-by-step example.

Compute: $(-7)(6)$

Step 1. Check the signs.

The signs are different.

Step 2. Multiply the absolute values of the two numbers.

$7 \cdot 6 = 42$

Step 3. Make the product negative.

$(-7)(6) = -42$

Here are additional examples.

$(-10)(3) = -30$

$\dfrac{1}{3} \cdot -\dfrac{2}{5} = -\dfrac{2}{15}$

$(-23.8)(9.1) = -216.58$

Using symbols, the sign rules for multiplication are as follows:

$+ \cdot + = +$

$- \cdot - = +$

$+ \cdot - = -$

$- \cdot + = -$

Tip: Read "$- \cdot - = +$" as "negative times negative equals positive," and read "$- \cdot + = -$" as "negative times positive equals negative."

Here are examples.

$(-20)(-5) = 100$ Because $(20)(5) = 100$ and $- \cdot - = +$.

$(-20)(5) = -100$ Because $(20)(5) = 100$ and $- \cdot + = -$.

$(20)(5) = 100$ Because $(20)(5) = 100$ and $+ \cdot + = +$.

$(20)(-5) = -100$ Because $(20)(5) = 100$ and $+ \cdot - = -$.

$\dfrac{3}{4} \cdot -\dfrac{5}{8} = -\dfrac{15}{32}$ Because $\dfrac{3}{4} \cdot \dfrac{5}{8} = \dfrac{15}{32}$ and $+ \cdot - = -$.

$(-45.2)(-7.5) = 339$ Because $(45.2)(7.5) = 339$ and $- \cdot - = +$.

Before going on to division, consider the following definition: If the product of two numbers is 1, the numbers are **reciprocals** of each other.

Tip: A number and its reciprocal always have the same sign.

Here are examples.

2 and $\dfrac{1}{2}$ are reciprocals because $2 \cdot \dfrac{1}{2} = 1$

-3 and $-\dfrac{1}{3}$ are reciprocals because $-3 \cdot -\dfrac{1}{3} = 1$

$\dfrac{3}{4}$ and $\dfrac{4}{3}$ are reciprocals because $\dfrac{3}{4} \cdot \dfrac{4}{3} = \dfrac{\cancel{3}^{1}}{\cancel{4}_{1}} \cdot \dfrac{\cancel{4}^{1}}{\cancel{3}_{1}} = \dfrac{1}{1} = 1$

-2.5 and $-\dfrac{1}{2.5}$ are reciprocals because $(-2.5)\left(-\dfrac{1}{2.5}\right) = 1$

Tip: Because zero times any number is 0, zero does not have a reciprocal.

Rule 4: To Divide by a Number, Multiply by Its Reciprocal.

This rule means that division of signed numbers follows the <u>same</u> rules as multiplication of signed numbers, except you divide the absolute values of the numbers instead of multiplying. Here are the sign rules for division in symbols.

$$\frac{+}{+} = +$$

$$\frac{-}{-} = +$$

$$\frac{+}{-} = -$$

$$\frac{-}{+} = -$$

Tip: Read "$\dfrac{-}{-} = +$" as "negative divided by negative equals positive," and read "$\dfrac{+}{-} = -$" as "positive divided by negative equals negative."

Here are examples.

$\dfrac{0}{6} = 0 \times \dfrac{1}{6} = 0$ Because 0 times any number is 0.

$-12 \div -3 = -12 \cdot -\dfrac{1}{3} = \dfrac{12}{3} = 4$ Because $\dfrac{12}{3} = 4$ and $\dfrac{-}{-} = +$.

$\dfrac{48}{-6} = 48 \cdot -\dfrac{1}{6} = -\dfrac{48}{6} = -8$ Because $\dfrac{48}{6} = 8$ and $\dfrac{+}{-} = -$.

$\dfrac{-1.03}{5.15} = -1.03 \cdot \dfrac{1}{5.15} = -\dfrac{1.03}{5.15} = -0.2$ Because $\dfrac{1.03}{5.15} = 0.2$ and $\dfrac{-}{+} = -$.

The previous examples illustrate that with integer and decimal division, it's okay to omit the step of writing the reciprocal.

Here are examples.

$$\frac{400}{-25} = -\frac{400}{25} = -16 \quad \text{Because} \quad \frac{400}{25} = 16 \text{ and } \frac{+}{-} = -.$$

$$\frac{-179.48}{-64.1} = 2.8 \quad \text{Because} \quad \frac{179.48}{64.1} = 2.8 \text{ and } \frac{-}{-} = +.$$

With fraction division, including the reciprocal step is helpful.

$$-\frac{3}{8} \div -\frac{3}{4} = -\frac{{}^{1}\cancel{3}}{{}_{2}\cancel{8}} \times -\frac{\cancel{4}^{1}}{\cancel{3}_{1}} = \frac{1}{2} \quad \text{Because} \quad \frac{3}{8} \div \frac{3}{4} = \frac{1}{2} \text{ and } \frac{-}{-} = +.$$

$$\frac{2\frac{1}{2}}{\frac{3}{8}} = \frac{5}{{}_{1}\cancel{2}} \cdot \frac{\cancel{8}^{4}}{3} = \frac{20}{3} = 6\frac{2}{3} \quad \text{Because} \quad \frac{2\frac{1}{2}}{\frac{3}{8}} = 6\frac{2}{3} \text{ and } \frac{+}{+} = +.$$

If a and b are nonzero integers, the fraction $\frac{a}{b}$ has three signs: the sign in front of the fraction, the sign of the numerator, and the sign of the denominator. You can change the signs *in pairs* without changing the fraction's value. In other words, the fraction's location on the number line stays the same. For instance, $\frac{a}{b} = -\frac{-a}{b} = -\frac{a}{-b} = \frac{-a}{-b}$ and $-\frac{a}{b} = \frac{-a}{b} = \frac{a}{-b} = -\frac{-a}{-b}$. A simple rule of thumb is a fraction with an even number of negative signs is positive, and one with an odd number of negative signs is negative.

Here are examples.

$$-\frac{-5}{6} = \frac{5}{6}$$

$$\frac{7}{-8} = -\frac{7}{8}$$

$$\frac{-12}{7} = -\frac{12}{7}$$

$$\frac{-2}{-3} = \frac{2}{3}$$

$$-\frac{-9}{-10} = -\frac{9}{10}$$

Rule 5: Division by Zero Cannot Be Done.

Division by zero is undefined because zero does not have a reciprocal. For instance, if you have $\frac{15}{0} = 15 \times (\text{zero's reciprocal})$, you are stuck. Zero's reciprocal does not exist. There is no number that multiplies by zero to give 1. Any number times zero is zero.

Here are examples.

$\dfrac{20}{0}$ is undefined.

$\dfrac{1}{2} \div 0$ is undefined.

$\dfrac{-6.25}{0}$ is undefined.

Here is a summary of the rules in this section.

> **Rule 1:** Zero times any number is zero.
>
> **Rule 2:** The product of two numbers with the same signs is positive.
>
> **Rule 3:** The product of two numbers with different signs is negative.
>
> **Rule 4:** To divide by a number, multiply by its reciprocal.
>
> **Rule 5:** Division by zero cannot be done.

☞ Try These

1. Fill in the blank(s).

   (a) The product of a number and zero is _____.

   (b) The product of two positive numbers is _____, and the product of two negative numbers is _____.

   (c) The quotient of two positive numbers is _____, and the quotient of two negative numbers is _____.

   (d) The product of a positive and a negative number is _____, and the quotient of a positive and a negative number is _____.

   (e) The product of a number and its reciprocal is _____.

   (f) The number _____ has no reciprocal.

   (g) To divide, multiply by the _____.

   (h) Zero divided by a nonzero number is _____ (zero, undefined).

   (i) Division by zero is _____ (zero, undefined).

2. Compute the product.

   (a) $(0)(95)$

   (b) $(-6)(-18)$

   (c) $(-16)(80)$

   (d) $(105.64)(-235)$

   (e) $\dfrac{2}{3} \cdot -\dfrac{3}{4}$

   (f) $(30.1)(9.58)$

   (g) $(-10.5)(-65.82)$

3. Compute the quotient.

   (a) $\dfrac{50}{-2}$

   (b) $\dfrac{-84}{-3}$

   (c) $\dfrac{-700}{1,000}$

   (d) $\dfrac{12.3}{8.2}$

   (e) $-2\dfrac{3}{4} \div -3\dfrac{1}{4}$

   (f) $\dfrac{-74.99}{-0.01}$

4. Write an equivalent positive or negative fraction.

   (a) $-\dfrac{-3}{-8}$

   (b) $\dfrac{-3}{-8}$

   (c) $\dfrac{-3}{8}$

   (d) $-\dfrac{-3}{8}$

   (e) $-\dfrac{3}{-8}$

   (f) $\dfrac{3}{-8}$

5. Model the problem using rational numbers, and then solve.

   (a) Every hour the outdoor temperature dropped 2°F. How many hours did it take for the outdoor temperature to drop a total of −18°F?

   (b) Josephine created a number-line diagram to show horizontal distance relative to her home. Her home corresponds to 0. A distance due east is labeled as positive, and a distance due west is labeled as negative. Yesterday, Josephine rode her bike −5 kilometers, and then returned home. Today, she rode three times −5 kilometers to her friend's house. What is the location of Josephine's friend's house on the number-line diagram? Describe the location in words.

   (c) How many times lower is an elevation of −420 meters compared to an elevation of −30 meters?

Solutions

1. (a) zero
    (b) positive; positive
    (c) positive; positive
    (d) negative; negative
    (e) 1
    (f) zero
    (g) reciprocal
    (h) zero
    (i) undefined

2. (a) $(0)(95) = 0$
    (b) $(-6)(-18) = 108$
    (c) $(-16)(80) = -1,280$
    (d) $(105.64)(-235) = -24,825.4$
    (e) $\dfrac{2}{3} \cdot -\dfrac{3}{4} = -\dfrac{6}{12} = -\dfrac{1}{2}$
    (f) $(30.1)(9.58) = 288.358$
    (g) $(-10.5)(-65.82) = 691.11$

3. (a) $\dfrac{50}{-2} = -25$

    (b) $\dfrac{-84}{-3} = 28$

    (c) $\dfrac{-700}{1,000} = -0.700 = -0.7$

    (d) $\dfrac{12.3}{8.2} = 1.5$

    (e) $-2\dfrac{3}{4} \div -3\dfrac{1}{4} = -\dfrac{11}{4} \div -\dfrac{13}{4} = -\dfrac{11}{{}_{1}\cancel{4}} \cdot -\dfrac{\cancel{4}^{1}}{13} = \dfrac{11}{13}$

    (f) $\dfrac{-74.99}{-0.01} = 7,499$

4. **(a)** $-\dfrac{-3}{-8} = -\dfrac{3}{8}$

   (b) $\dfrac{-3}{-8} = \dfrac{3}{8}$

   (c) $\dfrac{-3}{8} = -\dfrac{3}{8}$

   (d) $-\dfrac{-3}{8} = \dfrac{3}{8}$

   (e) $-\dfrac{3}{-8} = \dfrac{3}{8}$

   (f) $\dfrac{3}{-8} = -\dfrac{3}{8}$

5. **(a)** A drop of 2°F is –2°F. To find the number of hours, divide –18°F by –2°F per hour. Omitting units, $\dfrac{-18}{-2} = 9$. At the rate of –2°F per hour, it will take 9 hours for the outdoor temperature to drop a total of –18°F.

   (b) (3)(–5 kilometers) = –15 kilometers. Josephine's friend's house is located at –15 kilometers. The friend's house is 15 kilometers due west of Josephine's house.

   (c) Omitting units, $\dfrac{-420}{-30} = 14$. An elevation of –420 meters is 14 times lower than an elevation of 30 meters.

Understanding Properties of Operations with Rational Numbers

(CCSS.Math.Content.7.NS.A.1, CCSS.Math.Content.7.NS.A.2)

The operations of addition and multiplication with rational numbers have the following properties.

Properties of Addition

1. Commutative Property

The commutative property of addition allows you to switch the order of the numbers when you add, without changing the sum.

Here are examples.

$3 + -8 = -5$ and $-8 + 3 = -5$

$-\dfrac{3}{8} + -\dfrac{5}{8} = -\dfrac{8}{8} = -1$ and $-\dfrac{5}{8} + -\dfrac{3}{8} = -\dfrac{8}{8} = -1$

$-5.4 + 2.3 = -3.1$ and $2.3 + -5.4 = -3.1$

2. Associative Property

The associative property of addition says that when you have three numbers to add together, the final sum will be the same regardless of the way you group the numbers (two at a time) to perform the addition.

Here is an example.

Suppose you want to compute $3 + -8 + -2$. Without changing the order of the numbers, you have two ways to group the numbers for addition:

$$(3 + -8) + -2 = (-5) + -2 = -7 \text{ or } 3 + (-8 + -2) = 3 + (-10) = -7$$

Either way, -7 is the final sum.

Tip: The associative property of addition is needed when you have to add more than two numbers because you can do addition on only two numbers at a time. Thus, when you have three numbers, you must decide which two numbers you want to start with—the first two or the last two. Either way, your final answer is the same.

3. Additive Identity Property

The additive identity property guarantees that you have a rational number, namely zero, for which its sum with any rational number is the number itself.

Here are examples.

$0 + -8 = -8$ and $-8 + 0 = -8$

$\dfrac{5}{6} + 0 = \dfrac{5}{6}$ and $0 + \dfrac{5}{6} = \dfrac{5}{6}$

$-5.4 + 0 = -5.4$ and $0 + -5.4 = -5.4$

4. Additive Inverse Property

The additive inverse property guarantees that every rational number, a, has an additive inverse, $-a$, that is a rational number, which when added to the given number gives 0.

Here are examples.

$10 + -10 = 0$ and $-10 + 10 = 0$

$\dfrac{3}{4} + -\dfrac{3}{4} = 0$ and $-\dfrac{3}{4} + \dfrac{3}{4} = 0$

$-9.5 + 9.5 = 0$ and $9.5 + -9.5 = 0$

Tip: The additive inverse of a number is its opposite.

Properties of Multiplication

1. Commutative Property

The commutative property of multiplication allows you to switch the order of the numbers when you multiply, without changing the product.

Here are examples.

$3 \cdot 8 = 24$ and $8 \cdot 3 = 24$

$-\dfrac{1}{2} \cdot \dfrac{5}{6} = -\dfrac{5}{12}$ and $\dfrac{5}{6} \cdot -\dfrac{1}{2} = -\dfrac{5}{12}$

$(-5.4)(-2.3) = 12.42$ and $(-2.3)(-5.4) = 12.42$

2. Associative Property

The associative property of multiplication says that when you have three numbers to multiply together, the final product will be the same regardless of the way you group the numbers (two at a time) to perform the multiplication.

Here is an example.

Suppose you want to compute $3 \cdot -8 \cdot 5$. Without changing the order of the numbers, you have two ways to group the numbers for multiplication:

$$(3 \cdot -8) \cdot 5 = (-24)(5) = -120 \text{ or } 3 \cdot (-8 \cdot 5) = (3)(-40) = -120$$

Either way, –120 is the final product.

> **Tip: The associative property of multiplication is needed when you have to multiply more than two numbers because you can do multiplication on only two numbers at a time. Thus, when you have three numbers, you must decide which two numbers you want to start with—the first two or the last two. Either way, your final answer is the same.**

3. Multiplicative Identity Property

The multiplicative identity property guarantees that you have a rational number, namely 1, for which its product with any rational number is the number itself.

Here are examples.

$(-300)(1) = -300$ and $(1)(-300) = -300$

$\dfrac{8}{9} \cdot 1 = \dfrac{8}{9}$ and $1 \cdot \dfrac{8}{9} = \dfrac{8}{9}$

$(-2.15)(1) = -2.15$ and $(1)(-2.15) = -2.15$

4. Multiplicative Inverse Property

The multiplicative inverse property guarantees that every <u>nonzero</u> rational number, a, has a multiplicative inverse, $\dfrac{1}{a}$, that is a rational number, which when multiplied times the given number gives 1.

Tip: A number and its multiplicative inverse have the same sign.

Here are examples.

$$-4 \cdot -\frac{1}{4} = 1 \text{ and } -\frac{1}{4} \cdot -4 = 1$$

$$\frac{8}{9} \cdot \frac{9}{8} = 1 \text{ and } \frac{9}{8} \cdot \frac{8}{9} = 1$$

$$(-3.5)\left(-\frac{1}{3.5}\right) = 1 \text{ and } \left(-\frac{1}{3.5}\right)(-3.5) = 1$$

Tip: The multiplicative inverse of a number is its reciprocal.

The Distributive Property

The distributive property says that when you have a number times a sum (or a sum times a number), you can either add first and then multiply, or multiply first and then add. Either way, the final answer is the same.

Here are examples.

$3(10 + 5)$ can be computed two ways:

add first to obtain $3(10 + 5) = 3 \cdot 15 = 45$; or

multiply first to obtain $3(10 + 5) = 3 \cdot 10 + 3 \cdot 5 = 30 + 15 = 45$

Either way, the answer is 45.

$\left(\dfrac{1}{5} + \dfrac{4}{5}\right)20$ can be computed two ways:

add first to obtain $\left(\dfrac{1}{5} + \dfrac{4}{5}\right)20 = \left(\dfrac{5}{5}\right)(20) = (1)(20) = 20$; or

multiply first to obtain $\left(\dfrac{1}{5} + \dfrac{4}{5}\right)20 = \dfrac{1}{5} \cdot 20 + \dfrac{4}{5} \cdot 20 = 4 + 16 = 20$

Either way, the answer is 20.

Tip: The distributive property is the only property that involves both addition and multiplication at the same time. A common way to express the distributive property is to say *multiplication distributes over addition*.

You apply the properties along with the order of operations when you evaluate numerical expressions involving rational numbers.

1. Compute inside **Parentheses** (or other grouping symbols).

2. Do **Exponentiation** (that is, evaluate exponential expressions).

3. **Multiply** and **Divide** in the order in which they occur from left to right.

4. **Add** and **Subtract** in the order in which they occur from left to right.

Frequently, you have more than one way to perform computations. Use your own judgment to decide which way is more efficient.

Here are examples.

Evaluate $7.2 + -10 + 2.8$.

$$
\begin{aligned}
7.2 + -10 + 2.8 &= -10 + 7.2 + 2.8 && \text{By the commutative property of addition.} \\
&= -10 + (7.2 + 2.8) && \text{By the associative property of addition.} \\
&= -10 + (10.0) \\
&= 0 && \text{By the additive identity property.}
\end{aligned}
$$

Evaluate $(-200)(-9.34)\left(\dfrac{1}{2}\right)$.

$$
\begin{aligned}
(-200)(-9.34)\left(\tfrac{1}{2}\right) &= (-200)\left(\tfrac{1}{2}\right)(-9.34) && \text{By the commutative property of multiplication.} \\
&= \left(-200 \cdot \tfrac{1}{2}\right)(-9.34) && \text{By the associative property of multiplication.} \\
&= (-100)(-9.34) \\
&= 934
\end{aligned}
$$

Evaluate $21(89 + 11)$.

$$
\begin{aligned}
21(89 + 11) &= 21(100) && \text{Add first.} \\
&= 2{,}100 && \text{Then multiply.}
\end{aligned}
$$

Evaluate $50\left(-100 - \dfrac{1}{5}\right)$.

$$50\left(-100 - \frac{1}{5}\right) = 50\left(-100 + -\frac{1}{5}\right) \qquad \text{By the definition of subtraction.}$$

$$= (50)(-100) + (50)\left(-\frac{1}{5}\right) \quad \text{Multiply first.}$$

$$= (-5,000) + (-10)$$

$$= -5,010 \qquad\qquad\qquad \text{Then add.}$$

For a product of several numbers, multiply in pairs. You can keep track of the sign as you go along, or you can use the following guideline:

When zero is one of the factors, the product is *always* zero; otherwise, products that have an even number of *negative* factors are positive, whereas those that have an odd number of *negative* factors are negative.

Tip: Notice the sign of the product depends only on whether the number of negative factors is even or odd.

Here are examples.

Evaluate $(500)(-35)(-1,000)(0)(-40)$.

$$(500)(-35)(-1,000)(0)(-40) = 0 \quad \text{Because zero is a factor.}$$

Evaluate $\left(\dfrac{1}{2}\right)(-20)(-2.5)(-1)$.

$$\left(\frac{1}{2}\right)(-20)(-2.5)(-1) = (-10)(-2.5)(-1)$$

$$= (25)(-1)$$

$$= -25$$

Evaluate $(3.4)(-1)(-1)(-1)(-1)$.

$$(3.4)(-1)(-1)(-1)(-1) = 3.4 \quad \text{Because the number of negative factors is even.}$$

Evaluate $(-1)(-1)(-40)(-1)(-1)$.

$$(-1)(-1)(-40)(-1)(-1) = -40 \quad \text{Because the number of negative factors is odd.}$$

☞ Try These

1. Fill in the blank(s).

   (a) The _____ property of addition allows you to switch the order of the numbers when you add, without changing the sum.

   (b) The associate property is needed when you have to add or multiply more than two numbers because you can do addition or multiplication on only _____ numbers at a time.

   (c) The number _____ is the additive identity.

   (d) The additive inverse of −16 is _____.

   (e) The number _____ is the multiplicative identity.

   (f) A number and its multiplicative inverse have the _____ sign.

   (g) A common way to express the distributive property is to say _____ distributes over _____.

   (h) A product of nonzero factors that has an even number of negative factors is _____ (negative, positive). A product of nonzero factors that has an odd number of negative factors is _____ (negative, positive).

2. Evaluate.

   (a) $55.5 + -100 + 45.5$

   (b) $(400)(-6.25)\left(\dfrac{1}{4}\right)$

   (c) $70(135 - 35)$

   (d) $35\left(10 + \dfrac{1}{5}\right)$

   (e) $(250)(-36)(-100)(0)(-80)$

   (f) $\left(-\dfrac{1}{3}\right)(-60)\left(-\dfrac{1}{10}\right)(-2)$

   (g) $\left(-\dfrac{12}{25}\right)(-1)(-1)(-1)(-1)$

Solutions

1. **(a)** commutative

   (b) two

   (c) 0

   (d) 16

   (e) 1

   (f) same

   (g) multiplication; addition

   (h) positive; negative

2. **(a)** $55.5 + -100 + 45.5 = (55.5 + 45.5) + -100$
$$= (101) + (-100)$$
$$= 1$$

(b) $(400)(-6.25)\left(\dfrac{1}{4}\right) = (400)\left(\dfrac{1}{4}\right)(-6.25)$
$$= \left(400 \cdot \dfrac{1}{4}\right)(-6.25)$$
$$= (100)(-6.25)$$
$$= -625$$

(c) $70(135 - 35) = 70(135 + -35)$
$$= 70(100)$$
$$= 7,000$$

(d) $35\left(10 + \dfrac{1}{5}\right) = (35)(10) + (35)\left(\dfrac{1}{5}\right)$
$$= (350) + (7)$$
$$= 357$$

(e) $(250)(-36)(-100)(0)(-80) = 0$

(f) $\left(-\dfrac{1}{3}\right)(-60)\left(-\dfrac{1}{10}\right)(-2) = \left(-\dfrac{1}{3} \cdot -60\right)\left(-\dfrac{1}{10}\right)(-2)$
$$= (20)\left(-\dfrac{1}{10}\right)(-2)$$
$$= \left(20 \cdot -\dfrac{1}{10}\right)(-2)$$
$$= (-2)(-2)$$
$$= 4$$

(g) $\left(-\dfrac{12}{25}\right)(-1)(-1)(-1)(-1) = -\dfrac{12}{25}$

3. Expressions and Equations

In this chapter, you will expand, factor, add, and subtract linear expressions. You will solve one-variable linear equations and inequalities. And you will construct simple equations and inequalities to solve mathematical and real-world problems.

Expanding and Factoring Linear Expressions

(CCSS.Math.Content.7.EE.A.1)

In this section, you will expand and factor simple linear expressions.

Recognizing Linear Expressions

A **mathematical expression** uses symbols to represent a number. The symbols can be rational numbers, letters, and operation symbols. The rational numbers are **constants.** You know their values. The **letters** such as x, for example, stand for numbers. Without further information, you do not know the value of x. The **operation symbols** indicate calculations to be performed.

> **Tip: When the meaning is clear, refer to mathematical expressions as "expressions."**

A letter in an expression represents a **variable.** The letter is the variable's "name." You refer to variable x simply as "x," its letter representation. When you use letters in expressions, do not use the times ($\times$) symbol for multiplication. The $\times$ symbol can be confused with the letter x. To show $\frac{2}{5}$ times x, for example, do one of the following:

- Use the dot ($\cdot$) multiplication symbol between the factors, like this: $\frac{2}{5} \cdot x$.

- Enclose one or both factors in parentheses, like this: $\left(\frac{2}{5}\right)(x)$, $\left(\frac{2}{5}\right)x$, or $x\left(\frac{2}{5}\right)$. ***Tip:*** The commutative property of multiplication allows you to reverse the order of the two factors.

- Write the factors side by side with no symbols between them, like this: $\frac{2}{5}x$. ***Tip:*** The expression $\frac{2}{5}x$ is the result of multiplying $\frac{2}{5}$ times x. So, $\frac{2}{5} \cdot x = \frac{2}{5}x$, $\left(\frac{2}{5}\right)(x) = \frac{2}{5}x$, $\left(\frac{2}{5}\right)x = \frac{2}{5}x$, and $x\left(\frac{2}{5}\right) = \frac{2}{5}x$.

> **Tip: When you use the side-by-side form for the product of a number and a variable, write the number first, as in $\frac{2}{5}x$.**

In the product of a constant and a variable, the constant factor is the variable's **numerical coefficient.** For example, $\frac{2}{5}$ is the numerical coefficient of x in the expression $\frac{2}{5}x + 8$. If no number is shown as a factor times a variable, then the numerical coefficient of the variable is 1. For example, the numerical coefficient of x in the expression $x + 5$ is 1. If a variable is multiplied by several factors, their product is the numerical coefficient of the variable. For example, the numerical coefficient of x in the expression $(2)(3)x + 10$ is $(2)(3) = 6$. So, you can write the expression as $6x + 10$.

In an expression, **terms** are the parts connected to the other parts by plus or minus signs. If the expression has no plus or minus signs, then it consists of a single term.

A **linear expression** in the variable x is either one term that is a rational number times x, such as x, $3x$, $\frac{2}{5}x$, or $4.4x$, or it is an expression that can be written as several terms consisting of rational numbers and at least one term that is a rational number times x, such as $5x + 3$, $1.5x + 4.6 - 1.5x + 3.2$, $-\frac{1}{3} + 6x + \frac{5}{8} + 2x$, or $x + 5$.

The rational numbers that are multiplied times x are x's numerical coefficients.

> **Tip:** In a one-variable linear expression, the variable's exponent is 1, and no products of variables or variable divisors are allowed.

☞ Try These

1. Fill in the blank.

   (a) An expression uses symbols to represent a _____.
   (b) The rational numbers in an expression are _____.
   (c) The letters in an expression are _____.
   (d) In an expression, _____ are separated by plus or minus signs.
   (e) In a one-variable linear expression, the variable's exponent is _____.

2. State the coefficient of x in the expression.

   (a) $5x + 3$
   (b) $-\frac{3}{4}x + \frac{1}{2} - \frac{5}{8}$
   (c) $1.5x + 4.6$
   (d) $x + 5$
   (e) $25 + 3.75x$
   (f) $-1 + \frac{1}{2}x$
   (g) $(.25)(3)x + 90$

3. Indicate whether the expression is a linear expression by answering "Yes" or "No." If "No," explain why.

   (a) $3x^2 + 1$
   (b) $\frac{1}{3} + \frac{2}{x}$
   (c) $-1x + \frac{1}{5}$
   (d) $25 + 3.75x$
   (e) $9 + x^3$
   (f) $x \cdot x - 0.25x + 1$

Solutions

1. **(a)** number
   (b) constants
   (c) variables
   (d) terms
   (e) 1

2. **(a)** 5
   (b) $-\dfrac{3}{4}$
   (c) 1.5
   (d) 1
   (e) 3.75
   (f) $\dfrac{1}{2}$
   (g) $(.25)(3) = 0.75$

3. **(a)** No, because x's exponent is 2, not 1.
   (b) No, because x is a divisor.
   (c) Yes
   (d) Yes
   (e) No, because x's exponent is 3, not 1.
   (f) No, because $x \cdot x$ is a product of variables.

Using the Distributive Property to Expand an Expression

If a, b, and c are rational numbers, by the distributive property, then

$$a(b + c) = a \cdot b + a \cdot c = ab + ac$$

and

$$(b + c)a = b \cdot a + c \cdot a = ba + ca$$

When you use the distributive property to write $a(b + c)$ as the equivalent expression $ab + ac$, you are **expanding** the expression $a(b + c)$ by writing it as the sum of the two products ab and ac. Similarly, when you use the distributive property to write $(b + c)a$ as the equivalent expression $ba + ca$, you are expanding the expression $(b + c)a$ by writing it as the sum of the two products ba and ca.

Here are examples.

Expand $2(3x + 5)$.

$$
\begin{aligned}
2(3x + 5) &= 2 \cdot 3x + 2 \cdot 5 && \text{By the distributive property.} \\
&= (2 \cdot 3)x + 2 \cdot 5 && \text{By the associative property of multiplication.} \\
&= 6x + 10 && \text{By signed number multiplication.}
\end{aligned}
$$

Expand $-2(3x + 5)$.

$$-2(3x+5) = -2 \cdot 3x + -2 \cdot 5 \quad \text{By the distributive property.}$$
$$= (-2 \cdot 3)x + -2 \cdot 5 \quad \text{By the associative property of multiplication.}$$
$$= -6x + -10 \quad \text{By signed number multiplication.}$$

Expand $\dfrac{1}{2}\left(6x + \dfrac{2}{3}\right)$.

$$\frac{1}{2}\left(6x + \frac{2}{3}\right) = \frac{1}{2} \cdot 6x + \frac{1}{2} \cdot \frac{2}{3} \quad \text{By the distributive property.}$$
$$= \left(\frac{1}{2} \cdot 6\right)x + \frac{1}{{}_1\cancel{2}} \cdot \frac{\cancel{2}^{1}}{3} \quad \text{By the associative property of multiplication.}$$
$$= 3x + \frac{1}{3} \quad \text{By signed number multiplication.}$$

Expand $10 + 8(2x + 3)$.

$$10 + 8(2x + 3) = 10 + 8 \cdot 2x + 8 \cdot 3 \quad \text{By the distributive property.}$$
$$= 10 + (8 \cdot 2)x + 8 \cdot 3 \quad \text{By the associative property of multiplication.}$$
$$= 10 + 16x + 24 \quad \text{By signed number multiplication.}$$

Tip: Follow the order of operations. Do not begin by adding 10 and 8. You cannot detach the 8 from the indicated multiplication. Multiplication comes before addition in the order of operations.

Expand $-4(3x - 5)$.

$$-4(3x - 5) = -4(3x + -5) \quad \text{By the definition of subtraction.}$$
$$= -4 \cdot 3x + -4 \cdot -5 \quad \text{By the distributive property.}$$
$$= (-4 \cdot 3)x + -4 \cdot -5 \quad \text{By the associative property of multiplication.}$$
$$= -12x + 20 \quad \text{By signed number multiplication.}$$

Expand $7 - 2(5 - 8x)$.

$$7 - 2(5 - 8x) = 7 + -2(5 + -8x) \quad \text{By the definition of subtraction.}$$
$$= 7 + (-2)(5) + (-2)(-8x) \quad \text{By the distributive property.}$$
$$= 7 + (-2)(5) + (-2 \cdot -8)(x) \quad \text{By the associative property of multiplication.}$$
$$= 7 + -10 + 16x \quad \text{By signed number multiplication.}$$

Tip: Follow the order of operations. Do not begin by subtracting 2 from 7. You cannot detach the 2 from the indicated multiplication. Multiplication comes before subtraction in the order of operations.

If a plus sign comes immediately before an expression in parentheses, delete the parentheses and rewrite the expression inside without changing anything.

Here is an example.

Expand $20x + (5x + 9)$.

$$20x + (5x + 9) = 20x + 5x + 9$$

If a minus sign comes immediately before an expression in parentheses, change the minus sign to a plus sign, delete the parentheses, and rewrite the expression inside but change the sign of every term.

Here is an example.

Expand $20x - (5x + 9)$.

$$20x - (5x + 9) = 20x + -5x + -9$$

If a negative sign comes immediately before an expression in parentheses, delete the negative sign, delete the parentheses, and rewrite the expression inside but change the sign of every term.

Here is an example.

Expand $-(-2x + 7)$.

$$-(-2x + 7) = 2x + -7$$

Tip: Notice the results is the same whether the expression is preceded by a minus sign or a negative sign.

☞ Try These

1. Fill in the blank.

   (a) If a _____ sign comes immediately before an expression in parentheses, remove the parentheses and rewrite the expression inside without changing anything.

   (b) If a _____ sign comes immediately before an expression in parentheses, change the sign, remove the parentheses, and rewrite the expression inside but change the sign of every term.

2. Expand.

   (a) $4(6x + 3)$

   (b) $-5(2x + 1)$

   (c) $\dfrac{1}{3}\left(12x + \dfrac{3}{4}\right)$

   (d) $15 + 6(5x + 8)$

   (e) $-14x + 9(x - 2)$ ✓

   (f) $-5(10x - 3)$

   (g) $8 - 5(2 - 3x)$

   (h) $25x + (10x + 4)$

   (i) $25x - (10x + 4)$

   (j) $-(-8x - 6)$

Solutions

1. **(a)** plus

   (b) minus

2. **(a)** $4(6x+3) = 4 \cdot 6x + 4 \cdot 3$

   $\qquad = (4 \cdot 6)x + 4 \cdot 3$

   $\qquad = 24x + 12$

   (b) $-5(2x+1) = (-5)(2x) + (-5)(1)$

   $\qquad\quad = (-5 \cdot 2)(x) + (-5)(1)$

   $\qquad\quad = -10x + -5$

   (c) $\dfrac{1}{3}\left(12x + \dfrac{3}{4}\right) = \dfrac{1}{3} \cdot 12x + \dfrac{1}{3} \cdot \dfrac{3}{4}$

   $$= \left(\dfrac{1}{3} \cdot 12\right)x + \dfrac{1}{\cancel{3}_1} \cdot \dfrac{\cancel{3}^1}{4}$$

   $$= 4x + \dfrac{1}{4}$$

   (d) $15 + 6(5x+8) = 15 + 6 \cdot 5x + 6 \cdot 8$

   $\qquad\qquad = 15 + (6 \cdot 5)x + 6 \cdot 8$

   $\qquad\qquad = 15 + 30x + 48$

   (e) $-14x + 9(x-2) = -14x + 9(x + -2)$

   $\qquad\qquad = -14x + 9 \cdot x + 9 \cdot -2$

   $\qquad\qquad = -14x + 9x + -18$

   (f) $-5(10x - 3) = -5(10x + -3)$

   $\qquad\quad = -5 \cdot 10x + -5 \cdot -3$

   $\qquad\quad = (-5 \cdot 10)x + -5 \cdot -3$

   $\qquad\quad = -50x + 15$

   (g) $8 - 5(2 - 3x) = 8 + -5(2 + -3x)$

   $\qquad\qquad = 8 + -5 \cdot 2 + (-5 \cdot -3)x$

   $\qquad\qquad = 8 + -10 + 15x$

   (h) $25x + (10x + 4) = 25x + 10x + 4$

   (i) $25x - (10x + 4) = 25x + -10x + -4$

   (j) $-(-8x - 6) = -(-8x + -6)$

   $\qquad\quad = 8x + 6$

Using the Distributive Property to Factor an Expression

If a, b, and c are rational numbers, by the distributive property, then

$$ab + ac = a \cdot b + a \cdot c = a(b + c)$$

and

$$ba + ca = b \cdot a + c \cdot a = (b + c)a$$

When you use the distributive property to write $ab + ac$ as the equivalent expression $a(b + c)$, you are **factoring** the expression $ab + ac$ by writing it as the product of the common factor a and the sum $(b + c)$. The number a is a common factor because it is a factor of both ab and ac.

Similarly, when you use the distributive property to write $ba + ca$ as the equivalent expression $(b + c)a$, you are factoring the expression $ba + ca$. Again, a is the common factor.

When you factor an expression, the common factor can be a number or it can be a variable expression.

Here are examples.

Factor x from the expression $8x + 10x$.

$$
\begin{aligned}
8x + 10x &= 8 \cdot x + 10 \cdot x &&\text{By the definition of coefficient.} \\
&= (8 + 10)x &&\text{By the distributive property.}
\end{aligned}
$$

Factor x from the expression $7x - 5x$.

$$
\begin{aligned}
7x - 5x &= 7x + -5x &&\text{By the definition of subtraction.} \\
&= 7 \cdot x + -5 \cdot x &&\text{By the definition of coefficient.} \\
&= (7 + -5)x &&\text{By the distributive property.}
\end{aligned}
$$

Factor x from the expression $x + 0.085x$.

$$
\begin{aligned}
x + 0.085x &= 1 \cdot x + 0.085 \cdot x &&\text{By the definition of coefficient.} \\
&= (1 + 0.085)x &&\text{By the distributive property.}
\end{aligned}
$$

Factor x from the expression $x - 20\%x$.

$$
\begin{aligned}
x - 20\%x &= x - 0.20x &&\text{By the definition of percent.} \\
&= x + -0.20x &&\text{By the definition of subtraction.} \\
&= 1 \cdot x + -0.20 \cdot x &&\text{By the definition of coefficient.} \\
&= (1 + -0.20)x &&\text{By the distributive property.}
\end{aligned}
$$

Tip: Change percents to equivalent decimals or fractions for computations.

Factor the greatest common factor from the expression $6x + 15$. ***Tip:*** The greatest common factor (or GCF) of two numbers is the largest positive factor common to the two numbers.

$$6x + 15 = 3 \cdot 2x + 3 \cdot 5$$
$$= 3(2x + 5) \quad \text{By the distributive property.}$$

☞ Try These

1. Fill in the blank.

   (a) When you use the distributive property to write $ab + ac$ as the equivalent expression $a(b + c)$, you are _____ the expression $ab + ac$.

   (b) The greatest common factor of 8 and 12 is _____.

2. Factor the greatest common factor from the expression.

   (a) $8x + 12$
   (b) $10x - 35$

3. Factor x from the expression.

   (a) $5x + 9x$
   (b) $0.25x + 3.50x$
   (c) $x + 10\%x$

Solutions

1. **(a)** factoring
   (b) 4

2. **(a)** $8x + 12 = 4 \cdot 2x + 4 \cdot 3$
   $$= 4(2x + 3)$$
   (b) $10x - 35 = 10x + -35$
   $$= 5 \cdot 2x + 5 \cdot -7$$
   $$= 5(2x + -7)$$

3. **(a)** $5x + 9x = 5 \cdot x + 9 \cdot x$
   $$= (5 + 9)x$$
   (b) $0.25x + 3.50x = 0.25 \cdot x + 3.50 \cdot x$
   $$= (0.25 + 3.50)x$$
   (c) $x + 10\%x = x + 0.10x$
   $$= 1 \cdot x + 0.10 \cdot x$$
   $$= (1 + 0.10)x$$

Combining Like Terms

(CCSS.Math.Content.7.EE.A.1)

In an expression, **like terms** are terms that can be combined, using addition or subtraction, into a single term. In a linear expression in x, like terms are either constant terms or the terms that have x as a factor. For example, in the expression $20 + 8x + 10x + 25$, the constant terms 20 and 25 are like terms and the variable terms $8x$ and $10x$ are like terms.

To combine constant terms, add or subtract as indicated using the rules for **signed number computation (SNC).**

To combine x terms, use the distributive property as shown in the following examples.

$$8x + 10x = 8 \cdot x + 10 \cdot x \quad \text{By the definition of coefficient.}$$
$$= (8 + 10)x \quad \text{By the distributive property.}$$
$$= 18x \quad \text{By SNC.}$$

$$-8x - 10x = -8x + -10x \quad \text{By the definition of subtraction.}$$
$$= -8 \cdot x + -10 \cdot x \quad \text{By the definition of coefficient.}$$
$$= (-8 + -10)x \quad \text{By the distributive property.}$$
$$= -18x \quad \text{By SNC.}$$

$$-12x + 7x = -12 \cdot x + 7 \cdot x \quad \text{By the definition of coefficient.}$$
$$= (-12 + 7)x \quad \text{By the distributive property.}$$
$$= -5x \quad \text{By SNC.}$$

$$7x - 5x = 7x + -5x \quad \text{By the definition of subtraction.}$$
$$= 7 \cdot x + -5 \cdot x \quad \text{By the definition of coefficient.}$$
$$= (7 + -5)x \quad \text{By the distributive property.}$$
$$= 2x \quad \text{By SNC.}$$

$$x + 0.085x = 1 \cdot x + 0.085 \cdot x \quad \text{By the definition of coefficient.}$$
$$= (1 + 0.085)x \quad \text{By the distributive property.}$$
$$= 1.085x \quad \text{By SNC.}$$

$$x - 20\%x = x - 0.20x \quad \text{By the definition of percent.}$$
$$= x + -0.20x \quad \text{By the definition of subtraction.}$$
$$= 1 \cdot x + -0.20 \cdot x \quad \text{By the definition of coefficient.}$$
$$= (1 + -0.20)x \quad \text{By the distributive property.}$$
$$= 0.80x \quad \text{By SNC.}$$
$$= 80\%x \quad \text{By the definition of percent.}$$

Tip: A shortcut for combining x terms is to combine x's numerical coefficients and then attach the result to x. This shortcut will be used in later sections of this chapter.

When you use the properties of operations to combine like terms in an expression, you obtain an expression that is equivalent to the original expression.

Here is an example.

$$10 + 8x + 5 + 3x = 10 + 5 + 8x + 3x \qquad \text{By the commutative property of addition.}$$
$$= (10 + 5) + (8x + 3x) \qquad \text{Grouping like terms.}$$
$$= (10 + 5) + (8 + 3)x \qquad \text{By the distributive property.}$$
$$= 15 + 11x \qquad \text{By SNC.}$$

Therefore, $10 + 8x + 5 + 3x$ is equivalent to $15 + 11x$.

You might need to expand an expression before combining like terms.

Here is an example.

$$9 - 3(2 - 5x) = 9 + -3(2 + -5x) \qquad \text{By the definition of subtraction.}$$
$$= 9 + -3 \cdot 2 + -3 \cdot -5x \qquad \text{By the distributive property.}$$
$$= (9 + -6) + -3 \cdot -5x \qquad \text{By SNC and grouping like terms.}$$
$$= (9 + -6) + (-3 \cdot -5)x \qquad \text{By the associative property for multiplication.}$$
$$= 3 + 15x \qquad \text{By SNC.}$$

Therefore, $9 - 3(2 - 5x)$ is equivalent to $3 + 15x$.

☞ Try These

1. Fill in the blank(s).

   (a) In an expression, like terms are terms that can be combined, using addition or subtraction, into a _____ term.

   (b) In a linear expression in x, like terms are either _____ terms or the terms that have _____ as a factor.

   (c) When you use the properties of operations to combine like terms in an expression, you obtain an expression that is _____ to the original expression.

2. Combine x terms.

   (a) $5x + 9x$

   (b) $0.25x + 3.50x$

   (c) $x + 10\%x$

   (d) $-15x + 8x$

   (e) $\dfrac{3}{4}x + \dfrac{2}{3}x$

   (f) $-30x - 20x$

3. Combine like terms in the expression.

    (a) $6x + 3 + 5x + 2$

    (b) $-3x + 4 + 5x - 3$

    (c) $10 + 8(2x + 3)$

    (d) $7 - 2(5 - 8x)$

Solutions

1. **(a)** single

    (b) constant; x

    (c) equivalent

2. **(a)**
$$5x + 9x = 5 \cdot x + 9 \cdot x$$
$$= (5 + 9)x$$
$$= 14x$$

    (b)
$$0.25x + 3.50x = 0.25 \cdot x + 3.50 \cdot x$$
$$= (0.25 + 3.50)x$$
$$= 3.75x$$

    (c)
$$x + 10\%x = x + 0.10x$$
$$= 1 \cdot x + 0.10 \cdot x$$
$$= (1 + 0.10)x$$
$$= 1.10x$$
$$- 110\%x$$

    (d)
$$-15x + 8x = -15 \cdot x + 8 \cdot x$$
$$= (-15 + 8)x$$
$$= -7x$$

    (e)
$$\frac{3}{4}x + \frac{2}{3}x = \frac{3}{4} \cdot x + \frac{2}{3} \cdot x$$
$$= \left(\frac{3}{4} + \frac{2}{3}\right)x$$
$$= \left(\frac{9}{12} + \frac{8}{12}\right)x$$
$$= \frac{17}{12}x$$

    (f)
$$-30x - 20x = -30x + -20x$$
$$= -30 \cdot x + -20 \cdot x$$
$$= (-30 + -20)x$$
$$= -50x$$

3. **(a)** $6x + 3 + 5x + 2 = 6x + 5x + 3 + 2$
$$= (6x + 5x) + (3 + 2)$$
$$= (6 + 5)x + (3 + 2)$$
$$= 11x + 5$$

(b) $-3x + 4 + 5x - 3 = -3x + 4 + 5x + -3$
$$= -3x + 5x + 4 + -3$$
$$= (-3x + 5x) + (4 + -3)$$
$$= (-3 + 5)x + (4 + -3)$$
$$= 2x + 1$$

(c) $10 + 8(2x + 3) = 10 + 8 \cdot 2x + 8 \cdot 3$
$$= 10 + (8 \cdot 2)x + 8 \cdot 3$$
$$= 10 + 16x + 24$$
$$= 10 + 24 + 16x$$
$$= (10 + 24) + 16x$$
$$= 34 + 16x$$

(d) $7 - 2(5 - 8x) = 7 + -2(5 + -8x)$
$$= 7 + (-2)(5) + (-2)(-8x)$$
$$= 7 + (-2)(5) + (-2 \cdot -8)(x)$$
$$= 7 + -10 + 16x$$
$$= (7 + -10) + 16x$$
$$= -3 + 16x$$

Adding and Subtracting Linear Expressions

(CCSS.Math.Content.7.EE.A.1)

Use the properties of operations to add and subtract linear expressions.

Here are examples of adding linear expressions.

Find the sum of $3x + 4$ and $2x + 5$.

$$(3x + 4) + (2x + 5) = 3x + 4 + 2x + 5$$
$$= 3x + 2x + 4 + 5$$
$$= (3x + 2x) + (4 + 5)$$
$$= 5x + 9$$

Find the sum of $12x - 20$ and $-2x + 15$.

$$
\begin{aligned}
(12x - 20) + (-2x + 15) &= (12x + -20) + (-2x + 15) \\
&= 12x + -20 + -2x + 15 \\
&= 12x + -2x + -20 + 15 \\
&= (12x + -2x) + (-20 + 15) \\
&= 10x + -5 \\
&= 10x - 5
\end{aligned}
$$

Tip: Hereafter, in final answers, write "+ –" as simply "–."

Here are examples of subtracting linear expressions.

Find the difference of $3x + 4$ and $2x + 5$.

$$
\begin{aligned}
(3x + 4) - (2x + 5) &= 3x + 4 + -2x + -5 \\
&= 3x + -2x + 4 + -5 \\
&= (3x + -2x) + (4 + -5) \\
&= x + -1 \\
&= x - 1
\end{aligned}
$$

Find the difference of $12x - 20$ and $-2x + 15$.

$$
\begin{aligned}
(12x - 20) - (-2x + 15) &= (12x + -20) - (-2x + 15) \\
&= 12x + -20 + 2x + -15 \\
&= 12x + 2x + -20 + -15 \\
&= (12x + 2x) + (-20 + -15) \\
&= 14x + -35 \\
&= 14x - 35
\end{aligned}
$$

☞ Try These

1. Find the sum.

   (a) $(x + 8) + (4x + 15)$
   (b) $(24x - 30) + (-10x + 20)$

2. Find the difference.

   (a) $(x + 8) - (4x + 15)$
   (b) $(24x - 30) - (-10x + 20)$

Solutions

1. **(a)** $(x+8)+(4x+15) = x+8+4x+15$

$$= x+4x+8+15$$
$$= (x+4x)+(8+15)$$
$$= 5x+23$$

(b) $(24x-30)+(-10x+20) = (24x+-30)+(-10x+20)$

$$= 24x+-30+-10x+20$$
$$= 24x+-10x+-30+20$$
$$= (24x+-10x)+(-30+20)$$
$$= 14x+-10$$
$$= 14x-10$$

2. **(a)** $(x+8)-(4x+15) = x+8+-4x+-15$

$$= x+-4x+8+-15$$
$$= (x+-4x)+(8+-15)$$
$$= -3x+-7$$
$$= -3x-7$$

(b) $(24x-30)-(-10x+20) = (24x+-30)-(-10x+20)$

$$= 24x+-30+10x+-20$$
$$= 24x+10x+-30+-20$$
$$= (24x+10x)+(-30+-20)$$
$$= 34x+-50$$
$$= 34x-50$$

Solving Equations of the Forms $p(x + q) = r$ and $px + q = r$

(CCSS.Math.Content.7.EE.A.1, CCSS.Math.Content.7.EE.A.2, CCSS.Math.Content.7.EE.B.3, CCSS.Math.Content.7.EE.B.4.A)

In this section, you will solve multistep, one-variable equations that have the forms $p(x + q) = r$ and $px + q = r$, where x is a variable and p, q, and r are rational numbers.

An **equation** is a statement that two mathematical expressions are equal. An equation has two sides. Whatever is on the left side of the equal sign is the **left side (LS)** of the equation, and whatever is on the right side of the equal sign is the **right side (RS)** of the equation. An equation is true when the LS has the same value as the RS.

A **solution** to an equation that has one variable, x, is a number that when substituted for x makes the equation true. For example, 5 is the solution to the equation $2x + 8 = 18$. It is the number that when substituted for x makes the equation $2x + 8 = 18$ a true statement.

To determine whether a number is a solution to the equation, replace x with the number and perform the operations indicated on each side of the equation. If this results in a true equation, the number is a solution. This process is called **checking** a solution. For example, 5 is the solution to the equation $2x + 8 = 18$, because $2(5) + 8 = 18$ is a true statement.

The set consisting of all solutions to an equation is the equation's **solution set.** If the solution set is all real numbers, the equation is an **identity.** For example, $x + 5 = x + 2 + 3$ is an identity because any number substituted for x will make the equation true. If the solution set is empty, the equation has **no solution.** For example, $x + 5 = x + 2$ has no solution because there is no number that will make the equation true. Equations that have the same solution set are **equivalent equations.**

To **solve** a one-variable linear equation in x means to find its solution set. The strategy in solving the equation is to undo what has been done to x. You proceed through a series of steps until you produce an equivalent equation that has this form:

$$x = \text{solution}$$

The equation is solved when you succeed in getting x by itself on one side of the equation only and x's coefficient is understood to be 1, and on the other side of the equation there is a single number (the solution) all by itself.

Tip: Getting the x term by itself on one side of the equation is referred to as isolating the x term.

The equal sign in an equation is like a balance point. To keep the equation in balance, whatever you do to one side of the equation you must do to the other side of the equation.

> The main actions that will result in equivalent equations are
>
> - Adding the same number to both sides of the equation.
> - Subtracting the same number from both sides of the equation.
> - Multiplying both sides of the equation by the same *nonzero* number.
> - Dividing both sides of the equation by the same *nonzero* number.

Tip: *Never* multiply or divide both sides of an equation by 0.

What has been done to x determines the operation you choose to do. You do it to both sides to keep the equation balanced. You "undo" an operation by using the inverse of the operation. Addition and subtraction undo each other, as do multiplication and division (or multiplying by the reciprocal).

To solve an equation of the form $p(x + q) = r$ or $px + q = r$, follow these four steps:

1. Remove parentheses. If the equation has parentheses, use the distributive property to remove them.

2. Undo addition or subtraction. If a number is added to the x term, subtract that number from both sides of the equation. If a number is subtracted from the x term, add that number to both sides of the equation.

3. Combine like terms on each side of the equation.

4. Divide both sides of the equation by the coefficient of x. *Tip:* If the coefficient is a fraction, divide by multiplying both sides of the equation by its reciprocal.

> **Tip: Imagine solving an equation is a game in which you have to figure out the identity of x to win. Steps 1 through 4 are the moves you make to find out x's identity (value). Skip steps that are not needed for the equation you are solving.**

Here is an example.

Solve for x: $4(x + 10) = 30$

Before you start, think aloud about the equation. You might say, *"I see that x is a number that after it is first added to 10, and then that sum is multiplied by 4, the result is 30. I know x is not a positive number because if I add a positive number to 10, and then multiply the sum by 4, the answer will be greater than 30. I see x is inside a set of parentheses. A set of parentheses is like a fence. I will need to remove the parentheses. Then I will isolate x to obtain its value."*

As you solve the equation, continue your self-talk as illustrated here.

$4(x + 10) = 30$

"I will use the distributive property to remove parentheses."

$$4 \cdot x + 4 \cdot 10 = 30$$
$$4x + 40 = 30$$

"40 is added to the x term. I will subtract 40 from the left side of the equation to undo the addition. To keep the balance, I will subtract 40 from the right side, too."

$$4x + 40 - 40 = 30 - 40$$

"I will group like terms."

$$4x + (40 - 40) = (30 - 40)$$

"I will combine like terms. I know $(40 - 40)$ is 0, and $(30 - 40) = (30 + -40) = -10$."

$$4x + 0 = -10$$

"I know 4x + 0 is 4x."

$$4x = -10$$

"x is multiplied by 4. I want the coefficient of x to be 1. I will divide the left side of the equation by 4 to undo the multiplication. To keep the balance, I will divide the right side by 4, too."

$$\frac{4x}{4} = \frac{-10}{4}$$

"On the left side, the 4s will cancel out to give 1 as x's coefficient. On the right side, I have –10 ÷ 4, which is –2.5."

$$\frac{\cancel{4}x}{\cancel{4}} = -10 \div 4$$
$$1x = -2.5$$
$$x = -2.5$$

"I have solved the equation. I know x's value is –2.5. I can check my answer by substituting it into the original equation and evaluating."

$$4(x + 10) = 30$$
$$4(-2.5 + 10) \overset{?}{=} 30$$
$$4(7.5) \overset{?}{=} 30$$
$$30 \overset{\checkmark}{=} 30$$

"–2.5 makes the equation true, so it is the correct solution. I won!"

Tip: Make self-talk a habit. It is a proven comprehension strategy.

Here are additional examples with short comments. Do your self-talk mentally.

Solve for x: $3x + 8 = -46$

$3x + 8 = -46$	There are no parentheses, so skip to Step 2.
$3x + 8 - 8 = -46 - 8$	Subtract 8 from both sides of the equation.
$3x + 0 = -54$	Combine like terms.
$3x = -54$	Zero is the additive identity.
$\dfrac{3x}{3} = \dfrac{-54}{3}$	Divide both sides of the equation by 3.
$\dfrac{\cancel{3}x}{\cancel{3}} = -54 \div 3$	
$x = -18$	By SNC.

Check:

$$3x + 8 = -46$$

$$3(-18) + 8 \stackrel{?}{=} -46$$

$$-54 + 8 \stackrel{?}{=} -46$$

$$-46 \stackrel{\checkmark}{=} -46$$

Solve for x: $\dfrac{2}{3}(x + 15) = 18$

$$\frac{2}{3}(x + 15) = 18$$

$\dfrac{2}{3} \cdot x + \dfrac{2}{1\cancel{3}} \cdot \cancel{15}^{5} = 18$ Use the distributive property to remove parentheses.

$\dfrac{2}{3}x + 10 = 18$ By SNC.

$\dfrac{2}{3}x + 10 - 10 = 18 - 10$ Subtract 10 from both sides of the equation.

$\dfrac{2}{3}x + 0 = 8$ Combine like terms.

$\dfrac{2}{3}x = 8$ Zero is the additive identity.

$\dfrac{3}{2} \cdot \dfrac{2}{3}x = \dfrac{3}{2} \cdot 8$ Multiply both sides of the equation by $\dfrac{3}{2}$, the reciprocal of $\dfrac{2}{3}$.

$\dfrac{\cancel{3}}{\cancel{2}} \cdot \dfrac{\cancel{2}}{\cancel{3}}x = \dfrac{3}{1\cancel{2}} \cdot \cancel{8}^{4}$

$$1x = 12$$ By SNC.

$$x = 12$$

Check:

$$\frac{2}{3}(x + 15) = 18$$

$$\frac{2}{3}(12 + 15) \stackrel{?}{=} 18$$

$$\frac{2}{3}(27) \stackrel{?}{=} 18$$

$$\frac{2}{1\cancel{3}}\left(\cancel{27}^{9}\right) \stackrel{?}{=} 18$$

$$18 \stackrel{\checkmark}{=} 18$$

☞Try These

1. Fill in the blank.

   (a) An equation is a statement that two mathematical expressions are _____.
   (b) An equation has two _____.
   (c) To solve an equation that has one variable, x, means to find its _____ set.
   (d) A _____ to an equation is a number that when substituted for the variable makes the equation true.
   (e) To solve a one-variable linear equation in x, you _____ what has been done to x.
   (f) To keep an equation in balance, whatever you do to one side of the equation you must do to the _____ side of the equation.

2. Solve for x.

   (a) $3x - 4.5 = 1.8$
   (b) $5(x + 13) = 50$
   (c) $\frac{1}{2}x - 7 = 14$
   (d) $-4x + 9 = -5$
   (e) $-2(x - 1) = 20$

Solutions

1. **(a)** equal
   (b) sides
   (c) solution
   (d) solution
   (e) undo
   (f) other

2. **(a)**
$$3x - 4.5 = 1.8$$
$$3x - 4.5 + 4.5 = 1.8 + 4.5$$
$$3x + 0 = 6.3$$
$$3x = 6.3$$
$$\frac{3x}{3} = \frac{6.3}{3}$$
$$\frac{\cancel{3}x}{\cancel{3}} = 6.3 \div 3$$
$$x = 2.1$$

   Check:
$$3x - 4.5 = 1.8$$
$$3(2.1) - 4.5 \overset{?}{=} 1.8$$
$$6.3 - 4.5 \overset{?}{=} 1.8$$
$$1.8 \overset{\checkmark}{=} 1.8$$

(b) $5(x+13)=50$

$5 \cdot x + 5 \cdot 13 = 50$

$5x + 65 = 50$

$5x + 65 - 65 = 50 - 65$

$5x + 0 = 50 + -65$

$5x = -15$

$$\frac{5x}{5} = \frac{-15}{5}$$

$$\frac{\cancel{5}x}{\cancel{5}} = -15 \div 5$$

$x = -3$

Check:

$5(x+13)=50$

$5(-3+13)\overset{?}{=}50$

$5(10)\overset{?}{=}50$

$50\overset{\checkmark}{=}50$

(c) $\dfrac{1}{2}x - 7 = 14$

$\dfrac{1}{2}x - 7 + 7 = 14 + 7$

$\dfrac{1}{2}x + 0 = 21$

$\dfrac{1}{2}x = 21$

$\dfrac{2}{1} \cdot \dfrac{1}{2}x = 2 \cdot 21$

$\dfrac{\cancel{2}}{1} \cdot \dfrac{1}{\cancel{2}}x = 2 \cdot 21$

$1x = 42$

$x = 42$

Check:

$\dfrac{1}{2}x - 7 = 14$

$\dfrac{1}{2}(42) - 7 \overset{?}{=} 14$

$21 - 7 \overset{?}{=} 14$

$14 \overset{\checkmark}{=} 14$

(d) $-4x + 9 = -5$

$$-4x + 9 - 9 = -5 - 9$$

$$-4x + 0 = -14$$

$$\frac{-4x}{-4} = \frac{-14}{-4}$$

$$\frac{\cancel{-4}x}{\cancel{-4}} = -14 \div -4$$

$$x = 3.5$$

Check:

$$-4x + 9 = -5$$

$$-4(3.5) + 9 \overset{?}{=} -5$$

$$-14 + 9 \overset{?}{=} -5$$

$$-5 \overset{\checkmark}{=} -5$$

(e) $-2(x - 1) = 20$

$$-2(x + -1) = 20$$

$$-2 \cdot x + -2 \cdot -1 = 20$$

$$-2x + 2 = 20$$

$$-2x + 2 - 2 = 20 - 2$$

$$-2x + 0 = 18$$

$$-2x = 18$$

$$\frac{-2x}{-2} = \frac{18}{-2}$$

$$\frac{\cancel{-2}x}{\cancel{-2}} = 18 \div -2$$

$$x = -9$$

Check:

$$-2(x - 1) = 20$$

$$-2(-9 - 1) \overset{?}{=} 20$$

$$-2(-10) \overset{?}{=} 20$$

$$20 \overset{\checkmark}{=} 20$$

Using Equations of the Forms $px + q = r$ and $p(x + q) = r$ to Solve Mathematical and Real-World Problems

(CCSS.Math.Content.7.EE.A.1, CCSS.Math.Content.7.EE.A.2, CCSS.Math.Content.7.EE.B.3, CCSS.Math.Content.7.EE.B.4.A)

Many mathematical and real-world problems can be modeled and solved using multistep, single-variable equations that have the forms $px + q = r$ and $p(x + q) = r$. To solve such problems, read the problem carefully. Look for a sentence that contains words or phrases such as "what is," "what was," "find," "how many," and "determine" to help you identify what you are to find. Let the variable represent this unknown quantity. (*Tip:* Be precise in specifying a variable. State its units, if any.) Then write and solve an equation that represents the facts given in the problem.

Here are examples.

Three times the sum of a number and 25 is 99. What is the number?

Think: *"I need to find the number. Here's what I know. If I add 25 to the number, and then multiply the sum by 3, I will get 99."*

Let n = the number. (*Tip:* You might find it helpful to use the first letter of a key word to represent an unknown variable.)

Write an equation that represents the facts of the problem.

$3(n + 25) = 99$

Solve the equation.

$$3(n + 25) = 99$$
$$3 \cdot n + 3 \cdot 25 = 99$$
$$3n + 75 = 99$$
$$3n + 75 - 75 = 99 - 75$$
$$3n + 0 = 24$$
$$3n = 24$$
$$\frac{3n}{3} = \frac{24}{3}$$
$$\frac{\cancel{3}n}{\cancel{3}} = 24 \div 3$$
$$n = 8$$

The number is 8.

Check: The number is 8. If I add 25 to 8, I get 33. And then if I multiply 33 by 3, I get 99. ✓

The length of Kevin's lawn is 20 feet longer than its width. Kevin put a fence halfway around the lawn and planted bushes around the other half. The distance halfway around Kevin's lawn is 56 feet. What is the lawn's width?

In this problem, there are two unknown quantities. You don't know the width or the length of Kevin's lawn. You can use only one variable, so you have to describe both unknowns using just one letter as shown here.

Let w = the lawn's width in feet. Then $w + 20$ feet = the lawn's length.

Write an equation to represent the facts of the problem.

Think: *"I need to find the lawn's width. Here's what I know. The lawn's length is 20 feet longer than its width. Halfway around the lawn is 56 feet. So, the sum of the lawn's length and width is 56 feet."*

$w + (w + 20 \text{ feet}) = 56 \text{ feet}$

Solve the equation, omitting the units for convenience.

$$w + (w + 20) = 56$$
$$w + w + 20 = 56$$
$$2w + 20 = 56$$
$$2w + 20 - 20 = 56 - 20$$
$$2w + 0 = 36$$
$$2w = 36$$
$$\frac{2w}{2} = \frac{36}{2}$$
$$\frac{\cancel{2}w}{\cancel{2}} = 36 \div 2$$
$$w = 18$$

The lawn's width is 18 feet.

Check: The lawn's width is 18 feet. So the lawn's length is 18 feet + 20 feet = 38 feet. And 18 feet + 38 feet = 56 feet. ✓

👉 **Try These**

1. The original price of a watch is increased by $16.92. A customer buys two of the watches. The total price before sales tax is added is $118.44. What is the original price of the watch?

2. A car and a bus leave a location at exactly the same time, but travel in opposite directions. The car travels due west and the bus travels due east. After 3 hours, the two vehicles are 650 kilometers apart. The car has traveled x kilometers and the bus has traveled 50 kilometers farther in the opposite direction. How far has the car traveled at this time?

3. One-third of the school's seventh graders participated in the school mathematics Olympics competition. Twenty sixth graders and 25 eighth graders also participated. Altogether, 75 students participated. How many total students are in the seventh grade at the school?

4. Sumia is 4 years older than Clayton. The sum of their ages is 32. How old is Sumia?

Solutions

1. $42.30

   Let x = the original price of the watch in dollars.

   Write an equation to represent the facts of the problem.

   Think: *"I need to find the watch's original price. Here's what I know. If I add $16.92 to the watch's original price, and then multiply the sum by 2, I will get $118.44."*

   $$2(x + \$16.92) = \$118.44$$

   Solve the equation, omitting units for convenience.

   $$2(x+16.92)=118.44$$
   $$2 \cdot x + 2(16.92)=118.44$$
   $$2x+33.84=118.44$$
   $$2x+33.84-33.84=118.44-33.84$$
   $$2x=84.60$$
   $$\frac{2x}{2}=\frac{84.60}{2}$$
   $$\frac{\cancel{2}x}{\cancel{2}}=84.60 \div 2$$
   $$x=42.30$$

   The watch's original price is $42.30.

   Check: The watch's original price is $42.30. If I add $16.92 to it, I get $59.22. And then if I multiply $59.22 by 2, I get $118.44. ✓

2. 300 kilometers

   x = the distance the car has traveled in kilometers.

   Write an equation to represent the facts of the problem.

Think: *"I need to find x. Here's what I know. The car and the bus are 650 kilometers apart after 3 hours. The car traveled x kilometers going west and the bus traveled x + 50 kilometers going east. I think a sketch will help me understand the situation."*

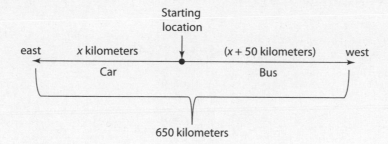

"From the sketch, I can see that the sum of the distances is 650 kilometers."

x kilometers + (x + 50 kilometers) = 650 kilometers.

Solve the equation, omitting units for convenience.

$$x + (x + 50) = 650$$
$$x + x + 50 = 650$$
$$2x + 50 = 650$$
$$2x + 50 - 50 = 650 - 50$$
$$2x + 0 = 600$$
$$2x = 600$$
$$\frac{2x}{2} = \frac{600}{2}$$
$$\frac{\cancel{2}x}{\cancel{2}} = 600 \div 2$$
$$x = 300$$

The car has traveled 300 kilometers.

Check: The car has traveled 300 kilometers. So, the bus has traveled 300 kilometers + 50 kilometers = 350 kilometers. And 300 kilometers + 350 kilometers = 650 kilometers. ✓

3. 90 students

Let x = the total number of students in the school's seventh grade.

Write an equation to represent the facts of the problem.

Think: *"I need to find how many students are in the seventh grade. Here's what I know. One-third of those students were in the competition with 20 sixth graders and 25 eighth graders. Altogether, 75 students participated in the competition."*

$$\frac{1}{3}x + 20 + 25 = 75$$

Solve the equation.

$$\frac{1}{3}x + 20 + 25 = 75$$

$$\frac{1}{3}x + 45 = 75$$

$$\frac{1}{3}x + 45 - 45 = 75 - 45$$

$$\frac{1}{3}x + 0 = 30$$

$$\frac{1}{3}x = 30$$

$$\frac{3}{1} \cdot \frac{1}{3}x = 3 \cdot 30$$

$$\frac{\cancel{3}}{1} \cdot \frac{1}{\cancel{3}}x = 3 \cdot 30$$

$$1x = 90$$

$$x = 90$$

There are 90 students in the school's seventh grade.

Check: There are 90 students in the school's seventh grade. One-third of 90 is 30. And 30 + 20 + 25 = 75. ✓

4. 18 years

Think: *"I have two unknowns. I don't know Clayton's age and I don't know Sumia's age. I can use only one variable, so I have to describe both unknowns using just one letter."*

Let c = Clayton's age in years. Then $c + 4$ years = Sumia's age in years.

Write an equation to represent the facts of the problem.

Think: *"I need to find Clayton's age. Here's what I know. Sumia is 4 years older than Clayton. The sum of Clayton's age and Sumia's age is 32."*

$$c + (c + 4 \text{ years}) = 32$$

Solve the equation, omitting units for convenience.

$$c + (c + 4) = 32$$

$$c + c + 4 = 32$$

$$2c + 4 = 32$$

$$2c + 4 - 4 = 32 - 4$$

$$2c + 0 = 28$$

$$2c = 28$$

$$\frac{2c}{2} = \frac{28}{2}$$

$$\frac{\cancel{2}c}{\cancel{2}} = 28 \div 2$$

$$c = 14$$

$$c + 4 = 18$$

Clayton is 14 years old and Sumia is 18 years old.

Tip: Make sure you answer the question asked. In this question, after you obtain Clayton's age, calculate Sumia's age.

Check: Clayton is 14 years old. So, Sumia's age is 14 years + 4 years = 18 years. And 14 years + 18 years = 32 years. ✓

Solving Mathematical and Real-World Inequalities of the Forms $px + q > r$ and $px + q < r$

(CCSS.Math.Content.7.EE.B.4.B)

You solve inequalities of the forms $px + q > r$ and $px + q < r$ basically the same way you solve equations of the same forms. However, there is one important difference.

> **When you multiply or divide both sides of an inequality by a *negative* number, you must *reverse* the direction of the inequality.**

To understand why you must do this, consider the following.

You know $5 > -2$ is a true inequality because 5 is to the right of -2 on the number line, as illustrated here.

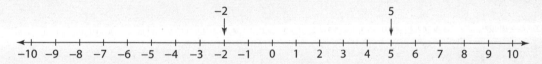

If both sides of the inequality $5 > -2$ are multiplied by a negative number, say -1, the direction of the inequality must be reversed, yielding the inequality $-5 < 2$. This is a true inequality because 2 is to the right of -5 on the number line, as illustrated here.

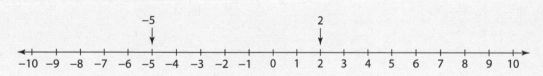

If you do not reverse the inequality symbol after multiplying both sides of $5 > -2$ by -1, you obtain $-5 > 2$, which is clearly false.

> Tip: The above example illustrates if $a < b$, it must be true that $-a > -b$, and if $a > b$, it must be true that $-a < -b$.

Here are examples.

Solve for x: $3x + 8 > -46$

$$3x + 8 > -46$$
$$3x + 8 - 8 > -46 - 8$$
$$3x + 0 > -54$$
$$3x > -54$$
$$\frac{3x}{3} > \frac{-54}{3}$$
$$\frac{\cancel{3}x}{\cancel{3}} > -54 \div 3$$
$$x > -18$$

The solution set consists of all numbers greater than –18. You can check by substituting a number from the solution set into the original inequality. For instance, you might let $x = 0$ (because 0 is greater than –18).

Check:

$3x + 8 > -46$

Is $3(0) + 8 > -46$?

Yes, because $3(0) + 8 = 8 > -46$. ✓

Solve for x: $-2(x - 15) < -36$

$$-2(x - 15) < -36$$
$$-2(x + -15) < -36$$
$$-2 \cdot x + -2 \cdot -15 < -36$$
$$-2x + 30 < -36$$
$$-2x + 30 - 30 < -36 - 30$$
$$-2x + 0 < -66$$
$$-2x < -66$$
$$\frac{-2x}{-2} > \frac{-66}{-2} \quad \text{Reverse the inequality symbol because of dividing both sides by a negative number.}$$
$$\frac{\cancel{-2}x}{\cancel{-2}} > -66 \div -2$$
$$1x > 33$$
$$x > 33$$

The solution set consists of all numbers greater than 33. You can check by substituting a number from the solution set into the original inequality. For instance, you might let $x = 40$ (because 40 is greater than 33).

Check:

$-2(x - 15) < -36$

Is $-2(40 - 15) < -36$?

Yes, because $-2(40 - 15) = -2(25) = -50 < -36$. ✓

Here is a real-world example.

> Inigo is paid \$300 per week, plus a commission of \$1.25 per sale. This week Inigo wants his pay to be more than \$500. What number of sales must Inigo make to achieve his goal?

Let n = the number of sales.

Write an inequality to represent the facts.

Think: *"I need to determine a range for the number of sales. Here's what I know. Inigo makes \$300 a week, plus what he makes as commission. His commission is \$1.25 times the number of sales he makes. He wants his weekly total to be greater than \$500."*

$$\$300 + \$1.25n > \$500$$

Solve the inequality for n, omitting units for convenience.

$$300 + 1.25n > 500$$
$$1.25n + 300 > 500$$
$$1.25n + 300 - 300 > 500 - 300$$
$$1.25n + 0 > 200$$
$$1.25n > 200$$
$$\frac{1.25n}{1.25} > \frac{200}{1.25}$$
$$\frac{1.25n}{1.25} > 200 \div 1.25$$
$$1n > 160$$
$$n > 160$$

Inigo will need to make more than 160 sales.

☞ Try These

1. Solve the inequality for x.

   (a) $3x - 4.5 < 1.8$

   (b) $5(x + 13) > 50$

   (c) $\frac{1}{2}x - 7 < 14$

   (d) $-4x + 9 > -5$

   (e) $-2(x - 1) > 20$

2. Chloe has $750, which she saved over the summer. She wants to have more than $200 of this money left by December. How many weeks can she spend $55 of her $750 savings and still have more than $200 left?

3. A company sells custom graphic t-shirts. It charges a one-time fee of $50 for creating the design for the t-shirts and then $15 for each shirt printed. Rafael is placing an order, but he wants to make sure he stays below $425. How many t-shirts can Rafael order?

4. If 20 times a number is increased by 35, the result is greater than 65. What are the possible values of the number?

Solutions

1. **(a)**

$$3x - 4.5 < 1.8$$
$$3x - 4.5 + 4.5 < 1.8 + 4.5$$
$$3x + 0 < 6.3$$
$$3x < 6.3$$
$$\frac{3x}{3} < \frac{6.3}{3}$$
$$\frac{\cancel{3}x}{\cancel{3}} < 6.3 \div 3$$
$$x < 2.1$$

(b)

$$5(x + 13) > 50$$
$$5 \cdot x + 5 \cdot 13 > 50$$
$$5x + 65 > 50$$
$$5x + 65 - 65 > 50 - 65$$
$$5x + 0 > 50 + -65$$
$$5x > -15$$
$$\frac{5x}{5} > \frac{-15}{5}$$
$$\frac{\cancel{5}x}{\cancel{5}} > -15 \div 5$$
$$x > -3$$

(c) $\dfrac{1}{2}x - 7 < 14$

$\dfrac{1}{2}x - 7 + 7 < 14 + 7$

$\dfrac{1}{2}x + 0 < 21$

$\dfrac{1}{2}x < 21$

$\dfrac{2}{1} \cdot \dfrac{1}{2}x < 2 \cdot 21$

$\dfrac{\cancel{2}}{1} \cdot \dfrac{1}{\cancel{2}}x < 2 \cdot 21$

$1x < 42$

$x < 42$

(d) $-4x + 9 > -5$

$-4x + 9 - 9 > -5 - 9$

$-4x + 0 > -14$

$\dfrac{-4x}{-4} < \dfrac{-14}{-4}$

$\dfrac{\cancel{-4}x}{\cancel{-4}} < -14 \div -4$

$x < 3.5$

(e) $-2(x - 1) > 20$

$-2(x + -1) > 20$

$-2 \cdot x + -2 \cdot -1 > 20$

$-2x + 2 > 20$

$-2x + 2 - 2 > 20 - 2$

$-2x + 0 > 18$

$-2x > 18$

$\dfrac{-2x}{-2} < \dfrac{18}{-2}$

$\dfrac{\cancel{-2}x}{\cancel{-2}} < 18 \div -2$

$x < -9$

2. Let n = the number of weeks Chloe can spend \$55 per week.

    Write an inequality to represent the facts.

    Think: *"I need to limit n so that Chloe will have more than \$200 left after n weeks. Here's what I know. She has \$750. She will spend \$55 a week for n weeks. I will multiply n by \$55 to obtain her total spending. She wants the difference between \$750 and her total spending to be more than \$200."*

$$\$750 - \$55n > \$200$$

Solve the inequality, omitting units for convenience.

$$750 - 55n > 200$$
$$750 + -55n > 200$$
$$-55n + 750 > 200$$
$$-55n + 750 - 750 > 200 - 750$$
$$-55n + 0 > -550$$
$$-55n > -550$$
$$\frac{-55n}{-55} < \frac{-550}{-55}$$
$$\frac{\cancel{-55}n}{\cancel{-55}} < -550 \div -55$$
$$n < 10$$

Chloe has less than 10 weeks to spend \$55 per week.

3. Let n = the number of t-shirts Rafael can order.

    Write an inequality to represent the facts.

    Think: *"I need to determine a range for n. Here's what I know. The company charges \$50 plus \$15 for every t-shirt. I will multiply n by \$15 to get the cost of n t-shirts. Rafael wants to make sure that the cost of n t-shirts plus the one-time \$50 fee stays below \$425."*

$$\$15n + \$50 < \$425$$

Solve the inequality, omitting units for convenience.

$$15n + 50 < 425$$
$$15n + 50 - 50 < 425 - 50$$
$$15n + 0 < 375$$
$$15n < 375$$
$$\frac{15n}{15} < \frac{375}{15}$$
$$\frac{\cancel{15}n}{\cancel{15}} < 375 \div 15$$
$$n < 25$$

If Rafael orders less than 25 t-shirts, the cost will be below \$425.

4. Let n = a possible value for the number.

    Write an inequality to represent the facts.

    Think: *"I need to determine a range for n. Here's what I know. If I multiply n by 20 and then add 35 to the product, the result is greater than 65."*

    $$20n + 35 > 65$$

Solve the inequality.

$$20n + 35 > 65$$
$$20n + 35 - 35 > 65 - 35$$
$$20n + 0 > 30$$
$$20n > 30$$
$$\frac{20n}{20} > \frac{30}{20}$$
$$\frac{\cancel{20}n}{\cancel{20}} > \frac{3}{2}$$
$$n > 1.5$$

Any number greater than 1.5 is a possible value of the number.

4. Geometry

In this chapter, you will solve problems involving scale drawings of geometric figures. You will decide conditions that determine a unique triangle, more than one triangle, or no triangle. And you will solve mathematical and real-life problems involving angle measure, area, surface area, and volume.

Solving Equations Involving Angle Measure

(CCSS.Math.Content.7.G.B.5)

A **ray** is a portion of a line extending from a point in one direction. When two rays meet at a common point, they form an **angle.** The point where the rays meet is the **vertex** of the angle, and the rays are its **sides** (or **arms**). *Tip:* The plural of *vertex* is *vertices.*

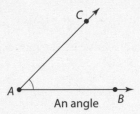

An angle

In the figure shown, A is the vertex and rays $\overrightarrow{AB}$ and $\overrightarrow{AC}$ are its sides. The symbol for angle is $\angle$. The angle in the figure is $\angle BAC$ or $\angle CAB$. *Tip:* $\overrightarrow{AB}$ is the ray that starts at A, goes through B, and continues on.

> **Tip: Read ∠BAC as "angle B, A, C." It does not matter which side you mention first, as long as the vertex label appears *between* the labels of the other two points. When it's clear what the sides are supposed to be, you can write simply ∠A to designate the angle.**

You also can designate an angle by writing a number or letter (usually lowercase) inside the angle. For example, as shown here, you can write $\angle 1$ for $\angle PQR$ and $\angle a$ for $\angle STU$.

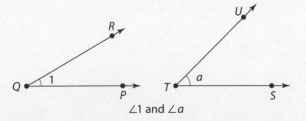

$\angle 1$ and $\angle a$

The two rays of an angle can be made to **coincide** (lie upon one another) by rotating one to the other around the vertex. The amount of rotation determines the size of the angle between the two rays. A counterclockwise rotation results in a positive measure. For example, a rotation from $\overrightarrow{QP}$ to $\overrightarrow{QR}$ is a counterclockwise rotation.

You measure an angle with reference to a circle with its center as the vertex of the angle. The amount of rotation required to form the angle can be expressed as a number of **degrees.** The symbol for degrees is °.

Tip: A full rotation around the circle is 360 degrees. An angle that turns $\frac{1}{360}$ of a complete rotation around the circle measures 1°.

In the figure shown, $\angle BAC$ is the result of ray $\overrightarrow{AC}$ turning $\frac{1}{8}$ of a complete rotation around the circle after starting in the same position as ray $\overrightarrow{AB}$. So the size of $\angle BAC$ is $\frac{1}{8}$ of 360°, or 45°.

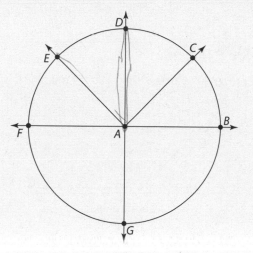

Similarly, ray $\overrightarrow{AD}$ has turned $\frac{1}{4}$ of a complete rotation. So the size of $\angle BAD$ is $\frac{1}{4}$ of 360°, or 90°. Ray $\overrightarrow{AE}$ has turned $\frac{3}{8}$ of a complete rotation. So the size of $\angle BAE$ is $\frac{3}{8}$ of 360°, or 135°. Ray $\overrightarrow{AF}$ has turned $\frac{1}{2}$ of a complete rotation. So the size of $\angle BAF$ is $\frac{1}{2}$ of 360°, or 180°. Ray $\overrightarrow{AG}$ has turned $\frac{3}{4}$ of a complete rotation. So the size of $\angle BAG$ is $\frac{3}{4}$ of 360°, or 270°.

Tip: The size of an angle depends on the amount of turning required to form it, NOT on the lengths of its sides.

An **acute angle** measures greater than 0°, but less than 90°. Angle BAC is an acute angle.

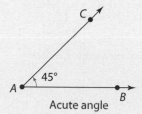

Acute angle

A **right angle** measures exactly 90°. Angle *BAD* is a right angle.

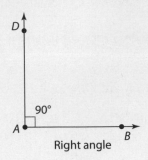

Right angle

Tip: The box in the corner denotes a right angle.

An **obtuse angle** measures greater than 90°, but less than 180°. Angle *BAE* is an obtuse angle.

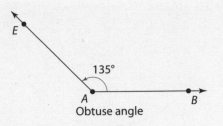

Obtuse angle

A **straight angle** measures exactly 180°. Angle *BAF* is a straight angle.

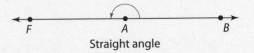

Straight angle

Two angles whose sum is 90° are **complementary angles.** Each angle is the other angle's **complement.**

Here is an example.

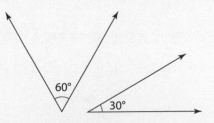

Complementary angles

Two angles whose sum is 180° are **supplementary angles.** Each angle is the other angle's **supplement.**

Here is an example.

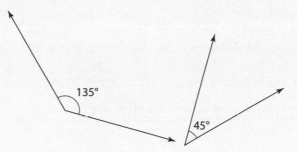

Supplementary angles

Adjacent angles are two angles that have a common vertex and a common side, with no overlap.

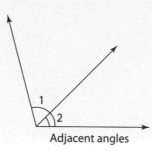

Adjacent angles

Two intersecting lines form four angles. **Vertical angles** are two *nonadjacent* angles formed by the two intersecting lines with a common vertex at the intersection of the two lines.

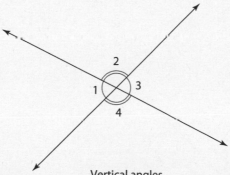

Vertical angles

Vertical angles formed by two intersecting lines are the same size.

Tip: Angles marked with the same number of strokes are the same size. In the figure, angles 1 and 3 are the same size, and angles 2 and 4 are the same size.

☞ Try These

1. Fill in the blank(s).

   (a) Two angles whose sum is 90° are _____ angles. Each angle is the other angle's_____.

   (b) Two angles whose sum is 180° are _____ angles. Each angle is the other angle's_____.

   (c) Two angles that have a common vertex and a common side, with no overlap, are _____ angles.

   (d) Two nonadjacent angles formed by two intersecting lines are _____ angles.

2. How many degrees are in the complement of the given angle?

   (a) 30°
   (b) 75°
   (c) 10°
   (d) 45°

3. How many degrees are in the supplement of the given angle?

   (a) 50°
   (b) 125°
   (c) 100°
   (d) 90°

4. Set up an equation and solve for x.

   (a)

   (b)

   (c)

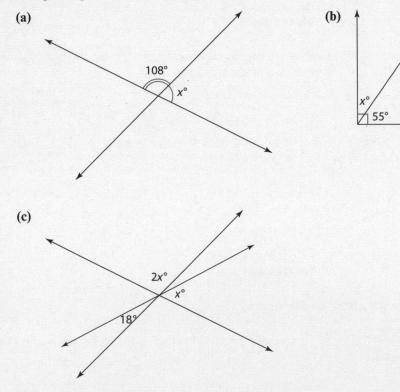

Solutions

1. **(a)** complementary; complement
    (b) supplementary; supplement
    (c) adjacent
    (d) vertical

2. **(a)** 60°
    (b) 15°
    (c) 80°
    (d) 45°

3. **(a)** 130°
    (b) 55°
    (c) 80°
    (d) 90°

4. **(a)** The two angles are supplementary, so their sum is 180°.

    $$x + 108 = 180 \quad \text{(omitting units)}$$
    $$x + 108 - 108 = 180 - 108$$
    $$x = 72$$

    (b) The two angles are complementary, so their sum is 90°.

    $$x + 55 = 90 \quad \text{(omitting units)}$$
    $$x + 55 - 55 = 90 - 55$$
    $$x = 35$$

    (c) Vertical angles have the same measure. So, the angle between $2x°$ and $x°$ measures 18°.

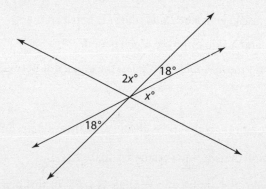

The sum of $2x°$, $18°$, and $x°$ is $180°$.

$$2x + 18 + x = 180 \quad \text{(omitting units)}$$
$$2x + x + 18 = 180$$
$$3x + 18 = 180$$
$$3x + 18 - 18 = 180 - 18$$
$$3x = 162$$
$$\frac{3x}{3} = \frac{162}{3}$$
$$\frac{\cancel{3}x}{\cancel{3}} = 162 \div 3$$
$$x = 54$$

Deciding Conditions That Determine a Unique Triangle, More Than One Triangle, or No Triangle

(CCSS.Math.Content.7.G.A.2)

The **parts** of a triangle are its three sides and three angles. If you are given three triangle parts, will the parts go together to form a triangle? And if they do, will the parts form one unique triangle or more than one triangle? How can you decide whether the parts do not go together to form a triangle?

Tip: Forming a unique triangle means the measures of the six parts of all triangles you form using the three given parts are the same.

Having only three parts of the six parts of a triangle leads to six situations:

1. You can have three sides.

2. You can have two sides and the *included angle* (the angle between them).

3. You can have two angles and the *included side* (the side between them).

4. You can have two angles and a side opposite a given angle.

5. You can have two sides and the *non-included angle* (the angle not between them).

6. You can have three angles.

Only in situations (1), (2), (3), and (4) do the three given parts always determine a unique triangle.

Here are explanations for each of these unique-triangle situations.

Note: The sum of the measures of the angles of a triangle is 180°. In this discussion, any given angle will measure between 0° and 180°.

(1) Three Sides Determine a Unique Triangle

If you are given three sides, you can put them together to form a unique triangle *provided* the length of the longest side is less than the sum of the lengths of the other two sides.

Here are examples.

Which sets of numbers could be the lengths of the sides of a triangle?

(a) 5, 6, 7
(b) 3, 3, 6
(c) 1, 3, 5

(a) The lengths 5, 6, and 7 can form a triangle because $7 < 5 + 6 = 11$. Here is a construction of the triangle.

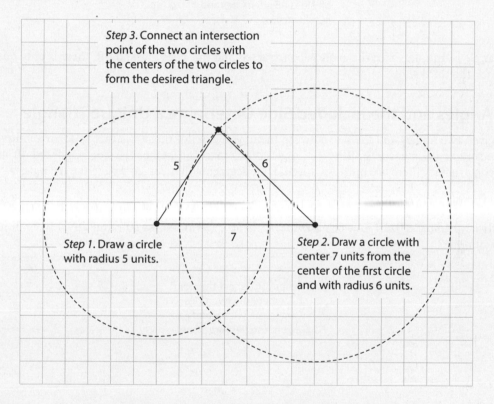

Step 3. Connect an intersection point of the two circles with the centers of the two circles to form the desired triangle.

Step 1. Draw a circle with radius 5 units.

Step 2. Draw a circle with center 7 units from the center of the first circle and with radius 6 units.

(b) The lengths 3, 3, and 6 do not satisfy the triangle inequality because $6 = 3 + 3$.

(c) The lengths 1, 3, 5 do not satisfy the triangle inequality because $5 > 1 + 3 = 4$.

(2) Two Sides and the Included Angle Determine a Unique Triangle

If you are given two sides and the angle between them, you can put them together to form a unique triangle. Once the angle is drawn and the sides are marked off, there is only one line segment that can complete the triangle.

Here is an example.

Construct triangle △*ABC*, in which *AB* is 5 inches, *AC* is 3 inches, and ∠*A* is 35°. Is △*ABC* unique?

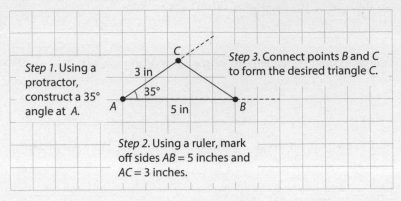

Yes, the triangle is unique. Once the angle is constructed and the sides marked off, there is only one location and length for the third side.

(3) Two Angles and the Included Side Determine a Unique Triangle

If you are given two angles and the side between them, you can put them together to form a unique triangle *provided* the sum of the measures of the two angles is less than 180°. Once the side is marked off and the angles are constructed, there are only two specific line segments that can complete the triangle.

Here is an example.

Construct triangle △*DEF*, in which ∠*D* measures 35°, ∠*F* measures 50°, and *DF* is 10 centimeters. Is △*DEF* unique?

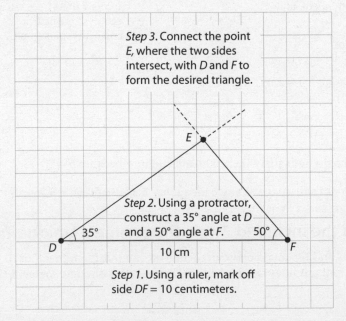

Yes, the triangle is unique. Once the included side is marked off and the angles are constructed, there are two specific line segments that complete the triangle.

(4) Two Angles and One Side Opposite a Given Angle Determine a Unique Triangle

If you are given two angles and one side opposite a given angle, you can put them together to form a unique triangle *provided* the sum of the measures of the two angles is less than 180°. A simple way to construct the triangle is to determine the third angle and proceed as in situation (3).

Here is an example.

Construct triangle $\triangle PQR$, in which $\angle P$ measures 50°, $\angle R$ measures 100°, and PQ is 12 feet. Is $\triangle PQR$ unique?

In $\triangle PQR$, $\angle Q$ measures $180° - 50° - 100° = 30°$. $\overline{PQ}$ is opposite $\angle R$. So $\overline{PQ}$ lies between $\angle P$ and $\angle Q$.

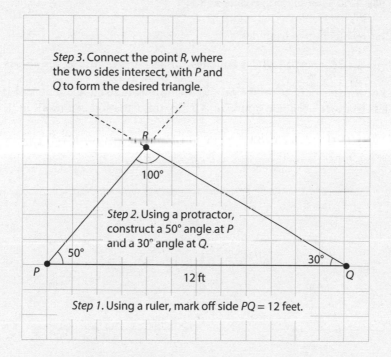

Step 3. Connect the point R, where the two sides intersect, with P and Q to form the desired triangle.

Step 2. Using a protractor, construct a 50° angle at P and a 30° angle at Q.

Step 1. Using a ruler, mark off side PQ = 12 feet.

Yes, the triangle is unique. Once the included side is marked off and the angles are constructed, there are two specific line segments that complete the triangle.

(5) Two Sides and an Angle That Is Not Between Them Do Not Determine a Unique Triangle

Suppose you know the measure of $\angle A$ and the length of side a, which is opposite $\angle A$, and you know the length of side b, which is opposite $\angle B$ (but you don't know $\angle B$'s measure). In this situation, you know two sides, a and b, and the non-included angle, $\angle A$. The following chart summarizes what can occur.

Number of Possible Distinct Triangles			
Situation	$a < b$	$a = b$	$a > b$
$\angle A$ is a right angle	none	none	1 unique triangle
$\angle A$ is obtuse	none	none	1 unique triangle
$\angle A$ is acute	0, 1, or 2	1 unique triangle	1 unique triangle

Tip: You shouldn't try to memorize this chart. Instead, you should spend time trying to construct various triangles given three parts. However, you should make a note that the possibility of two different triangles occurs in only one situation—when you have a non-included acute angle.

Here is an example that results in two triangles.

Construct triangle $\triangle ABC$, in which AC is 6 inches, CB is 4 inches, and $\angle A$ is 40°. Is $\triangle ABC$ unique?

In this problem, you know two sides, $\overline{AC}$ and $\overline{CB}$, and the non-included angle, $\angle A$. $\angle A$ is acute, and $\overline{CB}$, the side opposite $\angle A$, is less than $\overline{AC}$, the side opposite $\angle B$. So, this situation can result in 0, 1, or 2 triangles.

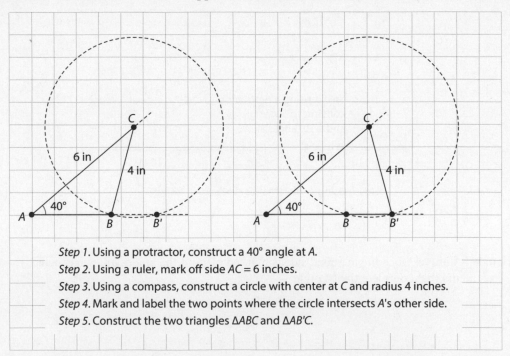

Step 1. Using a protractor, construct a 40° angle at A.
Step 2. Using a ruler, mark off side $AC = 6$ inches.
Step 3. Using a compass, construct a circle with center at C and radius 4 inches.
Step 4. Mark and label the two points where the circle intersects A's other side.
Step 5. Construct the two triangles $\triangle ABC$ and $\triangle AB'C$.

No, $\triangle ABC$ is not unique. From the information given, two different triangles can be constructed.

(6) Three Angles Do Not Determine a Unique Triangle

If you are given three angles of a triangle, there are infinitely many possibilities for the lengths of the sides of the triangle. You can construct infinitely many triangles whose angles are the same as those given. Here is an example.

Construct a triangle that has angles with measures 60°, 60°, and 60°.

Any equilateral triangle will have angles with measures 60°, 60°, and 60°. For example, equilateral triangles with sides 1, 1, and 1; 2, 2, and 2; 3, 3, and 3; and so on, have angles with measures 60°, 60°, and 60°.

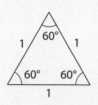

☞**Try These**

1. Fill in the blank(s).

   (a) The parts of a triangle are its three _____ and its three_____.

   (b) The length of the longest side of a triangle is _____ (greater, less) than the sum of the lengths of the other two sides.

   (c) The sum of the measures of the angles of a triangle is _____°.

   (d) Given three angles, _____ many triangles can be constructed whose angles are the same as those given.

2. Which sets of numbers could be the lengths of the sides of a triangle? Respond "Yes" or "No" and explain your answer.

   (a) 7, 24, 25

   (b) 1, 1, 1

   (c) 5, 5, 10

   (d) 5, 3, 18

   (e) 11, 12, 13

3. Label the three angles of a triangle $\angle P$, $\angle Q$, and $\angle R$. Label the three sides p, q, and r, where p is the side opposite $\angle P$, q is the side opposite $\angle Q$, and r is the side opposite $\angle R$. Which sets of conditions are certain to result in a unique triangle? Respond "Yes" or "No" and explain your answer.

   (a) Given the measures of p, q, and r
   (b) Given the measures of p, q, and $\angle R$
   (c) Given the measures of q, r, and $\angle P$
   (d) Given the measures of $\angle P$, $\angle R$, and q
   (e) Given the measures of $\angle P$, $\angle R$, and r
   (f) Given $p > q$, and $\angle P = 90°$
   (g) Given $p > q$, and $\angle P = 120°$
   (h) Given $p < q$, and $\angle P = 40°$

4. Using the labels given in Question 3, construct $\triangle PQR$, in which $p = 4$, $q = 6$, and $r = 9$. Is the triangle unique?

5. Using the labels given in Question 3, construct $\triangle PQR$, in which $p = 9$, $q = 12$, and the measure of $\angle R$ is 70°. Is the triangle unique?

Solutions

1. (a) sides; angles
   (b) less
   (c) 180
   (d) infinitely

2. (a) Yes, because $25 < 7 + 24 = 31$
   (b) Yes, because $1 < 1 + 1 = 2$
   (c) No, because $5 + 5 = 10$
   (d) No, because $5 + 3 < 18$
   (e) Yes, because $13 < 11 + 12 = 23$

3. (a) Yes, three sides
   (b) Yes, two sides and the included angle
   (c) Yes, two sides and the included angle
   (d) Yes, two angles and the included side
   (e) Yes, two angles and the side opposite a given angle
   (f) Yes, two sides and a right angle with the side opposite the angle greater than the other side
   (g) Yes, two sides and an obtuse angle with the side opposite the angle greater than the other side
   (h) No, two sides and an acute non-included acute angle with the side opposite the angle less than the other side.

4.

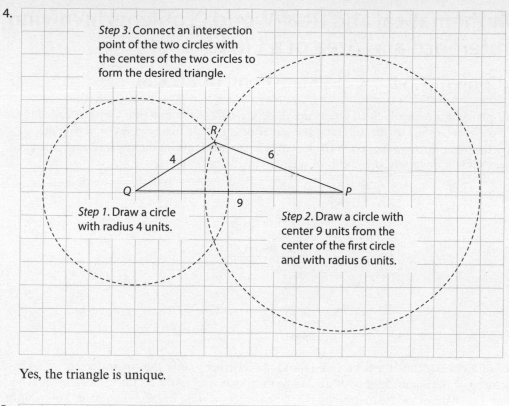

Step 3. Connect an intersection point of the two circles with the centers of the two circles to form the desired triangle.

Step 1. Draw a circle with radius 4 units.

Step 2. Draw a circle with center 9 units from the center of the first circle and with radius 6 units.

Yes, the triangle is unique.

5.

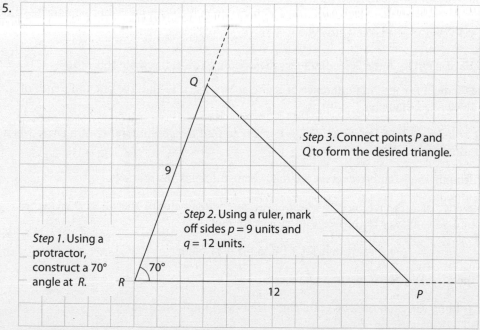

Step 3. Connect points *P* and *Q* to form the desired triangle.

Step 2. Using a ruler, mark off sides *p* = 9 units and *q* = 12 units.

Step 1. Using a protractor, construct a 70° angle at *R*.

Yes, the triangle is unique.

Solving Mathematical and Real-World Problems Involving the Circumference and Area of a Circle

(CCSS.Math.Content.7.G.B.4, CCSS.Math.Content.7.G.B.6)

A **circle** is a closed plane figure for which all points are the same distance from a point within, called the **center.** A **radius** of a circle is a line segment joining the center of the circle to any point on the circle. A **diameter** is a line segment through the center of the circle with endpoints on the circle. The diameter of a circle is twice the radius. Conversely, the radius of a circle is half the diameter.

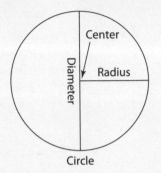

The **circumference** of a circle is the distance around the circle. In other words, the circumference of a circle is its perimeter. The ratio of the circumference of any circle to its diameter is always the same number. That number is called **pi.** The symbol for the number pi is π. The number π is an irrational number. You cannot write its exact value as a fraction or a terminating or repeating decimal. You can only approximate its value. For the problems in this book, use 3.14 as an approximate value for π.

If C is the circumference of a circle, and d is its diameter, then $\dfrac{C}{d} = \pi$. You can rewrite this ratio as $C = \pi d$.

This relationship is the formula for the circumference of a circle. You use it to find the circumference of a circle when you know the circle's diameter.

And, because $d = 2r$, $C = \pi d = \pi \cdot 2r = 2\pi r$. You can use $C = 2\pi r$ to find the circumference of a circle when you know the circle's radius.

Here is an example of finding the circumference of a circle when you know the diameter.

Find the circumference of a 26-inch bicycle wheel, meaning the diameter of the wheel is 26 inches. Use $\pi \approx 3.14$. Round your answer to the nearest tenth of an inch.

$$C = \pi d \approx \pi(26 \text{ in}) = 3.14(26 \text{ in}) = 81.64 \text{ in}$$

The circumference of the bicycle wheel is about 81.6 inches.

Here is an example of finding the circumference of a circle when you know the radius.

What is the distance around the edge of a dinner plate that has a radius of 11 centimeters? Use $\pi \approx 3.14$. Round your answer to the nearest centimeter.

$$C = 2\pi r \approx 2\pi(11 \text{ cm}) = 2(3.14)(11 \text{ cm}) = 69.08 \text{ cm}$$

The circumference of the plate is about 69 centimeters.

Here is an example of finding the diameter of a circle when you know its circumference. Use $\pi \approx 3.14$. Round your answer to the nearest tenth of an inch.

The distance around the edge of a circular disk is 15 inches. What is the diameter of the disk?

Substitute into the formula and solve for d, omitting units for convenience.

$$C = \pi d$$
$$15 = \pi d$$
$$15 = 3.14d$$
$$3.14d = 15$$
$$\frac{3.14d}{3.14} = \frac{15}{3.14}$$
$$\frac{\cancel{3.14}d}{\cancel{3.14}} = 15 \div 3.14$$
$$d \approx 4.77707$$

> **Tip: Read the symbol "≈" as "is approximately equal to."**

The diameter of the disk is about 4.8 inches.

The formula for the area of a circle is $A = \pi r^2$, where r is the radius of the circle. To see how this formula makes sense, cut a circle into 20 equal wedges.

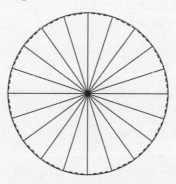

The area of each wedge is approximately the area of an isosceles triangle with sides r, base b, and height h. There are 20 wedges, so the base b of the triangle is approximately the circumference, C, of the circle divided by 20.

$$A = \frac{1}{2}bh = \frac{1}{2}\left(\frac{C}{20}\right)h$$

131

The area of the circle is approximately the total area of the 20 wedges. So, the area of the circle is approximately $20\left(\dfrac{1}{2}\left(\dfrac{C}{20}\right)h\right) = 2\!\!\!/0\left(\dfrac{1}{2}\left(\dfrac{C}{2\!\!\!/0}\right)h\right) = \dfrac{1}{2}Ch$. As you increase the number of wedges, the wedges get narrower and the sides of the triangles get closer together. As b gets smaller and smaller, the heights of the triangles get closer and closer to r. And the area, A, of the circle gets closer and closer to

$$A = \dfrac{1}{2}Cr = \dfrac{1}{2}(2\pi r)r = \dfrac{1}{2\!\!\!/}\left(2\!\!\!/\pi r\right)r = (\pi r)r = \pi r^2.$$

Here is an example of using the formula $A = \pi r^2$ to find the area of a circle.

> Find the area of a circular table that has a diameter of 3 feet. Use $\pi \approx 3.14$. Round your answer to the nearest square foot.

The diameter of the table is 3 feet, so the radius is $\dfrac{1}{2}$ of 3 feet, which is 1.5 feet.

$$A = \pi r^2 = \pi(1.5 \text{ ft})^2 \approx 3.14(1.5 \text{ ft})^2 = 3.14(2.25 \text{ ft}^2) = 7.065 \text{ ft}^2$$

Tip: Perform the exponentiation before multiplying by 3.14. Remember to follow the order of operations when performing calculations.

The area of the table is about 7 ft^2.

☞ Try These

1. Fill in the blank.

   (a) The circumference of a circle is _____.
   (b) The ratio of the circumference of any circle to its diameter is the number _____.
   (c) The formula for the circumference of a circle is _____ or _____.
   (d) The formula for the area of a circle is _____.

2. A circular wading pool has a diameter of 12 feet. What is its circumference, to the nearest foot? Use $\pi \approx 3.14$.

3. Gonzalo's bicycle has 28-inch wheels, meaning the diameter of each wheel is 28 inches. How far does his bike travel with each revolution of the wheels? Use $\pi \approx 3.14$. Give your answer to the nearest inch.

4. A tree trunk is 9 feet in circumference. What is its diameter, to the nearest tenth of a foot? Use $\pi \approx 3.14$.

5. Isla bought a circular rug for her bedroom. The rug has a radius of 3 feet. What is its area, to the nearest square foot? Use $\pi \approx 3.14$.

Solutions

1. (a) perimeter
   (b) π
   (c) $C = \pi d$; $C = 2\pi r$
   (d) $A = \pi r^2$

2. $C = \pi d \approx \pi(12 \text{ ft}) = 3.14(12 \text{ ft}) = 37.68 \text{ ft}$

   The pool's circumference is about 38 feet.

3. With each revolution of the wheels, the bike will travel a distance equal to the circumference of one wheel.

$$C = \pi d \approx \pi(28 \text{ in}) = 3.14(28 \text{ in}) = 87.92 \text{ in}$$

   The bike will travel about 88 inches with each revolution of the wheels.

4. Let $d =$ the tree trunk's diameter. Substitute into the formula and solve for d, omitting units for convenience.

$$C = \pi d$$
$$9 = \pi d$$
$$9 = 3.14d$$
$$3.14d = 9$$
$$\frac{3.14d}{3.14} = \frac{9}{3.14}$$
$$\frac{\cancel{3.14}d}{\cancel{3.14}} = 9 \div 3.14$$
$$d \approx 2.86624$$

   The tree trunk's diameter is about 2.9 feet.

5. $A = \pi r^2 = \pi(3 \text{ ft})^2 \approx 3.14(3 \text{ ft})^2 = 3.14(9 \text{ ft}^2) = 28.26 \text{ ft}^2$

   The rug's area is about 28 square feet.

Solving Mathematical and Real-World Problems Involving Area of Two-Dimensional Shapes and Surface Area and Volume of Three-Dimensional Figures

(CCSS.Math.Content.7.G.B.4, CCSS.Math.Content.7.G.B.6)

Success in solving problems involving area, surface area, and volume of geometric figures depends on an understanding of and ability to use formulas associated with common geometric figures.

Areas of Common Two-Dimensional Figures

The area of a triangle is $A = \frac{1}{2}bh$, where b is the measure of a base of the triangle, and h is the height for that base.

Here is an example.

Determine the area of the triangle.

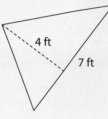

The area of the triangle shown is $A = \dfrac{1}{2}bh = \dfrac{1}{2}(7 \text{ ft})(4 \text{ ft}) = \dfrac{(7 \text{ ft})(\overset{2}{\cancel{4}} \text{ ft})}{\underset{1}{\cancel{2}}} = \dfrac{14 \text{ ft}^2}{1} = 14 \text{ ft}^2$.

The area of a parallelogram is $A = bh$, where b is the measure of a base of the parallelogram, and h is the height drawn to that base.

Here is an example.

Find the area of the parallelogram.

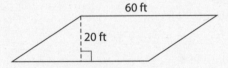

The area of the parallelogram shown is $A = bh = (60 \text{ ft})(20 \text{ ft}) = 1{,}200 \text{ ft}^2$.

Rhombuses, rectangles, and squares are parallelograms. Thus, the area of a rhombus is $A = bh$. The area of a rectangle is $A = bh = lw$, where l is the rectangle's length and w is its width. The area of a square is $A = bh = s \cdot s = s^2$, where s is the measure of a side of the square.

The area of a trapezoid is $A = \dfrac{(a+b)}{2}h$, where a and b are the measures of two parallel sides of the trapezoid, and h is the height between those two sides.

Here is an example.

Find the area of the trapezoid.

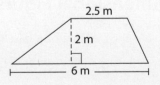

The area of the trapezoid shown is $A = \dfrac{(a+b)}{2}h = \dfrac{(2.5 \text{ m} + 6 \text{ m})}{2} \cdot 2 \text{ m} = \dfrac{(8.5 \text{ m})}{2} \cdot 2 \text{ m} = 4.25 \text{ m} \cdot 2 \text{ m} = 8.5 \text{ m}^2$.

☞ Try These

1. Find the area of the triangle.

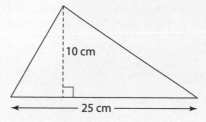

2. Find the area of the rhombus.

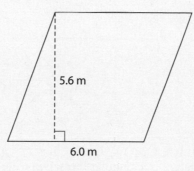

3. Find the area of the trapezoid.

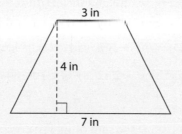

Solutions

1. $A = \dfrac{1}{2}bh = \dfrac{1}{2}(25 \text{ cm})(10 \text{ cm}) = \dfrac{(25 \text{ cm})(10 \text{ cm})}{2} = 125 \text{ cm}^2$

2. $A = bh = (6.0 \text{ m})(5.6 \text{ m}) = 33.6 \text{ m}^2$

3. $A = \dfrac{(a+b)}{2}h = \dfrac{(3 \text{ in} + 7 \text{ in})}{2} \cdot 4 \text{ in} = \dfrac{(10 \text{ in})}{2} \cdot 4 \text{ in} = 5 \text{ in} \cdot 4 \text{ in} = 20 \text{ in}^2$

Surface Areas of Right Prisms and Pyramids

A prism has two parallel congruent polygon-shaped bases and lateral (side) faces that are parallelograms. In a **right prism,** the two bases are directly across from each other and the lateral faces are rectangles. The surface area of a right prism is the sum of the areas of its two congruent bases and the areas of its lateral rectangular faces.

> **Tip: Congruent figures have the same size and shape.**

Here are examples.

A box is 16 inches in length, 12 inches in width, and 10 inches in height. What is its surface area?

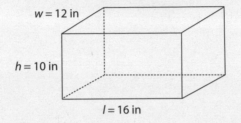

The box is a right rectangular prism. It has a top rectangular base and a bottom rectangular base that are exactly the same size. And it has four lateral rectangular faces. Opposite faces are the same size. Use the length and width to find the areas of the two congruent bases. Use the length and the height to find the areas of the two longer lateral faces. Use the width and the height to find the areas of the other two lateral faces.

The surface area of the box is $S.A. = 2lw + 2lh + 2wh,$ where l is its length, w is its width, and h is its height.

$$S.A. = 2(16 \text{ in})(12 \text{ in}) + 2(16 \text{ in})(10 \text{ in}) + 2(12 \text{ in})(10 \text{ in}) = 384 \text{ in}^2 + 320 \text{ in}^2 + 240 \text{ in}^2 = 944 \text{ in}^2$$

The surface area of the box is 944 in².

The surface area of a right triangular prism is the sum of its two congruent triangular bases and its three rectangular lateral faces.

Here is an example.

Find the surface area of the right triangular prism.

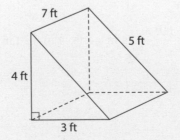

The bases of the prism shown are two congruent right triangles. The legs of the triangles are 3 feet and 4 feet. The three rectangular lateral faces have dimensions 7 feet by 5 feet, 7 feet by 4 feet, and 7 feet by 3 feet.

$$S.A. = 2\left(\frac{1}{2} \cdot 3 \text{ ft} \cdot 4 \text{ ft}\right) + (7 \text{ ft} \cdot 5 \text{ ft}) + (7 \text{ ft} \cdot 4 \text{ ft}) + (7 \text{ ft} \cdot 3 \text{ ft}) = 12 \text{ ft}^2 + 35 \text{ ft}^2 + 28 \text{ ft}^2 + 21 \text{ ft}^2 = 96 \text{ ft}^2$$

A pyramid has one polygon-shaped base and triangular lateral faces that meet at a point called the **apex**. In a **right pyramid,** the apex is directly above the center of the base. The surface area of a right pyramid is the sum of the area of its base and the areas of all its triangular faces.

Here is an example.

The sum of the areas of the four triangular lateral faces of the right rectangular pyramid shown is approximately 120 ft². Find its approximate surface area.

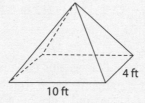

10 ft   4 ft

The surface area is the sum of the area of the pyramid's base and the areas of its four triangular lateral faces.

$$S.A. = (10 \text{ ft})(4 \text{ ft}) + 120 \text{ ft}^2 = 40 \text{ ft}^2 + 120 \text{ ft}^2 = 160 \text{ ft}^2$$

☞ Try These

1. How many square inches of wrapping paper will cover the box, without any overlap?

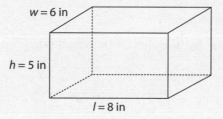

$w = 6$ in
$h = 5$ in
$l = 8$ in

2. Find the surface area of the right triangular prism.

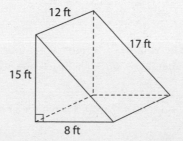

12 ft   17 ft   15 ft   8 ft

3. A square pyramid is composed of four equilateral triangles and a square base. Each triangle has sides of 8 inches and height of about 7 inches. What is the approximate surface area of the square pyramid?

Solutions

1. To answer the question, calculate the surface area of the box. The surface area of the box is $S.A. = 2lw + 2lh + 2wh$, where l is its length, w is its width, and h is its height.

   $S.A. = 2(8 \text{ in})(6 \text{ in}) + 2(8 \text{ in})(5 \text{ in}) + 2(6 \text{ in})(5 \text{ in}) = 96 \text{ in}^2 + 80 \text{ in}^2 + 60 \text{ in}^2 = 236 \text{ in}^2$

   236 square inches of wrapping paper will cover the box.

2. The surface area is the sum of the areas of the prism's two congruent triangular bases and its three rectangular lateral faces. The bases of the prism are two congruent right triangles. The legs of the triangles are 8 feet and 15 feet. The three rectangular lateral faces have dimensions 12 feet by 17 feet, 12 feet by 15 feet, and 12 feet by 8 feet.

   $$S.A. = 2\left(\frac{1}{2} \cdot 15 \text{ ft} \cdot 8 \text{ ft}\right) + (12 \text{ ft} \cdot 17 \text{ ft}) + (12 \text{ ft} \cdot 15 \text{ ft}) + (12 \text{ ft} \cdot 8 \text{ ft}) = 120 \text{ ft}^2 + 204 \text{ ft}^2 + 180 \text{ ft}^2 + 96 \text{ ft}^2$$

   $$= 600 \text{ ft}^2$$

3. The surface area is the area of the pyramid's base plus the sum of the areas of its four congruent triangular lateral faces. The base of the pyramid is an 8 inch by 8 inch square. Each of the four triangular lateral faces has a base of 8 inches and a height of about 7 inches.

   $$S.A. = (8 \text{ in} \cdot 8 \text{ in}) + 4\left(\frac{1}{2} \cdot 8 \text{ in} \cdot 7 \text{ in}\right) = 64 \text{ in}^2 + 112 \text{ in}^2 = 176 \text{ in}^2$$

Volume of Right Prisms and Pyramids

The volume of a right prism is the area of one of its congruent bases times the prism's height.

Here are examples.

A box has dimensions 16 inches by 12 inches by 10 inches. What is its volume?

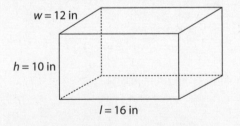

The box is a right rectangular prism. The volume of a right rectangular prism is $V = $ (area, B, of one of its congruent rectangular bases) times (its height) $= Bh = (lw)(h) = lwh$, where l is its length, w is its width, and h is its height.

$$V = (16 \text{ in})(12 \text{ in})(10 \text{ in}) = 1{,}920 \text{ in}^3$$

The volume of the box is 1,920 in³.

Find the volume of the right triangular prism.

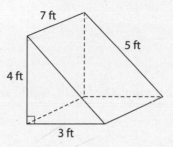

The volume of a right triangular prism is V = (area, B, of one of its congruent triangular bases) times (its height) = Bh. The bases of the prism shown are two right triangles. The legs of the triangles are 3 feet and 4 feet.

$$V = Bh = \left(\frac{1}{2} \cdot 3 \text{ ft} \cdot 4 \text{ ft}\right)(7 \text{ ft}) = \left(6 \text{ ft}^2\right)(7 \text{ ft}) = 42 \text{ ft}^3$$

The volume of a right pyramid is $V = \frac{1}{3} Bh$. (**Note:** B = area of base and h = height.)

Here is an example.

Find the volume of the right rectangular pyramid.

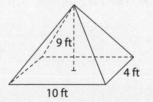

The base of the pyramid shown is a rectangle with dimensions 10 feet by 4 feet. The height of the pyramid is 9 feet.

$$V = \frac{1}{3} Bh = \frac{1}{3}(10 \text{ ft} \cdot 4 \text{ ft})(9 \text{ ft}) = \frac{1}{3}\left(40 \text{ ft}^2\right)(9 \text{ ft}) = 120 \text{ ft}^3$$

☞ Try These

1. Find the volume of a right rectangular prism with dimensions l = 8.5 m, w = 5 m, and h = 7 m.

2. Find the volume of a 2-inch cube.

3. A right triangular prism has a height of 9 centimeters. Its bases are right triangles with legs 5 centimeters and 12 centimeters. What is the prism's volume?

4. A right rectangular pyramid has a height of 4 inches. Its base has dimensions 12 inches by 4.5 inches. What is its volume?

Solutions

1. $V = lwh = (8.5 \text{ m})(5 \text{ m})(7 \text{ m}) = 297.5 \text{ m}^3$

2. A 2-inch cube is a right rectangular prism. The length, width, and height all have the same measure of 2 inches.

   $V = lwh = (2 \text{ in})(2 \text{ in})(2 \text{ in}) = 8 \text{ in}^3$

3. $V = Bh = \left(\dfrac{1}{2} \cdot 5 \text{ cm} \cdot 12 \text{ cm}\right)(9 \text{ cm}) = (30 \text{ cm}^2)(9 \text{ cm}) = 270 \text{ cm}^3$

4. $V = \dfrac{1}{3} Bh = \dfrac{1}{3}(12 \text{ in} \cdot 4.5 \text{ in})(4 \text{ in}) = \dfrac{1}{3}(54 \text{ in}^2)(4 \text{ in}) = 72 \text{ in}^3$

Multistep Problems Involving Area, Surface Area, and Volume

You can use what you know about the area of two-dimensional shapes and surface area and volume of three-dimensional figures to solve multistep problems.

Here is an example.

Elba wants to cover the box shown in colorful wrapping paper, with no overlap.

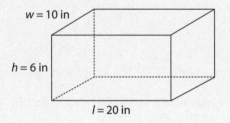

The wrapping paper costs $\dfrac{1}{2}$ cent per square inch. What is Elba's total cost for the box's wrapping paper?

To solve the problem, use two steps. First, find the surface area of the box. Next, find the total cost of the wrapping paper by using the unit rate of $\dfrac{1}{2}$ cent per square inch of wrapping paper.

Step 1. Find the box's surface area.

The box is a right rectangular prism. It has a top rectangular base and a bottom rectangular base that are exactly the same size. And it has four lateral rectangular faces. Opposite faces are the same size. Use the length and the width to find the areas of the two congruent bases. Use the length and the height to find the areas of the two longer lateral faces. Use the width and the height to find the areas of the other two lateral faces.

The surface area of the box is $S.A. = 2lw + 2lh + 2wh$, where l is its length, w is its width, and h is its height.

$$S.A. = 2(20 \text{ in})(10 \text{ in}) + 2(20 \text{ in})(6 \text{ in}) + 2(10 \text{ in})(6 \text{ in}) = 400 \text{ in}^2 + 240 \text{ in}^2 + 120 \text{ in}^2 = 760 \text{ in}^2$$

The surface area of the box is 760 in^2.

Step 2. Find the total cost of the wrapping paper.

Multiply 760 in^2 by the cost per in^2.

$$760 \text{ in}^2 \times \$0.005 \text{ per in}^2 = \frac{760 \text{ in}^2}{1} \times \frac{\$0.005}{\text{in}^2} = \$3.80$$

Tip: $\frac{1}{2}$ cent $= 0.5$ cent $= \$0.005$.

Elba's total cost for the wrapping paper is $3.80.

☞ Try These

1. What is the difference between the area of a 16-inch pizza and the area of an 8-inch pizza? (*Tip:* A pizza's diameter is used to describe its size.) Give your answer to the nearest square inch.

2. Taylor and Andreja's parents want to apply one coat of twilight blue paint to the walls in a large playroom in their home. The playroom is 20 feet long, 14 feet wide, and has a 10-foot-high ceiling. One gallon of paint will cover 320 square feet (ft^2). Twilight blue paint is sold in gallon containers only. How many gallons of paint will the parents need to buy?

3. Carpet is sold by the square yard (yd^2). How many square yards of carpet are needed to carpet a large room at school that is 22 feet long and 18 feet wide?

4. To determine the volume of a small crate, students in a seventh-grade math class pack the crate, leaving no empty space, with 125 cubes measuring 4 inches on each edge. What is the volume of the crate in cubic inches?

Solutions

1. To solve the problem, do three steps. First, find the area of a 16-inch pizza. Next, find the area of an 8-inch pizza. Then, find the difference by subtracting the area of an 8-inch pizza from the area of a 16-inch pizza.

   Step 1. Find the area of a 16-inch pizza.

   The radius of a 16-inch pizza is 8 inches. Its area is $A = \pi r^2 = \pi(8 \text{ in})^2 \approx 3.14(8 \text{ in})^2 = 3.14(64 \text{ in}^2) = 200.96 \text{ in}^2$.

Step 2. Find the area of an 8-inch pizza.

The radius of an 8-inch pizza is 4 inches. Its area is $A = \pi r^2 = \pi(4 \text{ in})^2 = 3.14(4 \text{ in})^2 \approx 3.14(16 \text{ in}^2) = 50.24 \text{ in}^2$.

Step 3. Find the difference.

The difference is $200.96 \text{ in}^2 - 50.24 \text{ in}^2 = 150.72 \text{ in}^2$, or about 151 in^2.

2. To solve the problem, do two steps. First, find the surface area of the walls to be painted. Second, find the number of gallons needed to cover the walls by using the unit rate of 320 ft² per gallon of paint.

Step 1. Find the surface area of the walls to be painted.

The room is a rectangular prism, so opposite walls are the same size. Use the length and the height to find the areas of the two longer walls. Use the width and the height to find the area of the other two walls.

Surface area to be painted $= 2(20 \text{ ft})(10 \text{ ft}) + 2(14 \text{ ft})(10 \text{ ft}) = 400 \text{ ft}^2 + 280 \text{ ft}^2 = 680 \text{ ft}^2$

Step 2. Find the number of gallons of paint needed.

Write the unit rate as a fraction: $320 \text{ ft}^2 \text{ per gallon} = \dfrac{320 \text{ ft}^2}{1 \text{ gal}}$.

$$\text{number of gallons needed} = 680 \text{ ft}^2 \div \frac{320 \text{ ft}^2}{1 \text{ gal}} = \frac{680 \text{ ft}^2}{1} \times \frac{1 \text{ gal}}{320 \text{ ft}^2} = \frac{680 \cancel{\text{ ft}^2}}{1} \times \frac{1 \text{ gal}}{320 \cancel{\text{ ft}^2}} = \frac{680 \text{ gal}}{320}$$

$$= 2.125 \text{ gal}$$

The parents will need to buy 3 gallons of paint.

3. Sketch a diagram to illustrate the problem.

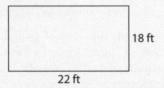

18 ft

22 ft

Square yards are units of area, so find the area of the room in square yards. To solve the problem, do two steps. First, convert the dimensions of the room's floor to yards. Next, find the area of the floor in square yards.

Step 1. Convert the dimensions of the floor to yards. (See Appendix A for measurement conversions.)

1 yard = 3 feet. You can write this relationship as $\dfrac{3 \text{ ft}}{1 \text{ yd}}$ or $\dfrac{1 \text{ yd}}{3 \text{ ft}}$.

Write each dimension of the floor as a fraction with denominator 1 and let the units tell you whether to multiply by $\dfrac{3 \text{ ft}}{1 \text{ yd}}$ or $\dfrac{1 \text{ yd}}{3 \text{ ft}}$. Because you want the feet to divide out, multiply by $\dfrac{1 \text{ yd}}{3 \text{ ft}}$.

Tip: Keep in mind you are converting from *a smaller unit to a larger unit*. You should expect it will take *less* of the larger units to equal the same amount.

$$\frac{22 \text{ ft}}{1} \cdot \frac{1 \text{ yd}}{3 \text{ ft}} = \frac{22 \cancel{\text{ ft}}}{1} \cdot \frac{1 \text{ yd}}{3 \cancel{\text{ ft}}} = \frac{22 \text{ yd}}{3} = 7\frac{1}{3} \text{ yd}$$

$$\frac{18 \text{ ft}}{1} \cdot \frac{1 \text{ yd}}{3 \text{ ft}} = \frac{\cancel{18}^{6} \cancel{\text{ ft}}}{1} \cdot \frac{1 \text{ yd}}{\cancel{3}_{1}\cancel{\text{ ft}}} = 6 \text{ yd}$$

Step 2. Find the area of the room's floor in square yards.

$$A = lw = \left(7\frac{1}{3} \text{ yd}\right)(6 \text{ yd}) = \left(\frac{22}{3} \text{ yd}\right)\left(\frac{6}{1} \text{ yd}\right) = \left(\frac{22}{\cancel{3}_1} \text{ yd}\right)\left(\frac{\cancel{6}^2}{1} \text{ yd}\right) = 44 \text{ yd}^2$$

44 square yards of carpet are needed.

4. To solve the problem, do two steps. First, find the volume of one 4-inch cube. Then, find the volume of the crate by multiplying the volume of one 4-inch cube by 125.

Step 1. Find the volume of one 4-inch cube.

A 4-inch cube is a right rectangular prism. The length, width, and height all have the same measure of 4 inches. The volume of a 4-inch cube is

$$V = lwh = (4 \text{ in})(4 \text{ in})(4 \text{ in}) = 64 \text{ in}^3$$

Step 2. Find the volume of the crate.

It took 125 of the 4-inch cubes to fill the crate, so the volume of the crate is

125 times (the volume of one 4-inch cube) = $125(64 \text{ in}^3)$ = 8,000 in^3

Solving Problems Involving Scale Drawings of Geometric Figures

(CCSS.Math.Content.7.G.A.1, CCSS.Math.Content.7.G.B.4, CCSS.Math. Content.7.G.B.6)

A drawing (or diagram) is a **scale drawing** (or diagram), if corresponding parts of the drawing and the original object have a proportional relationship. The constant of proportionality is the **scale factor.** To find the scale factor, compute the ratio of one part of the scale drawing to the corresponding part of the original object. The drawing is an **enlargement,** if $r > 1$; and a **reduction,** if $r < 1$.

Here is an example.

The diagram shown represents the first-floor plan of Luli's house. It is drawn to **scale.**

In the diagram, $\frac{1}{8}$ inch in length corresponds to 1 foot of actual length.

(a) What is the scale factor r for the diagram?

(b) Is the diagram an enlargement or a reduction?

(c) If the actual dimensions of the living room are 12 feet by 16 feet, what are the dimensions of the living room on the scale drawing?

(a) The scale factor, r, is the constant of proportionality between the corresponding parts of the diagram and the actual house. The scale factor, r, is the ratio of $\frac{1}{8}$ inch to 12 inches (1 foot):

$$r = \frac{\frac{1}{8} \text{ in}}{12 \text{ in}} = \frac{\left(\frac{1}{8}\right) \cdot \frac{8}{1}}{12 \cdot 8} = \frac{1}{96}$$

(b) The diagram is a reduction because $r < 1$.

(c) Method 1: Multiply each dimension by the scale factor.

First, change the dimensions to inches. (See Appendix A for measurement conversions.)

$$12 \text{ ft} \times \frac{12 \text{ in}}{1 \text{ ft}} = 144 \text{ in}; \ 16 \text{ ft} \times \frac{12 \text{ in}}{1 \text{ ft}} = 192 \text{ in}$$

Next, multiply by the scale factor.

$$144 \text{ in} \times \frac{1}{96} = \frac{144}{96} \text{ in} = \left(\frac{144 \div 48}{96 \div 48}\right) \text{ in} = \frac{3}{2} \text{ in} = 1\frac{1}{2} \text{ in}$$

$$192 \text{ in} \times \frac{1}{96} = \frac{192}{96} \text{ in} = \left(\frac{192 \div 96}{96 \div 96}\right) \text{ in} = \frac{2}{1} \text{ in} = 2 \text{ in}$$

On the scale drawing, the dimensions of the living room are $1\frac{1}{2}$ inches by 2 inches.

Method 2: Use mathematical reasoning.

If $\frac{1}{8}$ inch in length corresponds to 1 foot, then 12 times $\frac{1}{8}$ inch corresponds to 12 feet;

$$12 \cdot \frac{1}{8} \text{ in} = \frac{12}{8} \text{ in} = 1\frac{1}{2} \text{ in}.$$

Similarly, $16 \cdot \frac{1}{8}$ inch corresponds to 16 feet; $16 \cdot \frac{1}{8}$ in $= 2$ in.

Here is another example.

The dimensions of a 5-by-5-inch square are enlarged by a scale factor of r.

(a) What is the ratio of the perimeter of the enlargement to the perimeter of the original square?
(b) What is the ratio of the area of the enlargement to the area of the original square?

(a) $\dfrac{\text{perimeter of enlargement}}{\text{perimeter of original}} = \dfrac{4 \cdot 5r}{4 \cdot 5} = \dfrac{4 \cdot 5r}{4 \cdot 5} = \dfrac{r}{1}$

The ratio of the perimeter of the enlargement to the perimeter of the original square is r to 1.

(b) $\dfrac{\text{area of enlargement}}{\text{area of original}} = \dfrac{(5 \cdot r)^2}{(5)^2} = \dfrac{25r^2}{25} = \dfrac{r^2}{1}$

The ratio of the area of the enlargement to the area of the original square is r^2.

The results of this second example hold true regardless of the shape of the figure.

> If a two-dimensional figure is enlarged by a scale factor of r, the ratio of the perimeter of the enlargement to the perimeter of the original figure is r to 1, and the ratio of the area of the enlargement to the area of the original figure is r^2 to 1.

☞ Try These

1. Fill in the blank(s).

(a) In a scale drawing, corresponding parts of the drawing and the original object have a _____ relationship.
(b) In a scale drawing, the constant of proportionality for corresponding parts is the _____ (two words).
(c) A scale drawing is an enlargement if _____, where r is the _____ (two words).
(d) A scale drawing is a reduction if _____, where r is the _____ (two words).

2. A picture book has scale drawings of various animals. The scale shows that $\frac{1}{4}$ inch in the drawing represents 5 inches of actual length.

   (a) What is the scale factor of the drawing?
   (b) Is the drawing an enlargement or a reduction?
   (c) Suppose a dog is actually 20 inches long. What is the length (in inches) of the dog in the scale drawing?

3. In the diagram, $ABCD$ and $WXYZ$ are squares. Square $WXYZ$ is a scale drawing of square $ABCD$.

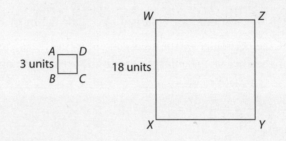

   (a) What is the scale factor?
   (b) Is $WXYZ$ an enlargement or a reduction?
   (c) What is the ratio of the area of $WXYZ$ to the area of $ABCD$?

Solutions

1. **(a)** proportional
   (b) scale factor
   (c) $r > 1$; scale factor
   (d) $r < 1$; scale factor

2. **(a)** $r = \dfrac{\frac{1}{4} \text{ in}}{5 \text{ in}} = \dfrac{\left(\frac{1}{4}\right) \cdot \frac{4}{1}}{(5) \cdot 4} = \dfrac{1}{20}$

   The scale factor is $\dfrac{1}{20}$.

   (b) The diagram is a reduction because $r < 1$.
   (c) Multiply 20 inches by the scale factor.

   $$20 \text{ in} \times \frac{1}{20} = \frac{20 \text{ in}}{1} \times \frac{1}{20} = 1 \text{ in}$$

   In the scale drawing, the dog is 1 inch long.

3. **(a)** $r = \dfrac{18 \text{ in}}{3 \text{ in}} = \dfrac{6}{1} = 6$

The scale factor is 6.

(b) $WXYZ$ is an enlargement because $r > 6$.

(c) The ratio of the area of $WXYZ$ to the area of $ABCD$ is 6^2 to 1^2 or 36 to 1.

Describing Two-Dimensional Figures That Result from Slicing Right Rectangular Prisms and Pyramids

(CCSS.Math.Content.7.G.A.3)

If you "slice" through a right rectangular prism or pyramid with a plane, you obtain plane (two-dimensional) cross sections of the figures.

Here are guidelines.

Right rectangular prisms

- Slices made parallel to a base will result in cross sections that have the same shape and size of the base.
- Slices made perpendicular to a base will result in rectangular cross sections with a height equal to the height of the prism.
- Slices made parallel to a lateral face will result in cross sections that have the same shape and size of the lateral face.

Right rectangular pyramids

- Slices made parallel to a base will result in cross sections that have the shape of the base.
- Slices made perpendicular to a base and passing through the apex will result in cross sections that have the shape of a lateral triangular face.
- Slices made perpendicular to a base but not passing through the apex will result in cross sections that have the shape of an isosceles trapezoid.

You should practice confirming the guidelines.

Here is an example.

What is the shape of a cross section when a plane perpendicular to the base of a right rectangular pyramid passes through the pyramid, but not through the pyramid's apex?

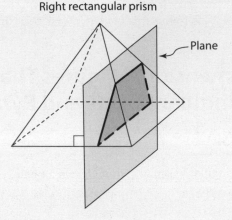

Right rectangular prism

Plane

The shape is an isosceles trapezoid.

☞ Try These

1. Describe the shape of the cross section that results when a plane passes through a right rectangular prism as described.

   (a) Parallel to a base
   (b) Parallel to a lateral side
   (c) Perpendicular to a base

2. Describe the shape of the cross section that results when a plane passes through a right rectangular pyramid as described.

   (a) Parallel to the base
   (b) Perpendicular to the base and passing through the apex
   (c) Perpendicular to the base but not passing through the apex

Solutions

1. **(a)** The same size and shape as the base
   (b) The same size and shape as the lateral side
   (c) A rectangle with the same height as the prism

2. **(a)** The same shape as the base
   (b) The shape of a lateral triangle
   (c) The shape of an isosceles trapezoid

5. Statistics and Probability

In this chapter, you will learn about probability, generate probability models, and compute probabilities. You will learn about the importance of random sampling in statistics, visually compare data distributions, and draw informal inferences about two populations.

Understanding Basic Probability Terms and Definitions

(CCSS.Math.Content.7.SP.C.8.B)

Probability is part of everyday life. In industry and technology, probability is used to estimate how long component parts will last. In medicine, probability is used to assess the chances of infections. In biology, probability is used to predict how genes are passed on from parents to children. In meteorology, probability is used to forecast the weather. These examples are just a few of the endless ways probability is used in numerous and various fields.

This section introduces the basic terminology and definitions you must know in order to understand and calculate probabilities.

Determining Sample Spaces

A **chance process** gives results that cannot be determined with certainty beforehand. A **random experiment** is a chance process that has a single result. Here are examples of random experiments:

> Flipping a coin one time and observing the up face
>
> Tossing a number cube one time and observing the up face
>
> Drawing a card without looking from a well-shuffled deck of 52 standard playing cards and observing which card was drawn

Tip: When you draw "without looking," you are making a *random selection*.

For each of these experiments you get a single **outcome** that occurs by chance. You cannot determine with certainty the outcome beforehand. That is, you cannot say for certain what the exact outcome will be. However, for each experiment you have an idea of the *possible* outcomes.

For instance, in the random experiment of flipping a coin, the two possible outcomes are H (representing heads on the up face) or T (representing tails on the up face).

Suppose a number cube has one number from 1 to 6 on each face. In the random experiment of tossing the number cube and observing the up face, the six possible outcomes are 1 (representing the number 1 on the up face), 2 (representing the number 2 on the up face), 3 (representing the number 3 on the up face), 4 (representing the number 4 on the up face), 5 (representing the number 5 on the up face), and 6 (representing the number 6 on the up face).

In the random experiment of drawing a card from a well-shuffled deck of playing cards, there are 52 possible outcomes: ace, 2, 3, 4, 5, 6, 7, 8, 9, 10, jack, queen, and king of clubs (♣); ace, 2, 3, 4, 5, 6, 7, 8, 9, 10, jack, queen, and king of spades (♠); ace, 2, 3, 4, 5, 6, 7, 8, 9, 10, jack, queen, and king of hearts (♥); and ace, 2, 3, 4, 5, 6, 7, 8, 9, 10, jack, queen, and king of diamonds (♦). Here is a black and white illustration of a standard deck of playing cards.

Source: *www.jfitz.com/cards/*

Clubs, spades, hearts, and diamonds are called "suits." Commonly, clubs (♣) and spades (♠) have black coloring and hearts (♥) and diamonds (♦) have red coloring.

The set of all possible outcomes of a random experiment is its **sample space, *S*.** Here are examples.

S = {H, T} is the sample space for flipping a coin and observing the up face.

S = {1, 2, 3, 4, 5, 6} is the sample space for tossing a number cube (with faces numbered 1 to 6) one time and observing the up face.

S = {♣A, ♣2, ♣3, ♣4, ♣5, ♣6, ♣7, ♣8, ♣9, ♣10, ♣J, ♣Q, ♣K, ♠A, ♠2, ♠3, ♠4, ♠5, ♠6, ♠7, ♠8, ♠9, ♠10, ♠J, ♠Q, ♠K, ♥A, ♥2, ♥3, ♥4, ♥5, ♥6, ♥7, ♥8, ♥9, ♥10, ♥J, ♥Q, ♥K, ♦A, ♦2, ♦3, ♦4, ♦5, ♦6, ♦7, ♦8, ♦9, ♦10, ♦J, ♦Q, ♦K}—where ♣A represents the ace of clubs, ♣2 represents the 2 of clubs, ... ♣J represents the jack of clubs, ♣Q represents the queen of clubs, ♣K represents the king of clubs, and so on—is the sample space for drawing one card at random from a well-shuffled deck of 52 standard playing cards and observing which card was drawn.

Tip: To show the elements in the sample space, use the roster notation for sets. That is, enclose in curly braces, a list of the elements in the sample space, separated by commas.

Sometimes random experiments have several stages. For instance, consider the experiment of flipping two coins and observing the up faces. Think of the experiment as having two stages. First, flip the first coin and observe the up face. Next, flip the second coin and observe the up face. Three common methods for generating the possible outcomes for such an experiment are **organized lists, tables,** and **tree diagrams.**

Here is an example of using an organized list to generate the possible outcomes. Let H represent heads or face up; let T represent tails or face down.

Proceed systematically. First, list H twice on the first coin with each of the possibilities (H, T) for the second coin. Next, list T twice on the first coin with each of the possibilities (H, T) for the second coin.

First Coin	Second Coin
H	H
H	T
T	H
T	T

Tip: When you use an organized list to count possibilities, be careful to proceed in a systematic manner, as illustrated in this example. Otherwise, you might overlook a possibility or count one more than once.

Here is an example of using a table to generate the possible outcomes.

	First Coin	
Second Coin	**H**	**T**
H	HH	HT
T	TH	TT

Here is an example of using a tree diagram to generate the possible outcomes.

First, draw a branch for each possibility for the first stage (in this case, the first coin).

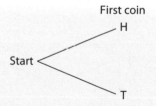

Next, attach branches for each possibility for the second stage (in this case, the second coin) to each of the possibilities for the first stage.

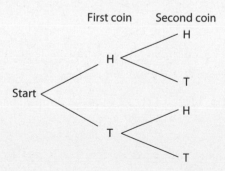

Then, list the possible outcomes by tracing along the branches.

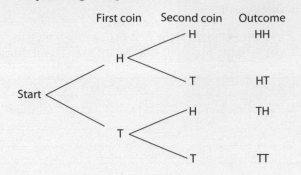

Each of the three methods results in the same four outcomes. The possible outcomes when two coins are flipped are HH (representing heads on the first coin and heads on the second coin), HT (representing heads on the first coin and tails on the second coin), TH (representing tails on the first coin and heads on the second coin), and TT (representing tails on the first coin and tails on the second coin). Therefore, S = {HH, HT, TH, TT} is the sample space for flipping two coins.

Tip: Notice that HT and TH are NOT the same outcome. HT is the outcome of heads on the first coin and tails on the second coin, but TH is the outcome of tails on the first coin and heads on the second coin.

You can extend organized lists and tree diagrams to three or more stages. Here is a tree diagram for flipping three coins.

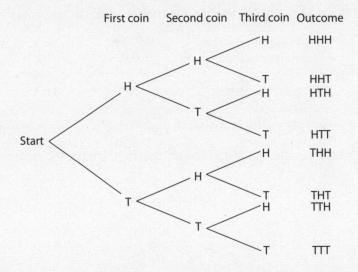

S = {HHH, HHT, HTH, HTT, THH, THT, TTH, TTT} is the sample space for flipping three coins. The number of possible outcomes is 8.

☞ Try These

1. Fill in the blank.

   (a) A chance process is one that gives results that _____ (can, cannot) be determined beforehand.

   (b) A random experiment is a chance process that has a _____ result.

   (c) The set of all possible outcomes of a random experiment is its _____ (two words).

2. Random experiment: A coin is flipped and then a number cube (with faces numbered 1 to 6) is tossed. The up faces are observed.

   (a) Use an organized list to generate the possible outcomes.

   (b) Use a table to generate the possible outcomes.

   (c) Use a tree diagram to generate the possible outcomes.

   (d) Specify the sample space.

3. Specify the sample space of the random experiment.

   (a) One marble is drawn without looking from a box containing 3 marbles, all identical except for color. One marble is red, 1 marble is black, and 1 marble is white.

   (b) One spin on the spinner shown: The spinner has five equal sectors numbered 10, 20, 30, 40, and 50. In one spin, the pointer will turn a random number of times and stop.

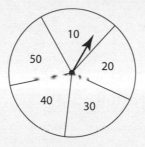

   (c) Two spins on the spinner shown: The spinner has four equal sectors colored yellow (Y), blue (B), red (R), and green (G). In one spin, the pointer will turn a random number of times and stop.

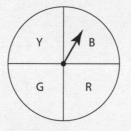

Solutions

1. **(a)** cannot
   (b) single
   (c) sample space

2. The coin can come up as heads (H) or tails (T). The number cube can come up as 1, 2, 3, 4, 5, or 6.

    (a) Organized list of possible outcomes:

Coin	Number Cube
H	1
H	2
H	3
H	4
H	5
H	6
T	1
T	2
T	3
T	4
T	5
T	6

(b) Table of possible outcomes:

	Coin	
Number Cube	**H**	**T**
1	H1	T1
2	H2	T2
3	H3	T3
4	H4	T4
5	H5	T5
6	H6	T6

(c) Tree diagram of possible outcomes:

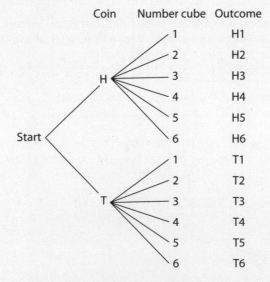

(d) S = {H1, H2, H3, H4, H5, H6, T1, T2, T3, T4, T5, T6}

3. **(a)** Let R represent that a red marble is drawn, B represent that a black marble is drawn, and W represent that a white marble is drawn.

$$S = \{R, B, W\}$$

(b) Let 10 represent that the pointer stops on 10, 20 represent that the pointer stops on 20, and so on.

$$S = \{10, 20, 30, 40, 50\}$$

(c) Let YY represent yellow on the first spin and yellow on the second spin, YB represent yellow on the first spin and blue on the second spin, and so on.

$$S = \{YY, YB, YR, YG, RY, RB, RR, RG, BY, BB, BR, BG, GY, GB, GR, GG\}$$

Counting the Number of Possible Outcomes

For many random experiments, you can determine the number of possible outcomes by using the Counting Principle.

> **The Counting Principle:** If a first activity can be done in m different ways, and, for each of these ways, a second activity can be done in n different ways, then both activities can be done, in the order given, in $m \times n$ different ways.

Tip: You can extend the Counting Principle to any number of activities.

Here are examples.

A coin is flipped and a number cube is tossed. How many possible outcomes are in the sample space for this random experiment?

The coin can come up 2 ways, and the number cube can come up 6 ways. So, there are $2 \times 6 = 12$ possible outcomes in the sample space.

Two cards are drawn without looking, one after the other *with replacement,* from a standard deck of 52 playing cards. How many possible outcomes are in the sample space for this random experiment? *Tip:* "With replacement" means an item is put back before the next item is selected.

The first card can come up 52 ways, and the second card can come up 52 ways (because the first card is put back into the deck). So, there are $52 \times 52 = 2,704$ possible outcomes in the sample space.

Two cards are drawn without looking, one after the other *without replacement,* from a standard deck of 52 playing cards. How many possible outcomes are in the sample space for this random experiment? *Tip:* "Without replacement" means an item is NOT put back before the next item is selected.

The first card can come up 52 ways, and the second card can come up 51 ways (because the first card is not put back into the deck). So, there are $52 \times 51 = 2,652$ possible outcomes in the sample space.

☞ Try These

1. Fill in the blank.

   (a) If a first activity can be done in m different ways, and, for each of these ways, a second activity can be done in n different ways, then both activities can be done, in the order given, in _____ different ways.

   (b) "With replacement" means an item _____ (is, is not) put back before the next item is selected.

   (c) "Without replacement" means an item _____ (is, is not) put back before the next item is selected.

2. Determine the number of outcomes in the sample space of the random experiment.

   (a) A coin is flipped three times.

   (b) Two number cubes (with faces numbered 1 to 6) are tossed.

   (c) Two marbles are drawn without looking, one after the other with replacement, from a box containing 3 marbles, all identical except for color. One marble is red, 1 marble is black, and 1 marble is white.

   (d) Two marbles are drawn without looking, one after the other without replacement, from a box containing 3 marbles, all identical except for color. One marble is red, 1 marble is black, and 1 marble is white.

Solutions

1. (a) $m \times n$
   (b) is
   (c) is not

2. (a) $2 \times 2 \times 2 = 8$
   (b) $6 \times 6 = 36$
   (c) $3 \times 3 = 9$
   (d) $3 \times 2 = 6$

Determining Probabilities of Events Using Uniform Probability Models

(CCSS.Math.Content.7.SP.C.5, CCSS.Math.Content.7.SP.C.7.A)

A **probability model** associated with a sample space assigns a number between 0 and 1 to each outcome in the sample space. The number assigned to an outcome in S is the **probability** of that outcome. The numbers assigned to all the possible outcomes in S must sum to 1.

When each of the possible outcomes in a sample space has an equal chance of occurring, the sample space has **equally likely outcomes.** The probability model for a sample space with equally likely outcomes is a

uniform probability model. The probability of each outcome is $\frac{1}{n}$, where n is the number of possible outcomes. You write $P(\text{outcome}) = \frac{1}{n}$ to mean "the probability of an outcome is $\frac{1}{n}$."

Here are examples.

When a coin is flipped, each of the possible outcomes in the sample space, $S = \{H, T\}$, has an equal chance of occurring. The probability of each outcome is $\frac{1}{2}$. The sum of the probabilities of the outcomes in S is $P(H) + P(T) = \frac{1}{2} + \frac{1}{2} = 1$.

> **Tip:** Read $P(H)$ as "the probability of heads," and read $P(T)$ as "the probability of tails."

When a number cube (with faces numbered 1 to 6) is tossed, each of the possible outcomes in the sample space, $S = \{1, 2, 3, 4, 5, 6\}$, has an equal chance of occurring. The probability of each outcome is $\frac{1}{6}$. The sum of the probabilities of the outcomes in S is

$$P(1) + P(2) + P(3) + P(4) + P(5) + P(6) = \frac{1}{6} + \frac{1}{6} + \frac{1}{6} + \frac{1}{6} + \frac{1}{6} + \frac{1}{6} = 1 \cdot$$

> **Tip:** In theoretical probability, objects such as coins, number cubes, and spinners are considered to be *fair objects*. The outcomes from fair objects are equally likely.

An **event, *E*,** is a subset of a sample space, *S*. (***Tip:*** Use uppercase letters to represent events.) For example, consider the experiment of tossing a number cube (with faces numbered 1 to 6) and observing the up face. You can define many different events for this experiment that has sample space $S = \{1, 2, 3, 4, 5, 6\}$.

Here are examples.

The event the up face is a number less than 3. This event contains two outcomes: $\{1, 2\}$.
The event the up face is an even number. This event contains three outcomes: $\{2, 4, 6\}$.
The event the up face is a number greater than 2. This event contains four outcomes: $\{3, 4, 5, 6\}$.
The event the up face is the number 5. This event has one outcome: $\{5\}$.
The event the up face is a whole number. This event has six outcomes: $\{1, 2, 3, 4, 5, 6\}$.
An event, *E*, **occurs** if an outcome in *E* is observed when the experiment is performed.

> The **probability of an event *E*,** denoted $P(E)$, is the sum of the probabilities of the individual outcomes that make up the event *E*.

An event's probability is a number ranging from 0 to 1 that quantifies the likelihood of the event occurring. A probability near zero indicates an unlikely event; a probability around $\frac{1}{2}$ is neither likely nor unlikely; and a probability near 1 indicates a likely event.

Here is an example.

For the experiment of tossing a number cube (with faces numbered 1 to 6) and the event the up face is a number less than 3:

$$P(\text{number} < 3) = P(\{1,\ 2\}) = P(1) + P(2) = \frac{1}{6} + \frac{1}{6} = \frac{2}{6} = \frac{1}{3}$$

The probability of this event is between 0 and $\frac{1}{2}$. It is closer to $\frac{1}{2}$ (because $\frac{1}{2} - \frac{1}{3} = \frac{3}{6} - \frac{2}{6} = \frac{1}{6}$), so it is neither likely nor unlikely.

☞ Try These

1. Fill in the blank(s).

   (a) A probability model associated with a sample space assigns a number between _____ and _____ to each outcome in the sample space.

   (b) The number assigned to an outcome in a sample space is the _____ of that outcome.

   (c) The numbers assigned to all the possible outcomes in a sample space must sum to _____.

   (d) "Equally likely" outcomes means each of the possible outcomes in a sample space has a(n) _____ chance of occurring.

   (e) The probability model for a sample space with n equally likely outcomes is a _____ probability model. The probability of each outcome is _____.

   (f) An event, E, is a _____ of a sample space.

   (g) An event, E, _____ if an outcome in E is observed when the experiment is performed.

   (h) The probability of an event E, denoted $P(E)$, is the _____ of the probabilities of the individual outcomes that make up the event E.

   (i) A probability is a number ranging from 0 to 1 that quantifies the _____ of the event occurring.

   (j) A probability near _____ indicates an unlikely event; a probability around _____ is neither likely nor unlikely; and a probability near _____ indicates a likely event.

2. Consider the experiment of tossing a number cube (with faces numbered 1 to 6) and observing the up face. Find the probability of the event.

   (a) The up face is an odd prime number.

   (b) The up face is an even number.

   (c) The up face is a number greater than 2.

   (d) The up face is the number 5.

   (e) The up face is a whole number.

3. Consider the experiment of drawing a card without looking from a well-shuffled deck of playing cards (see illustration below) and observing the card drawn.

Source: *www.jfitz.com/cards/*

Find the probability of the event.

(a) The card drawn is a face card. (*Tip:* Face cards are jacks, queens, and kings.)

(b) The card drawn is a number greater than 2 and less than 5.

(c) The card drawn has red coloring.

(d) The card drawn is a 10.

(e) The card drawn is the ace of hearts.

4. Consider the experiment of flipping three coins and observing the up faces. Find the probability of the event.

(a) The coins show exactly one head.

(b) The coins show at least one head.

(c) The coins show three tails.

(d) The coins show at least two tails.

(e) The coins show no tails.

Solutions

1. **(a)** 0; 1
   (b) probability
   (c) 1
   (d) equal
   (e) uniform; $\dfrac{1}{n}$
   (f) subset
   (g) occurs
   (h) sum
   (i) likelihood
   (j) zero; $\dfrac{1}{2}$; 1

2. $S = \{1, 2, 3, 4, 5, 6\}$. The probability of each outcome in S is $\dfrac{1}{6}$.

(a) $P(\text{odd prime number}) = P(\{3, 5\}) = P(3) + P(5) = \dfrac{1}{6} + \dfrac{1}{6} = \dfrac{2}{6} = \dfrac{1}{3}$

(b) $P(\text{even number}) = P(\{2, 4, 6\}) = P(2) + P(4) + P(6) = \dfrac{1}{6} + \dfrac{1}{6} + \dfrac{1}{6} = \dfrac{3}{6} = \dfrac{1}{2}$

(c) $P(\text{number} > 2) = P(\{3, 4, 5, 6\}) = P(3) + P(4) + P(5) + P(6) = \dfrac{1}{6} + \dfrac{1}{6} + \dfrac{1}{6} + \dfrac{1}{6} = \dfrac{4}{6} = \dfrac{2}{3}$

(d) $P(5) = P(\{5\}) = P(5) = \dfrac{1}{6}$

(e) $P(\text{whole number}) = P(\{1, 2, 3, 4, 5, 6\})$

$= P(1) + P(2) + P(3) + P(4) + P(5) + P(6)$

$= \dfrac{1}{6} + \dfrac{1}{6} + \dfrac{1}{6} + \dfrac{1}{6} + \dfrac{1}{6} + \dfrac{1}{6} = \dfrac{6}{6} = 1$

3. $S = \{\clubsuit A, \clubsuit 2, \clubsuit 3, \clubsuit 4, \clubsuit 5, \clubsuit 6, \clubsuit 7, \clubsuit 8, \clubsuit 9, \clubsuit 10, \clubsuit J, \clubsuit Q, \clubsuit K, \spadesuit A, \spadesuit 2, \spadesuit 3, \spadesuit 4, \spadesuit 5, \spadesuit 6, \spadesuit 7, \spadesuit 8, \spadesuit 9, \spadesuit 10, \spadesuit J, \spadesuit Q, \spadesuit K, \heartsuit A, \heartsuit 2, \heartsuit 3, \heartsuit 4, \heartsuit 5, \heartsuit 6, \heartsuit 7, \heartsuit 8, \heartsuit 9, \heartsuit 10, \heartsuit J, \heartsuit Q, \heartsuit K, \diamondsuit A, \diamondsuit 2, \diamondsuit 3, \diamondsuit 4, \diamondsuit 5, \diamondsuit 6, \diamondsuit 7, \diamondsuit 8, \diamondsuit 9, \diamondsuit 10, \diamondsuit J, \diamondsuit Q, \diamondsuit K\}$

The probability of each outcome in S is $\dfrac{1}{52}$.

(a) $P(\text{face card}) = P(\{\clubsuit J, \clubsuit Q, \clubsuit K, \spadesuit J, \spadesuit Q, \spadesuit K, \heartsuit J, \heartsuit Q, \heartsuit K, \diamondsuit J, \diamondsuit Q, \diamondsuit K\})$

$= P(\clubsuit J) + P(\clubsuit Q) + P(\clubsuit K) + P(\spadesuit J) + P(\spadesuit Q) + P(\spadesuit K) + P(\heartsuit J) + P(\heartsuit Q) + P(\heartsuit K) + P(\diamondsuit J) +$
$P(\diamondsuit Q) + P(\diamondsuit K)$

$= \dfrac{1}{52} + \dfrac{1}{52} + \dfrac{1}{52} + \dfrac{1}{52} + \dfrac{1}{52} + \dfrac{1}{52} + \dfrac{1}{52} + \dfrac{1}{52} + \dfrac{1}{52} + \dfrac{1}{52} + \dfrac{1}{52} + \dfrac{1}{52} = \dfrac{12}{52} = \dfrac{3}{13}$

(b) $P(2 < \text{number} < 5) = P(\{\clubsuit 3, \clubsuit 4, \spadesuit 3, \spadesuit 4, \heartsuit 3, \heartsuit 4, \diamondsuit 3, \diamondsuit 4\})$

$= P(\clubsuit 3) + P(\clubsuit 4) + P(\spadesuit 3) + P(\spadesuit 4) + P(\heartsuit 3) + P(\heartsuit 4) + P(\diamondsuit 3) + P(\diamondsuit 4)$

$= \dfrac{1}{52} + \dfrac{1}{52} + \dfrac{1}{52} + \dfrac{1}{52} + \dfrac{1}{52} + \dfrac{1}{52} + \dfrac{1}{52} + \dfrac{1}{52} = \dfrac{8}{52} = \dfrac{2}{13}$

(c) $P(\text{red suit}) = P(\{\heartsuit A, \heartsuit 2, \ldots, \heartsuit J, \heartsuit Q, \heartsuit K, \diamondsuit A, \diamondsuit 2, \ldots, \diamondsuit J, \diamondsuit Q, \diamondsuit K\})$

$= P(\heartsuit A) + P(\heartsuit 2) + \cdots + P(\heartsuit J) + P(\heartsuit Q) + P(\heartsuit K) + P(\diamondsuit A) + P(\diamondsuit 2) + \cdots + P(\diamondsuit J) + P(\diamondsuit Q) + P(\diamondsuit K)$

$= \dfrac{1}{52} + \dfrac{1}{52} + \cdots + \dfrac{1}{52} + \dfrac{1}{52} + \dfrac{1}{52} + \dfrac{1}{52} + \dfrac{1}{52} + \cdots + \dfrac{1}{52} + \dfrac{1}{52} + \dfrac{1}{52} = \dfrac{26}{52} = \dfrac{1}{2}$

(d) $P(10) = P(\{\clubsuit 10, \spadesuit 10, \heartsuit 10, \diamondsuit 10\}) = P(\clubsuit 10) + P(\spadesuit 10) + P(\heartsuit 10) + P(\diamondsuit 10) = \dfrac{1}{52} + \dfrac{1}{52} + \dfrac{1}{52} + \dfrac{1}{52} = \dfrac{4}{52} = \dfrac{1}{13}$

(e) $P(\text{ace of hearts}) = P(\{\heartsuit A\}) = P(\heartsuit A) = \dfrac{1}{52}$

4. $S = \{$HHH, HHT, HTH, HTT, THH, THT, TTH, TTT$\}$. The probability of each outcome is $\dfrac{1}{8}$.

(a) $P(\text{exactly one head}) = P(\{\text{HTT}, \text{THT}, \text{TTH}\}) = P(\text{HTT}) + P(\text{THT}) + P(\text{TTH}) = \dfrac{1}{8} + \dfrac{1}{8} + \dfrac{1}{8} = \dfrac{3}{8}$

(b) $P(\text{at least one head}) = P(\{\text{HHH, HHT, HTH, HTT, THH, THT, TTH}\})$

$= P(\text{HHH}) + P(\text{HHT}) + P(\text{HTH}) + P(\text{HTT}) + P(\text{THH}) + P(\text{THT}) + P(\text{TTH})$

$= \dfrac{1}{8} + \dfrac{1}{8} + \dfrac{1}{8} + \dfrac{1}{8} + \dfrac{1}{8} + \dfrac{1}{8} + \dfrac{1}{8} = \dfrac{7}{8}$

(c) $P(\text{three tails}) = P(\{\text{TTT}\}) = P(\text{TTT}) = \dfrac{1}{8}$

(d) $P(\text{at least two tails}) = P(\{\text{HTT}, \text{THT}, \text{TTH}, \text{TTT}\})$

$= P(\text{HTT}) + P(\text{THT}) + P(\text{TTH}) + P(\text{TTT})$

$= \dfrac{1}{8} + \dfrac{1}{8} + \dfrac{1}{8} + \dfrac{1}{8} = \dfrac{4}{8} = \dfrac{1}{2}$

(e) $P(\text{no tails}) = P(\{\text{HHH}\}) = P(\text{HHH}) = \dfrac{1}{8}$

Determining Theoretical Probabilities

(CCSS.Math.Content.7.SP.C.5, CCSS.Math.Content.7.SP.C.7.A, CCSS.Math.Content.7.SP.C.8.A, CCSS.Math.Content.7.SP.C.8.B)

Theoretical probability is an approach that depends on being able to count the number of ways various occurrences can happen.

If all outcomes in the sample space are *equally likely*, the **theoretical probability** of an event E is

$$P(E) = \frac{\text{number of outcomes in } E}{\text{total number of outcomes in } S}.$$

Tip: When using the formula for the theoretical probability of an event, the denominator will always be *larger than* or *equal to* the numerator. Check for this when you plug numbers into the formula.

Finding Probabilities for Single Events

Consider the experiment of tossing a number cube (with faces numbered 1 to 6) and observing the up face. The experiment has sample space $S = \{1, 2, 3, 4, 5, 6\}$. Determine the probabilities for the following single events.

Event A: The up face is a number less than 3.

$$P(A) = P(\{1, 2\}) = \frac{\text{number of outcomes in } A}{\text{total number of outcomes in } S} = \frac{2}{6} = \frac{1}{3}$$

Event B: The up face is a number greater than 2.

$$P(B) = P(\{3, 4, 5, 6\}) = \frac{\text{number of outcomes in } B}{\text{total number of outcomes in } S} = \frac{4}{6} = \frac{2}{3}$$

Event C: The up face is an even number.

$$P(C) = P(\{2, 4, 6\}) = \frac{\text{number of outcomes in } C}{\text{total number of outcomes in } S} = \frac{3}{6} = \frac{1}{2}$$

> **Tip:** Probabilities can be expressed as fractions, decimals, or percents. For event C, the probability can be expressed as $\frac{1}{2}$, 0.5, or 50%.

Look at this special case.

Event D: The up face is a number less than 1. There are no outcomes in event D.

$$P(D) = P(\{\ \}) = \frac{\text{number of outcomes in } D}{\text{total number of outcomes in } S} = \frac{0}{6} = 0$$

The event D is impossible. An **impossible event** is one that cannot occur.

> The probability of an impossible event is 0.

Here is another special case.

Event F: The up face is a whole number. The event F contains all the possible outcomes in S.

$$P(F) = P(\{1, 2, 3, 4, 5, 6\}) = \frac{\text{number of outcomes in } F}{\text{total number of outcomes in } S} = \frac{6}{6} = 1$$

The event F is certain to occur. A **certain event** is one that is guaranteed to occur.

> The probability of a certain event is 1.

Probabilities of events range from 0 to 1. The lowest probability you can have is 0, and the highest probability you can have is 1. All other probabilities fall between 0 and 1.

> For any event E, $0 \le P(E) \le 1$.

Be careful. Do not use the formula $P(E) = \dfrac{\text{number of outcomes in } E}{\text{total number of outcomes in } S}$ for sample spaces in which the events are not equally likely. Consider the spinner shown.

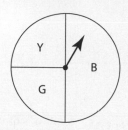

$S = \{Y, B, G\}$. The probabilities for the three different outcomes are $P(Y) = \dfrac{1}{4}$, $\left(\text{not } \dfrac{1}{3}\right)$; $P(B) = \dfrac{1}{2}$, $\left(\text{not } \dfrac{1}{3}\right)$; and $P(G) = \dfrac{1}{4}$, $\left(\text{not } \dfrac{1}{3}\right)$.

☞ Try These

1. Fill in the blank(s).

   (a) Theoretical probability is an approach that depends on being able to _____ the number of ways various occurrences can happen.

   (b) If all outcomes in the sample space are equally likely, the theoretical probability of an event E is $P(E) =$ _____.

   (c) The probability of an impossible event is _____.

   (d) The probability of a certain event is _____.

   (e) The probability of any event E must be equal to or greater than _____ and less than or equal to _____.

2. To win a game, Kate must obtain a number less than 3 on one toss of a number cube (with faces numbered 1 to 6). What is the probability Kate will win the game?

3. Kailash spins once on the spinner shown. In one spin, the pointer will turn a random number of times and stop.

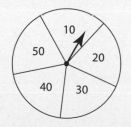

   (a) What is the probability the pointer will stop on a number divisible by 4?
   (b) What is the probability the pointer will stop on a number divisible by 7?
   (c) What is the probability the pointer will stop on a number divisible by 10?

Solutions

1. **(a)** count

   (b) $\dfrac{\text{number of outcomes in } E}{\text{total number of outcomes in } S}$

   (c) 0

   (d) 1

   (e) 0; 1

2. Let event E be the number is less than 3.

$$P(\text{number less than 3}) = P(\{1,\ 2\}) = \frac{\text{number of outcomes less than 3}}{\text{total number of outcomes in } S} = \frac{2}{6} = \frac{1}{3}$$

   The probability Kate will win is $\dfrac{1}{3}$.

3. **(a)** $P(\text{number divisible by 4}) = P(\{20,\ 40\}) = \dfrac{\text{number of outcomes divisible by 4}}{\text{total number of outcomes in } S} = \dfrac{2}{5}$

   (b) $P(\text{number divisible by 7}) = P(\{\ \}) = \dfrac{\text{number of outcomes divisible by 7}}{\text{total number of outcomes in } S} = \dfrac{0}{5} = 0$

   (c) $P(\text{number divisible by 10}) = P(\{10,\ 20,\ 30,\ 40,\ 50\}) = \dfrac{\text{number of outcomes divisible by 10}}{\text{total number of outcomes in } S} = \dfrac{5}{5} = 1$

Finding Probabilities of Events Not Occurring

If you know the probability that an event E does occur, you can find the probability that the event E does not occur.

The probability the event E does NOT occur is $1 - P(E)$.

Here are examples.

A box contains 20 marbles, all identical except for color. Each marble is either green, blue, or purple. The probability of drawing a green marble is $\dfrac{3}{5}$. Alina draws one marble out of the box without looking. What is the probability that Alina's marble is not green?

$$P(\text{not green}) = 1 - P(\text{green}) = 1 - \left(\frac{3}{5}\right) = \frac{2}{5}$$

Armand and Jenna are going on a picnic today. According to the weather forecast, the probability of rain is 20%. What is the probability it will not rain? Give your answer as a percent.

$$P(\text{not rain}) = 1 - P(\text{rain}) = 100\% - 20\% = 80\%$$

Tip: Recall that 1 = 100%.

☞Try These

1. The probability of an event happening is $\frac{2}{9}$. What is the probability of the event not happening?

2. The probability of an event happening is 0.875. What is the probability of the event not happening?

3. A box contains 100 numbered tiles, all identical in size and shape. The probability of drawing an even-numbered tile is $\frac{5}{8}$. Clayton draws one tile out of the box without looking. Clayton will win a prize if the number on his tile is odd. What is the probability that Clayton will win a prize?

4. The baseball coaches are concerned because, according to the weather forecast, the probability of rain on game day is 35%. What is the probability it will not rain on game day? Give your answer as a percent.

Solutions

1. $P(\text{not event}) = 1 - P(\text{event}) = 1 - \left(\frac{2}{9}\right) = \frac{7}{9}$

2. $P(\text{not event}) = 1 - P(\text{event}) = 1 - 0.875 = 0.125$

3. $P(\text{odd}) = P(\text{not even}) = 1 - P(\text{even}) = 1 - \left(\frac{5}{8}\right) = \frac{3}{8}$

   The probability that Clayton will win a prize is $\frac{3}{8}$.

4. $P(\text{not rain}) = 1 - P(\text{rain}) = 100\% - 35\% = 65\%$

Finding Probabilities for Compound Events *A* or *B*

A **compound event** is a combination of two or more events. The compound event (*A* **or** *B*) is the event that *A* occurs or *B* occurs or that both occur at the same time on *one* trial of an experiment.

To find *P* (*A* **or** *B*), sum the number of ways that *A* can occur and the number of ways that *B* can occur, *being sure to add in such a way that* no outcome is counted twice, and then divide by the number of outcomes in the sample space.

Here is an example.

    Andrei spins once on the spinner shown. In one spin, the pointer will turn a random number of times and stop.

    What is the probability the pointer will stop on a number divisible by 4 or a number greater than 30?

Let A be the event the pointer will stop on a number divisible by 4. Let B be the event the pointer will stop on a number greater than 30. You want to find the probability of the compound event $(A$ or $B) = P(A$ or $B) =$

P (number divisible by 4 or number greater than 30) $= \dfrac{\text{number of outcomes in the compound event } (A \text{ or } B)}{\text{number of outcomes in the sample space}}$.

To find the probability, do three steps.

Step 1. Determine the number of outcomes in the sample space.

$S = \{10, 20, 30, 40, 50\}$. The number of outcomes is 5.

Step 2. Determine the number of outcomes in the compound event $(A$ or $B)$.

Event $A = \{20, 40\}$ and event $B = \{40, 50\}$. Looking at the outcomes in the two events, you can see that 40 is an outcome in both events. You do not want to count 40 twice, so the compound event $(A$ or $B) = \{20, 40, 50\}$. Thus, there are 3 outcomes in the compound event $(A$ or $B)$.

Step 3. Divide the number of outcomes in the compound event $(A$ or $B)$ by the number of outcomes in the sample space.

$$P(A \text{ or } B) = P(\text{number divisible by 4 or number greater than 30}) = \frac{3}{5}$$

Here is another example.

    Suppose one card is drawn at random from a standard deck of 52 playing cards. Find the probability that the card is a king or a heart.

Let A be the event the card drawn is a king. Let B be the event the card drawn is a heart. You want to find the probability of the compound event $(A$ or $B) = P(A$ or $B) = P(\text{king or heart}) =$

$\dfrac{\text{number of outcomes in the compound event } (A \text{ or } B)}{\text{number of outcomes in the sample space}}$.

Step 1. Determine the number of outcomes in the sample space.

There are 52 outcomes (one outcome for each card in the deck) in the sample space.

Step 2. Determine the number of outcomes in the compound event (*A* or *B*).

There are 4 kings in the deck. One of these kings is the king of hearts. There are 12 other hearts that are *not* kings. See illustration below.

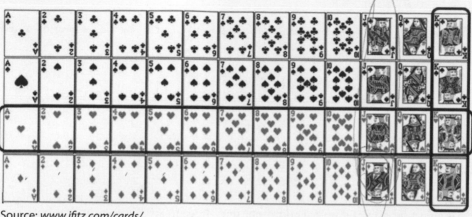

Source: *www.jfitz.com/cards/*

Thus, there are 4 + 12 = 16 distinct cards in the compound event (*A* or *B*).

Step 3. Divide the number of outcomes in the compound event (*A* or *B*) by the number of outcomes in the sample space.

$$P(A \text{ or } B) = P(\text{king or heart}) = \frac{16}{52} = \frac{4}{13}$$

From these examples, you can see you must be extra careful when events overlap. If there is no overlap, you simply sum the outcomes in the two events.

Here is an example.

A bag contains 5 black marbles, 3 green marbles, and 2 red marbles, all identical except for color. Lupita draws one marble from the bag without looking. What is the probability that Lupita's marble is green or red?

Tip: A sample space might contain two or more objects that are exactly alike. You must count each of such like objects as a separate outcome.

Let *A* be the event the marble drawn is green. Let *B* be the event the marble drawn is red. You want to find the probability of the compound event (*A* or *B*) = *P*(*A* or *B*) = *P*(green or red) =

$$\frac{\text{number of outcomes in the compound event } (A \text{ or } B)}{\text{number of outcomes in the sample space}}.$$

Step 1. Determine the number of outcomes in the sample space.

There are 10 outcomes in the sample space.

Step 2. Determine the number of outcomes in the compound event (*A* or *B*).

There are 3 green marbles in the bag, so event *A* contains 3 outcomes. There are 2 red marbles in the bag, so event *B* contains 2 outcomes. These two events have no overlap. Thus, the number of outcomes in the compound event (*A* or *B*) is 3 + 2 = 5.

Step 3. Divide the number of outcomes in the compound event (*A* or *B*) by the number of outcomes in the sample space.

$$P(A \text{ or } B) = P(\text{green or red}) = \frac{5}{10} = \frac{1}{2}$$

☞ Try These

1. Fill in the blank.

   (a) A compound event is a _____ of two or more events.

   (b) The compound event (*A* or *B*) is the event that *A* occurs or *B* occurs or that both occur at the same time on _____ trial of an experiment.

2. State "yes" or "no" as to whether the given events have overlapping outcomes. Explain your answer.

   (a) Drawing a red card or drawing a queen on one draw from a standard deck of 52 playing cards

   (b) Getting a 2 or a number greater than 4 on one toss of a number cube (with faces numbered 1 to 6)

   (c) Drawing a red marble or drawing a green marble in one draw from a box containing 9 black marbles, 6 green marbles, and 20 red marbles

   (d) Getting a multiple of 6 or a number less than 40 on one spin of the spinner shown

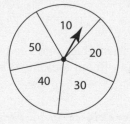

   (e) Drawing a face card or drawing a king on one draw from a standard deck of 52 playing cards

3. A bag contains 8 white marbles, 2 red marbles, and 5 yellow marbles, all identical except for color. Josie draws one marble from the bag without looking. What is the probability that Josie's marble is white or yellow?

4. Benjamin tosses a number cube (with faces numbered 1 to 6). What is the probability the up face will show 2 or a number greater than 4?

5. Birdie draws one card without looking from a well-shuffled standard deck of 52 playing cards. Find the probability that Birdie draws a jack or a diamond.

Solutions

1. **(a)** combination
   (b) one
2. **(a)** Yes, the queen of diamonds and the queen of hearts are common to both events.
   (b) No, 2 is not greater than 4.
   (c) No, only one color can be drawn at a time.
   (d) Yes, 30 is a common outcome in both events.
   (e) Yes, the four kings are common to both events.

3. $P(\text{white or yellow}) = \dfrac{13}{15}$

4. $P(2 \text{ or} > 4) = \dfrac{3}{6} = \dfrac{1}{2}$

5. $P(\text{jack or diamond}) = \dfrac{16}{52} = \dfrac{4}{13}$

Finding Probabilities for Compound Events *A* and *B*

The compound event (*A* **and** *B*) is the event that *A* occurs on the first trial and *B* occurs on the second trial of an experiment.

> To find the probability that event *A* occurs on the first trial and event *B* occurs on the second trial of an experiment, multiply the probability of event *A* times the probability of event *B*, *where you have determined the* **conditional probability** *of event B by taking into account that* **event A has already occurred.**

Tip: Conditional probability of event *B* is the probability of *B* after taking into account that a previous event has occurred.

Here is an example.

> Suppose Keoki draws two marbles without looking from a box containing 10 black marbles and 5 blue marbles. She draws the first marble, replaces it, and then draws the second marble. Find the probability Keoki draws a black marble on the first draw and a blue marble on the second draw.

Let *A* be the event a black marble is drawn first. Let *B* be the event a blue marble is drawn second. You want to find the probability of the compound event (*A* and *B*) = *P*(*A* and *B*) = *P*(black on the first draw and blue on the second draw) = *P*(black on first draw) · *P*(blue on second draw given black drawn on first draw with replacement).

Tip: Recall that "with replacement" means an item is put back before the next item is selected.

To find the probability, do three steps.

Step 1. Find the probability Keoki draws a black marble on the first draw.

$$P(\text{black on first draw}) = \frac{\text{number of black marbles}}{\text{total number of marbles in box}} = \frac{10}{15} = \frac{2}{3}$$

Step 2. Find the probability Keoki draws a blue marble on the second draw, *taking into account that she drew a black marble on the first draw and put it back.*

Keoki drew a black marble and put it back. So there are still 15 total marbles in the box, 5 of which are blue.

$$P(\text{blue on second draw given black drawn on first draw with replacement})$$

$$= \frac{\text{number of blue marbles}}{\text{total number of marbles in box}} = \frac{5}{15} = \frac{1}{3}$$

Step 3. Multiply the probabilities obtained in steps 1 and 2.

$$P(\text{black on first draw}) \cdot P(\text{blue on second draw given black drawn on first draw with replacement})$$

$$= \frac{2}{3} \cdot \frac{1}{3} = \frac{2}{9}$$

Here is another example.

> Suppose Benicio draws two marbles without looking from a box containing 10 black marbles and 5 blue marbles. He draws the first marble without replacement, and then draws the second marble. Find the probability that Benicio draws a black marble on the first draw and a blue marble on the second draw.

Let A be the event a black marble is drawn first. Let B be the event a blue marble is drawn second. You want to find the probability of the compound event $(A \text{ and } B) = P(A \text{ and } B) = P(\text{black on the first draw and blue on the second draw}) = P(\text{black on the first draw}) \cdot P(\text{blue on the second draw given black drawn on first draw without replacement}).$

Tip: Recall that "without replacement" means an item is *not* put back before the next item is selected.

To find the probability, do three steps.

Step 1. Find the probability Benicio draws a black marble on the first draw.

$$P(\text{black on first draw}) = \frac{\text{number of black marbles}}{\text{total number of marbles in box}} = \frac{10}{15} = \frac{2}{3}$$

Step 2. Find the probability Benicio draws a blue marble on the second draw. Remember, Benicio drew a black marble and did not put it back. So there are 14 total marbles left, 5 of which are blue.

$$P(\text{blue on second draw given black drawn on first draw without replacement})$$

$$= \frac{\text{number of blue marbles}}{\text{total number of marbles left in box}} = \frac{5}{14}$$

Step 3. Multiply the probabilities obtained in steps 1 and 2.

$$P(\text{black on first draw}) \cdot P(\text{blue on second draw given black drawn on first draw without replacement})$$

$$= \frac{2}{3} \cdot \frac{5}{14} = \frac{\overset{1}{\cancel{2}}}{3} \cdot \frac{5}{\cancel{14}_7} = \frac{5}{21}$$

The previous examples illustrate *independent* and *dependent* events.

Two events, *A* and *B*, are **independent** if the occurrence of one does not affect the probability of the occurrence of the other. For instance, if a box contains 10 black marbles and 5 blue marbles, the event of drawing a black marble *with replacement* on the first draw and the event of drawing a blue marble on the second draw are independent events. The probability of drawing a blue marble remains the same $\left(\dfrac{5}{15} = \dfrac{1}{3}\right)$ because the first marble is replaced.

If events *A* and *B* are not independent, they are **dependent.** For example, if a box contains 10 black marbles and 5 blue marbles, the event of drawing a black marble *without replacement* on the first draw and the event of drawing a blue marble on the second draw are dependent events. The probability of a drawing a blue marble changes from $\dfrac{1}{3}$ to $\dfrac{5}{14}$ because the first marble is not replaced.

Here is an example of using a tree diagram to find the probability of a compound event (*A* and *B*).

Sadi flips a coin and then tosses a number cube (with faces numbered 1 to 6). Find the probability that the coin turns up heads and the number cube turns up 4.

A tree diagram shows the possible outcomes.

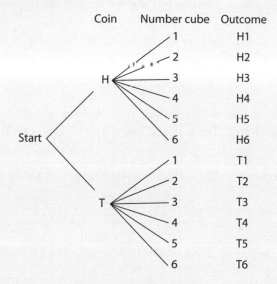

$S = \{H1, H2, H3, H4, H5, H6, T1, T2, T3, T4, T5, T6\}$

The probability of heads on the coin and 4 on the number cube is $P(H4) = \dfrac{1}{12}$.

The event of heads on the coin and the event of 4 on the number cube are independent events. So the probability of heads on the coin and 4 on the number cube is $P(H \text{ and } 4) = P(H) \cdot P(4) = \dfrac{1}{2} \cdot \dfrac{1}{6} = \dfrac{1}{12}$, the same answer you get with the tree diagram.

☞ Try These

1. Fill in the blank(s).

   (a) The compound event (A and B) is the event that A occurs on the _____ trial and B occurs on the _____ trial of an experiment.

   (b) Two events are independent if the occurrence of one _____ (does, does not) affect the probability of the occurrence of the other.

   (c) Two events are dependent if the occurrence of one _____ (does, does not) affect the probability of the occurrence of the other.

2. Dragana tosses a number cube (with faces numbered 1 to 6) two times. What is the probability she will get an odd number and then a number less than 3 on the two tosses?

3. Diego draws two cards without looking from a well-shuffled standard deck of 52 playing cards. He draws the first card, replaces it, and then draws the second card. Find the probability that the first card drawn is an ace and the second card drawn is a face card.

4. A fair coin is flipped three times and the up face is observed. Find the probability of observing all heads.

5. Suppose Ines draws two jelly beans without looking from a bag containing 8 red jelly beans and 6 blue jelly beans. She draws the first jelly bean, eats it, and then draws the second jelly bean. Find the probability that the first jelly bean drawn is red and the second one drawn is blue.

Solutions

1. **(a)** first; second
   (b) does not
   (c) does

2. These two events are independent. Thus, $P(\text{odd and} < 3) = P(\text{odd}) \cdot P(< 3) = \dfrac{3}{6} \cdot \dfrac{2}{6} = \dfrac{\cancel{3}^{1}}{{}_{2}\cancel{6}} \cdot \dfrac{\cancel{2}^{1}}{\cancel{6}_{3}} = \dfrac{1}{6}$.

3. These two events are independent. Thus, $P(\text{ace and face card}) = P(\text{ace on first draw}) \cdot P(\text{face card on second draw given first card ace and put back}) = \dfrac{4}{52} \cdot \dfrac{12}{52} = \dfrac{\cancel{4}^{1}}{{}_{13}\cancel{52}} \cdot \dfrac{\cancel{12}^{3}}{\cancel{52}_{13}} = \dfrac{3}{169}$.

4. These three events are independent. Thus, $P(\text{HHH}) = P(\text{H on the first coin}) \cdot P(\text{H on the second coin}) \cdot P(\text{H on the third coin}) = \dfrac{1}{2} \cdot \dfrac{1}{2} \cdot \dfrac{1}{2} = \dfrac{1}{8}$.

5. These two events are dependent. Thus, $P(\text{red and blue}) = P(\text{red on first draw}) \cdot P(\text{blue on second draw given first draw red and not put back}) = \dfrac{8}{14} \cdot \dfrac{6}{13} = \dfrac{\cancel{8}^{4}}{{}_{7}\cancel{14}} \cdot \dfrac{6}{13} = \dfrac{24}{91}$.

Understanding and Applying Empirical Probability

(CCSS.Math.Content.7.SP.C.6, CCSS.Math.Content.7.SP.C.7.B, CCSS.Math.Content.7.SP.C.8.C)

In **empirical probability,** a probability is assigned to an event E by conducting the experiment a large number of times, called **trials,** and counting the number of times that event E actually occurs.

> The **empirical probability** of an event E is estimated as $P(E) = \dfrac{\text{number of times event } E \text{ occurs}}{\text{total number of trials}}$.

Tip: The empirical probability of an event is also called its **relative frequency probability** or **experimental probability.**

In some situations, empirical probability is the only feasible way to assign a probability to an event.

Here is an example.

> Out of 100 light bulbs tested at Company X, 2 are defective.
>
> **(a)** What is the empirical probability that a randomly selected Company X light bulb is defective?
> **(b)** Based on the result in part (a), what is the probability a randomly selected Company X light bulb is *not* defective?

(a) P(Company X light bulb is defective) $= \dfrac{2}{100} = 0.02$

(b) Based on the result in part (a), the probability a randomly selected Company X light bulb is *not* defective is $1 - 0.02 = 0.98$.

Empirical probabilities are needed to develop probability models for **biased objects** such as unbalanced coins or other objects for which one result is more likely to happen than another. You cannot reliably assign probabilities to the outcomes without collecting data to support your claims.

Here is an example.

> Ashley and Dijana suspect a coin is unbalanced. They decide to take turns flipping the coin. Each of them completes 50 tosses and records the number of heads as shown in the table.

	Number of Heads	Number of Tosses
Ashley	33	50
Dijana	29	50
Total	62	100

> **(a)** Using the data in the table, develop an empirical probability model for flipping the coin.
> **(b)** What will Ashley and Dijana likely conclude about the coin?
> **(c)** Based on the probability model, predict the number of heads that will come up in 350 tosses of the coin.

(a) Using the combined data, the empirical probability model is $P(H) = \dfrac{62}{100} = 0.62$ and $P(T) = 1 - 0.62 = 0.38$.

(b) The theoretical probabilities are $P(H) = 0.5$ and $P(T) = 0.5$. So, Ashley and Dijana likely will conclude the coin is unbalanced.

(c) The number of heads in 350 tosses will be roughly, but probably not exactly, 217, which is 0.62×350.

You can generate data from a chance process by performing simulations. A **simulation** is a well-designed imitation of a chance process. Here are the steps using a real-world situation.

> It is known that 10% of blood donors have type B blood. Suppose 10 donors come to a particular blood center one morning. Find the probability of at least 2 type B blood donors among the 10 donors.

Step 1. Assuming the donors arrive randomly and independently, set up a model for the simulation that matches the probability of a donor having type B blood, which is 10%.

To model 10%, set up a 1-in-10 model. For this example, use a 10-sided numbered die and designate 1 on the die as representing a donor with type B blood. *Tip:* There are many other appropriate models. For instance, you could use random digits from 0 to 9 and designate the digit 1 as a donor with type B blood (see Appendix B for a table of random digits). Or you could use a bag with 10 marbles, 9 blue and 1 red, with red representing a donor with type B blood.

Step 2. Define a trial (or run) in the simulation.

One trial would be to roll the die ten times and count the number of 1s rolled.

Step 3. Define what is meant by a "success" when a trial is performed.

A success is getting 2 or more 1s in a trial. *Tip:* A **success** is the particular outcome of a trial that you want to keep count of.

Step 4. Perform a large number of trials ($n \geq 100$) and count the total number of successes.

Step 5. Compute the proportion of successes in the n trials as the estimate of the probability of at least 2 type B blood donors out of 10 donors.

☞ Try These

1. Fill in the blank.

   (a) In empirical probability, a probability is assigned to an event E by conducting the experiment a large number of times, called _____, and counting the number of times that event E actually occurs.

   (b) A _____ object is an object in an experiment for which one result is more likely to happen than another.

   (c) A simulation is a well-designed _____ of a chance process.

2. In a survey of 150 randomly selected seventh graders in a large middle school, 96 responded that they listen to a certain popular teen music channel.

   (a) What is the empirical probability that a randomly selected seventh grader in the middle school listens to this music channel?

   (b) Based on the result in part (a), what is the probability a randomly selected seventh grader does *not* listen to this music channel?

3. Dembe, Sameen, Thomas, and Zoe test whether the spinner shown is biased in favor of the letter C.

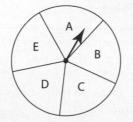

   Taking turns, each completes 25 spins and records the outcome as shown in the table.

	Number of As	Number of Bs	Number of Cs	Number of Ds	Number of Es	Number of Spins
Dembe	2	7	11	2	3	25
Sameen	4	5	8	1	7	25
Thomas	4	6	6	3	6	25
Zoe	3	6	8	2	6	25
Total	13	24	33	8	22	100

   (a) Using the data in the table, develop an empirical probability model for spinning the spinner.

   (b) What will the students likely conclude about the spinner?

   (c) Based on the probability model, predict the number of times the pointer will land on C in 500 spins.

4. According to a recent poll, 40% of teenagers in the United States have an iPhone. A school administrator wants to answer the following question using a simulation: In a group of 10 randomly selected teenagers, what is the probability at least 2 have an iPhone?

   (a) Describe a model that matches the probability that 40% of teenagers have an iPhone.

   (b) Describe a trial in the simulation.

   (c) Describe a success in a trial.

Solutions

1. (a) trials
   (b) biased
   (c) imitation

2. (a) P(seventh-grader listens to this music channel) $= \dfrac{96}{150} = 0.64$

   (b) Based on the result in part (a), the probability that a randomly selected seventh grader does *not* listen to this music channel is $1 - 0.64 = 0.36$.

3. **(a)** Using the combined data, the empirical probability model is

$$P(A) = \frac{13}{100} = 0.13, \ P(B) = \frac{24}{100} = 0.24, \ P(C) = \frac{33}{100} = 0.33, \ P(D) = \frac{8}{100} = 0.08, \text{ and } P(E) = \frac{22}{100} = 0.22$$

(b) The theoretical probabilities are $P(A) = P(B) = P(C) = P(D) = P(E) = 0.20$. So, the students will likely conclude the spinner is biased in favor of C.

(c) The number of Cs in 500 spins will be roughly, but probably not exactly, 165, which is 0.33×500.

4. **(a)** Answers may vary. To model 40%, set up a 4-in-10 model or a 2-in-5 model. There are many appropriate models: a 10-sided numbered die with 1, 2, 3, and 4 on the die representing a teenager with an iPhone; random digits from 0 to 9 with 1, 2, 3, and 4 representing a teenager with an iPhone; a bag with 5 marbles, 3 blue and 2 red, with red representing a teenager with an iPhone.

(b) Answers may vary. As an example, a trial is randomly drawing one marble 10 times from the bag of 5 marbles (3 blue and 2 red) and recording the number of times a red marble is drawn.

(c) Answers may vary. As an example, a success is two or more times a red marble is drawn in 10 draws from the bag of 5 marbles (3 blue and 2 red).

Understanding Statistical Inference

(CCSS.Math.Content.7.SP.A.1, CCSS.Math.Content.7.SP.A.2)

This section will present basic terminology and concepts of statistical inference. In statistical inference, data are collected, summarized, and analyzed to answer questions or to inform decision making. The data provide information about the world around you.

Tip: The word *data* is the plural form of the word *datum*.

Recognizing Populations and Samples

A **statistical question** is one that anticipates the data collected to answer it will vary. It does not have a specific pre-determined answer. For instance, "How tall are the seventh-grade students in your school?" is a statistical question. You expect the heights of seventh graders to vary from student to student. But "How tall is your best friend?" is *not* a statistical question. Your best friend has a specific height. There is no variability in the answer at the time of the question.

Tip: Statistical questions are answered by collecting data that vary.

When you have a statistical question, you need data to answer it. To answer the statistical question "How tall are the seventh-grade students in your school?" you could measure the height of every seventh grader in your school and summarize the results. Undoubtedly, obtaining the heights of all the seventh graders would be a challenging and time-consuming task.

Instead, you might measure a portion of your school's seventh graders to find out information that you could use to conjecture the heights of all seventh graders at your school. In this scenario, the portion of students you measure is a *sample*, and all seventh graders at your school is a *population*.

A **population** is the set of all persons or things (such as seventh graders, teachers, light bulbs, pine seedlings, batteries, and so forth) that you want information about. A **sample** is a subset of the population.

A **parameter** is a number that describes a population. It is a fixed number. However, in many situations, its value is *unknown*. A **statistic** is a number that describes a sample. Once you have data from a sample, the value of a statistic is *known*, because you can compute it. However, its value can change from sample to sample.

A **statistical inference** is a conclusion about a population based on information from a sample of the population. You use statistics from samples to *estimate* parameters of populations. The following diagram illustrates the process of statistical inference.

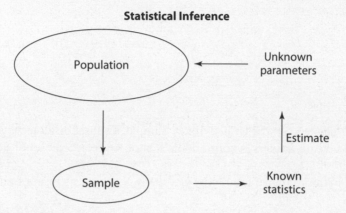

It is important for you to realize that conclusions of statistical inference are *always* about populations, NOT about samples.

☞ Try These

1. Fill in the blank(s).

   (a) A statistical question is one that anticipates the data collected to answer it will _____.
   (b) In a statistical study, the _____ is the set of all persons or things of interest to you.
   (c) A sample is a subset of the _____.
   (d) Numerical descriptions of a population are _____.
   (e) Numerical descriptions of a sample are _____.
   (f) A statistical inference is a _____ about a population based on information from a sample of the population.
   (g) Conclusions of statistical inference are *always* about _____, NOT about _____.

2. Describe the population and sample for the statistical question.

   (a) What percentage of teenagers in the United States have iPhones?
   (b) What is the mean height of seventh graders in your middle school?
   (c) What percentage of batteries manufactured by Company X are defective?
   (d) How many pets do students in your school own?

3. State whether the boldface number in the paragraph is a parameter or a statistic. *Note:* For purposes of this question, the parameters are known values.

    (a) School records show that **35%** of the 1,800 students in the school district's two middle schools are seventh graders. Of 125 students selected from all middle-school students in the district, **38%** are seventh graders.

    (b) In a group of 30 students from Middle School *X*, the mean age is **12.6 years.** School records show the mean age of all students at Middle School *X* is **12.5 years.**

Solutions

1. **(a)** vary
    (b) population
    (c) population
    (d) parameters
    (e) statistics
    (f) conclusion
    (g) populations; samples

2. **(a)** population: all teenagers in the United States; sample: a subset of all teenagers in the United States
    (b) population: all seventh graders in your middle school; sample: a subset of all seventh graders in your middle school
    (c) population: all batteries manufactured by Company X; sample: subset of all batteries manufactured by Company X
    (d) population: all students in your school; sample: a subset of all students in your school

3. **(a)** **35%** is a parameter; **38%** is a statistic.
    (b) **12.5 years** is a parameter; **12.6 years** is a statistic.

Understanding Random Sampling

When you select a sample from a population, you use a **random sample** of **adequate size** so that it will be *representative* of the population from which it was selected. A **representative sample** has characteristics that mimic those of the population from which it was selected. Suppose your population is all seventh graders in your school. Your sample, for instance, should have a similar age, race, and gender makeup. It also should be of adequate size. Conclusions about populations should not be based on samples that are far too small (for example, an opinion survey that uses fewer than 10 subjects).

In a **simple random sample** (or just **random sample**), every member of the population has an equal chance of being selected. Drawing names from a bowl is a way to obtain a random sample. For many situations, however, this method is impractical. Computer-generated random digits or a table of random digits can be used to choose a random sample (see Appendix B).

The powerful techniques of inferential statistics allow you to take sample data and draw inferences about the entire population. Of course, you can't be positive your conclusions are correct because your data are not from the entire population. Fortunately, though, random sampling tends to produce representative samples. Representative samples provide meaningful results that will support valid inferences you make about the population.

Tip: Making inferences about the population from information in a sample is known as *generalizing* to the population.

☞ Try These

1. Fill in the blank(s).

   (a) Samples should be _____ and of _____ size.

   (b) A representative sample has characteristics that _____ those of the population from which it was selected.

   (c) In a random sample, every member of the population has a(n) _____ chance of being selected.

   (d) Random sampling tends to produce _____ samples.

   (e) Making inferences about the population from information in a sample is known as _____ to the population.

2. State whether the sample method likely will produce a representative sample. Explain your answer.

   (a) Taraji and Hayden want to know the opinions of the 658 students in their middle school on whether students should be required to wear uniforms. They survey 100 of the students who attend the next after-school spirit rally.

   (b) Kevin and Isla want to know the average years of teaching experience of the 124 teachers in their middle school. They ask all the mathematics teachers in the middle school.

   (c) Annet and Jony want to know the favorite academic subject (math, English language arts, social studies, or science) of the 356 seventh graders in their school. They survey 100 randomly selected seventh graders in their school.

   (d) A television station manager wants to know which local shows are popular with viewers in the station's viewing area. The station manager sets up a website where viewers can click to select their favorites shows. The website collects data from 20,502 viewers.

   (e) Oliver and Shuja do a survey at their school of students' favorite school lunches. They ask 8 randomly selected students from their school's 425 students.

Solutions

1. **(a)** random; adequate
   (b) mimic
   (c) equal
   (d) representative
   (e) generalizing

2. **(a)** This method is unlikely to produce a representative sample because students who do not attend the after-school spirit rally do not have a chance of being selected.
   (b) This method is unlikely to produce a representative sample because teachers who do not teach math do not have a chance of being selected.
   (c) This method is likely to produce a representative sample because all seventh graders in the school have an equal chance of being chosen.
   (d) This method is unlikely to produce a representative sample because the 20,502 viewers voluntarily responded. They were not randomly selected.
   (e) This method is unlikely to produce a representative sample because the sample size is too small to provide useful information.

Using Sample Data to Estimate a Population Parameter

(CCSS.Math.Content.7.SP.A.2)

Estimating a Population Mean from Sample Data

What is the mean age of all students in your middle school? To answer this statistical question, you randomly select a sample of 30 students in your school. You ask each student in the sample the same question, "What is your age in years?" You collect the responses and calculate the mean of the sample to be 12.6 years. If you select a second random sample of 30 students and calculate the mean, the new sample will have different students in it. And it is just about certain that the mean of the second sample will be different from the mean of your first sample. That is, the value of the sample mean will vary from sample to sample.

Now, imagine that you could repeat this process until you have taken all possible samples of size 30 and computed the mean age of each. A big idea of statistical inference is that if you create a histogram of all those means from the many, many samples, the histogram will be symmetric with a large cluster in the middle. And the mean of all those sample means will be the same as the mean of the population from which you selected them. In this case, the mean of the sample means will be the true mean age of all students in your middle school. What's more, the sample means will cluster more tightly around the true mean age of the students, than do the ages of students in the population.

Suppose that in fact (unknown to you) the true mean age of all students in your middle school is 12.5 years. Here is a graphical illustration of the population distribution and the sample means distribution for 10,000 samples of size 30.

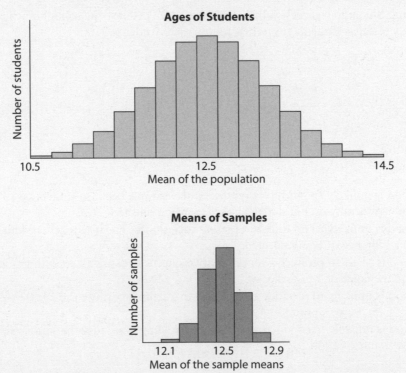

Both distributions have a mean of 12.5. The values of the sample means vary from sample to sample; some are less than the true mean of the population and some are greater. But the distribution is relatively symmetrical, so there is no tendency to be always less or always greater. And, most important, the values of the sample means are centered at 12.5, the true mean age of the population, and clustered close to it.

The distribution of the sample means has much less variability (spread) than the population distribution. Observe that $12.5 - 12.1 = 0.4$ and $12.9 - 12.5 = 0.4$. It appears that random samples of size 30 are likely to produce sample means that are within 0.4 units of the true mean.

The result is that the value of the mean of 12.6 you calculated from the sample you took is close to the true mean age of the students. It is a trustworthy estimate of the mean age of all students at your middle school.

In practice, when you want to estimate an unknown population mean, you select just *one* sample from the population. You calculate the mean of the sample and use it as your best estimate of the population mean. Statisticians generally agree that if you used a random sample of size 30 or more, your estimate should be close to the true value of the population parameter. Thus, it would be a trustworthy estimate of the population mean.

Here is an example.

A teacher wants to know the mean time it take students to complete a weekly 10-problem math quiz. She randomly selects 30 of the 98 total students in her classes and records their quiz times. The following data shows the times, in minutes. Estimate the mean time for all the teacher's students. Is the estimate trustworthy?

11, 12, 12, 13, 15, 15, 15, 16, 17, 20, 21, 21, 21, 22, 22,
22, 23, 24, 26, 27, 27, 28, 29, 29, 30, 31, 32, 34, 35, 37

The mean of the sample is 22.9 minutes. Thus, the teacher's best estimate of the mean time for all her students to complete a weekly 10-problem math quiz is 22.9 minutes. The sample is random and the sample size is 30, so this estimate is trustworthy.

Tip: Generally, if the sample is random and the sample size is 30 or more, the mean of the sample is a trustworthy estimate of the mean of the population.

☞ Try These

1. Fill in the blank(s).

   (a) The value of the sample mean will _____ from sample to sample.

   (b) The shape of the distribution of the means of all possible samples selected from a population is _____.

   (c) The mean of the means of all possible samples selected from a population is the _____ as the mean of the population from which the samples were selected.

   (d) The mean of the sample is the _____ estimate of the mean of the population.

   (e) Generally, if the sample is _____ and the sample size is _____ or more, the mean of the sample is a trustworthy estimate of the mean of the population.

2. The dot plot shows the scores of 35 randomly selected seventh graders on the school district's benchmark social studies test. Estimate the mean score of all seventh graders in the district. Round your estimate to the nearest tenth. Is the estimate trustworthy? *Tip:* Each dot represents a student's score.

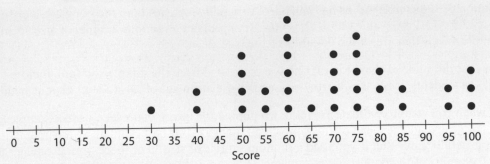

Benchmark Social Studies Test Scores of 35 Seventh-grade Students

3. A local deli chain advertises a "heart-healthy" sandwich on the menu. To estimate the average number of fat grams in the heart-healthy sandwiches, a nutritionist selects a random sample of 40 heart-healthy sandwiches. The mean number of fat grams in the sample of sandwiches is 11 grams. What is the nutritionist's best estimate of the average number of fat grams in heart-healthy sandwiches? Is the estimate trustworthy?

Solutions

1. **(a)** vary
   (b) symmetric
   (c) same
   (d) best
   (e) random; 30

2. The mean of the sample is $\frac{2,400}{35} \approx 68.6$. Thus, the best estimate of the mean score of all seventh graders in the district is 68.6. This estimate is trustworthy because the sample is random and the sample size is greater than 30.

3. The mean of the sample is 11 grams. Thus, the best estimate of the average number of fat grams in the heart-healthy sandwiches is 11 grams. The sample is random and the sample size is greater than 30, so this estimate is trustworthy.

Estimating a Population Proportion from Sample Data

What proportion of students in your middle school own a cat or a dog? To answer this statistical question, you randomly select a sample of 100 students in your middle school. You ask each student in the sample the same question, "Do you own a cat, a dog, or both?" You collect the responses and calculate the proportion of students who responded "yes" as 0.59 or 59%. You can use this sample proportion as an estimate of the population proportion.

The question you should ask yourself is, "How trustworthy is this estimate?" When estimating population means, you know that if your sample is randomly selected and is 30 or more in size, the sample mean likely is close to the true population mean. Unfortunately, when estimating proportions from large populations, the accuracy of the sample proportion is low unless you take a very large random sample of 1,000 or more.

The percentage points that your estimate misses the true proportion in the population is the **margin of error.** Survey results by polling organizations (you might have heard of the Gallup Poll or the Zogby Poll) include a statement of the margin of error. For example, a poll might report that 40% of teenagers in the United States own an iPhone, with a margin of error of 3%. This information tells you that the true proportion of teenagers who own an iPhone is likely between 37% and 43%. You get the lower number by subtracting the margin of error (40% – 3% = 37%) and the upper number by adding the margin of error (40% + 3% = 43%).

A rough idea of the margin of error for survey results from a sample of size n is $\dfrac{1}{\sqrt{n}}$. For your survey about cat or dog ownership, the margin of error is around $\dfrac{1}{\sqrt{100}} = \dfrac{1}{10} = 10\%$. So you would report the percentage of students in your middle school who own a cat or a dog is 59%, with a margin of error of 10%. Or you could simply say the percentage is between 49% and 69%.

> **Tip:** In the real world, margins of error above 10% commonly are considered too high, because they compromise the accuracy of the estimate. Some authorities suggest that acceptable margins of error fall between 3% and 8%.

Margins of error also can be calculated for estimates of means. But the formulas for doing so are a bit complicated. For now, you can simply report the mean of the sample as your best estimate of the mean of the population. As a rule, when the sample is random and of adequate size (30 or more), this estimate will be trustworthy.

> **Warning:** One very important caution you should keep in mind is that even when you report results with margins of error, you still could be wrong! Your conclusions about a population based on data from a sample are NEVER completely certain.

Also, the size of the population has little to do with the accuracy of your estimate of a population parameter. The *most important factor is the size of the sample*. Larger samples result in less variability in the distribution of the sample statistic. So the value of the sample mean you calculate is closer to the true value of the population mean as the sample size increases. And the value of the sample proportion you calculate is closer to the true value of the population proportion as the sample size increases.

☞ Try These

1. Fill in the blank(s).

   (a) When estimating population proportions, the accuracy of the sample proportion is low unless you take a very large random sample of _____ or more.

   (b) The percentage points that an estimate misses the true proportion in the population is the margin of _____, which can be determined as roughly _____ for a sample of size n.

   (c) Conclusions about a population based on data from a sample are _____ completely certain.

   (d) The most important factor that affects the accuracy of an estimate of a population parameter is the size of the _____ (population, sample).

2. Annet and Esteban ask 50 randomly selected seventh graders in their middle school whether they live within 5 miles of the school. Eight of the students responded "yes" to the survey question.

   (a) Using Annet and Esteban's data, estimate the proportion of seventh graders in their middle school who live within 5 miles of the school.

   (b) What is your assessment of Annet and Esteban's survey?

3. Andrew and Meera ask a randomly selected sample of students in their middle school whether they have a nighttime curfew. Of the 200 students in the sample, 142 answered "yes."

   (a) Using Andrew and Meera's data, estimate the proportion of students in their middle school who have a nighttime curfew.

   (b) What is your assessment of Andrew and Meera's survey?

Solutions

1. (a) 1,000

   (b) error; $\dfrac{1}{\sqrt{n}}$

   (c) never
   (d) sample

2. (a) The proportion of students in the sample who said "yes" is $\dfrac{8}{50} = 0.16 = 16\%$. Using a margin of error of $\dfrac{1}{\sqrt{50}} \approx 0.14 = 14\%$, the proportion of seventh graders in the middle school who live within 5 miles of the school is between 2% and 30%.

   (b) Answers may vary. The margin of error is too high. So, the results are not very useful. They should take a larger sample.

3. (a) The proportion of students in the sample who said "yes" is $\dfrac{142}{200} = 0.71 = 71\%$. Using a margin of error of $\dfrac{1}{\sqrt{200}} \approx 0.07 = 7\%$, the proportion of students in their middle school who have a nighttime curfew is between 64% and 78%.

   (b) Answers may vary. The margin of error is acceptable, and the results are informative. However, if they had the time and resources, they could consider taking a larger sample to improve the accuracy of their estimate.

Informally Comparing Two Population Parameters

(CCSS.Math.Content.7.SP.B.3, CCSS.Math.Content.7.SP.B.4)

When you have population data, questions about differences in population means are indisputable because you have the known values. You don't need samples to estimate them. However, you might want to give additional information about the differences.

Here is an example.

The dot plots show the scores of 30 seventh graders on the mathematics beginning-of-year (BOY) assessment and on the mathematics end-of-year (EOY) assessment. Analyze the differences in these two populations of scores.

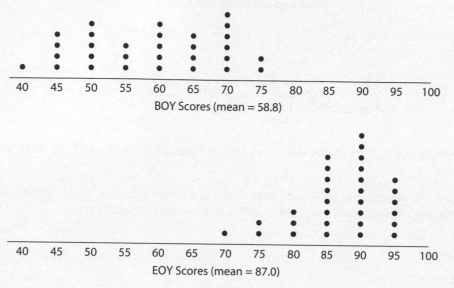

The end-of-year scores, on average, are 28.2 points higher than the beginning-of-year scores (because 87.0 – 58.8 = 28.2). This difference indicates much improvement from the beginning of the year to the end of the year. The scores on the mathematics end-of-year assessment range from 70 to 95, a 25-point spread, and have less variability than the scores on the mathematics beginning of year assessment, which range from 40 to 75, a 35-point spread.

When you don't have population data, you need samples from those populations to determine differences. To make informal inferences about the population means, you must consider the differences between the two sample mean distributions. Each population mean has a sample mean distribution. (See the section "Estimating a Population Mean from Sample Data" earlier in this chapter for a discussion of sample mean distributions.) You must base your decision about the difference in the population means on the difference in the sample mean distributions.

Here is an example.

A manager at a popular retail store wants to know whether the store's Internet sales exceed its in-store sales. The manager took a random sample of 30 Internet sales and a random sample of 30 in-store sales. The mean of the sample of Internet sales was $86.40, with a MAD of $8.75. The mean of the in-store sales was $75.20 with a MAD of $9.25. According to these data, is the average of all Internet sales of the store greater than the average of all the in-store sales? Explain your answer.

Tip: Recall that the mean absolute deviation (MAD) is the average distance between each data value and the mean of the data values.

The difference in the sample means is $86.40 – $75.20 = $11.20. The MADs in the two populations are $8.75 and $9.25. From the discussion of sample mean distributions in the section "Estimating a Population Mean from

Sample Data" (earlier in this chapter), you know that the variability in the sample means of each of these two populations is much smaller than their corresponding MAD values. A sketch of the two sampling distributions would show that the two sampling distributions are $11.20 apart with little or no overlap (see below).

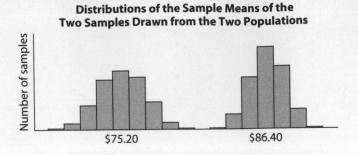

Distributions of the Sample Means of the Two Samples Drawn from the Two Populations

So, you can informally conclude the average of all Internet sales of the store is greater than the average of all the in-store sales.

If it appears that two sampling distributions might overlap a great deal, then you should *not* conclude that the means of the populations from which the samples were drawn are different.

☞ Try These

1. Fill in the blank.

   (a) When you have population data, you _____ (do, do not) need samples to determine differences.

   (b) When you do not have population data, you _____ (do, do not) need samples to determine differences.

   (c) If it appears that two sampling distributions might overlap a great deal, then you _____ (should, should not) conclude that the means of the populations from which the samples were drawn are different.

2. The histograms show the years of experience of teachers at Middle School X and teachers at Middle School Y. Analyze the differences in these two populations.

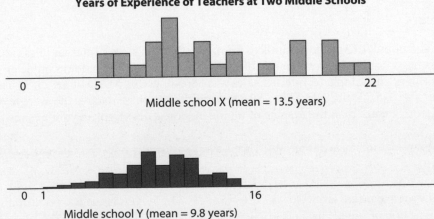

Years of Experience of Teachers at Two Middle Schools

Middle school X (mean = 13.5 years)

Middle school Y (mean = 9.8 years)

3. Ignacio and Margo want to know whether the number of hours seventh-grade boys in their school play video games each week is fewer than the number of hours eighth-grade boys in their school play video games. Ignacio selects a random sample of 50 seventh-grade boys and determines that the mean number of hours the boys in the sample play video games is 10.4 hours, with a MAD of 3.2 hours. Margo selects a random sample of 50 eighth-grade boys and determines that the mean number of hours the boys in the sample play video games is 13.2 hours, with a MAD of 2.6 hours. According to the data, is the number of hours seventh-grade boys in their school play video games each week fewer than the number of hours eighth-grade boys in their school play video games ? Explain your answer.

4. Below are two sample mean distributions from data regarding the prices of shirts at two different stores. Should you conclude the mean costs of shirts at the two stores are different? Explain your answer.

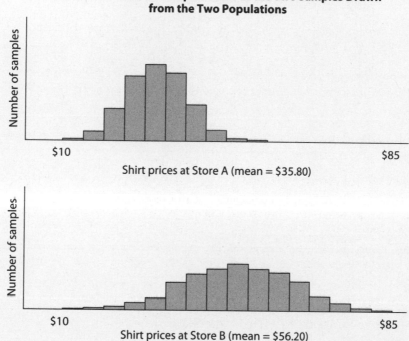

Distributions of the Sample Means of the Two Samples Drawn from the Two Populations

Shirt prices at Store A (mean = $35.80)

Shirt prices at Store B (mean = $56.20)

Solutions

1. **(a)** do not
   (b) do
   (c) should not

2. Answers may vary. The years of experience of teachers at Middle School X is, on average, 3.7 years higher than the years of experience of teachers at Middle School Y (because 13.5 − 9.8 = 3.7). This difference means that, on average, the teachers at Middle School X are slightly more experienced. Both populations show noticeable variability in experience. Experience at Middle School X ranges from 5 years to 22 years, a 17-year spread. Experience at Middle School Y ranges from 1 year to 16 years, a 15-year spread.

3. Answer may vary. The difference in the sample means is 13.2 hours – 10.4 hours = 2.8 hours. The MADs in the two populations are 3.2 hours and 2.6 hours. The variability in the sample means of each of these two populations is much smaller than their corresponding MAD values. So, informally, it appears the two sampling distributions are 2.8 hours apart with little or no overlap. So, Ignacio and Margo can informally conclude that, on average, the number of hours seventh-grade boys in their school play video games each week is fewer than the number of hours eighth-grade boys in their school play video games.

4. Answers may vary. The difference in the means of the samples is $20.40, which is $56.20 – $35.80. But there is too much overlap in the two sample mean distributions to conclude the average costs of all shirts at the two stores are different.

6. Practice Test 1

Directions: For questions 1–30, select the best answer choice.

1. Simplify the complex fraction: $\dfrac{\frac{9}{16}}{\frac{1}{4}}$

   A. $\dfrac{9}{64}$

   B. $\dfrac{4}{9}$

   C. $\dfrac{9}{4}$

   D. $\dfrac{16}{4}$

2. Connor walked $1\frac{1}{8}$ miles in $\frac{1}{4}$ hour. What is Connor's rate of miles per hour?

   A. 4.4 miles per hour
   B. 4.5 miles per hour
   C. 4.6 miles per hour
   D. 4.7 miles per hour

3. Olivia typed 140 words in 2 minutes 20 seconds. At this rate, how many words can Olivia type in 10 minutes?

   A. 300 words
   B. 308 words
   C. 600 words
   D. 616 words

4. Which pair of points represents a proportional relationship?

   A. (2, 2) and (5, 5)
   B. (1, 3) and (3, 6)
   C. (2, 0) and (4, 8)
   D. (6, 1) and (1, 6)

5. Which graph represents a proportional relationship containing the plotted points?

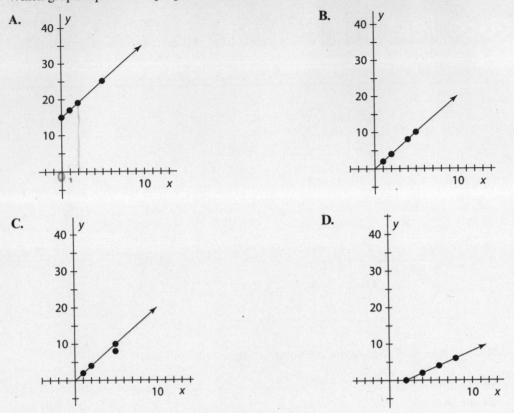

6. The table shows a proportional relationship between the cost, c (in dollars), and the number, n, of used books purchased.

Number, n, of Books Purchased	Cost, c (in Dollars)
4	24
7	42
8	48
11	66

Write an equation that represents the proportional relationship between n and c.

A. $n = c - 6$

B. $n = 6c$

C. $c = n + 6$

D. $c = 6n$

7. The ratio of boys in the band to the number of the girls in the band is 3 to 5. There are 18 boys in the band. How many students are in the band?

    A. 30
    B. 48
    C. 60
    D. 78

8. Forty percent of 200 spectators are students. How many of the spectators are students?

    A. 40
    B. 60
    C. 80
    D. 100

9. Express $-\dfrac{5}{8}$ as an equivalent decimal.

    A. −0.0625
    B. −0.580
    C. −0.625
    D. −1.600

10. Express $37\dfrac{1}{2}\%$ as an equivalent fraction in reduced form.

    A. $\dfrac{1}{8}$

    B. $\dfrac{3}{8}$

    C. $\dfrac{5}{8}$

    D. $\dfrac{7}{8}$

11. Express 108% as an equivalent decimal.

    A. 0.108
    B. 1.08
    C. 10.8
    D. 108

12. Compute: $-\dfrac{4}{5} + -\dfrac{3}{5}$

   A. $-\dfrac{7}{5}$

   B. $-\dfrac{1}{5}$

   C. $\dfrac{1}{5}$

   D. $\dfrac{7}{5}$

13. Compute: $25 + -17$

   A. -42
   B. -8
   C. 8
   D. 42

14. Compute: $6.135 - 9.4$

   A. -15.535
   B. -3.265
   C. 3.265
   D. 15.535

15. Compute: $7.95 - -19.34$

   A. -27.29
   B. -11.39
   C. 11.39
   D. 27.29

16. Which statement is TRUE?

   A. $(-40)(-50) = -2,000$
   B. $(-40)(50) = 2,000$
   C. $(40)(-50) = 2,000$
   D. $(-40)(-50) = 2,000$

17. Which statement is TRUE?

    A. $\dfrac{-24}{8} = -3$

    B. $\dfrac{-24}{-8} = -3$

    C. $\dfrac{24}{-8} = 3$

    D. $\dfrac{-24}{8} = 3$

18. Find the vertical distance between an elevation of –345 feet and an elevation of –762 feet.

    A. –1,107 feet
    B. –417 feet
    C. 417 feet
    D. 1,107 feet

19. Evaluate: $7.4 - 15 + 2.6$

    A. –25
    B. –5
    C. 5
    D. 25

20. Which statement is TRUE?

    A. $\dfrac{-45}{0} = 0$

    B. $\left(\dfrac{1}{2}\right)(-20)(-2.5)(-1) = 25$

    C. $(-1)(-1)(-60)(-1)(-1) = -60$

    D. $\dfrac{-100}{-100} = -1$

21. Expand: $2(5x + 3)$

    A. $11x$
    B. $16x$
    C. $10x + 3$
    D. $10x + 6$

22. Find the sum of $3x + 5$ and $2x - 5$.

    A. x
    B. $5x$
    C. $x - 10$
    D. $5x - 10$

23. Find the difference of $15x - 20$ and $-3x + 25$.

    A. $13x - 5$
    B. $13x - 45$
    C. $18x - 45$
    D. $18x - 5$

24. In triangle ABC, $\angle A$ measures $25°$ and $\angle C$ measures $60°$. What type of angle is angle B?

    A.   acute
    B.   obtuse
    C.   right
    D.   straight

25. Which set of numbers could be the lengths of the sides of a triangle?

    A.   8, 14, 18
    B.   6, 16, 24
    C.   6, 15, 7
    D.   2, 3, 5

26. Use the diagram below to answer the question that follows.

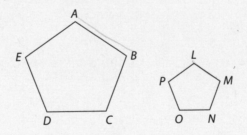

    $ABCDE$ and $LMNOP$ are regular pentagons. If $AB = 12$ units and $LM = 6$ units, what is the ratio of the area of $ABCDE$ to the area of $LMNOP$?

    A.   1:2
    B.   2:1
    C.   4:1
    D.   24:1

27. A science textbook has scale drawings of various insects. The scale shows that 1 centimeter in the drawing represents 2.5 centimeters of actual length. What is the length (in centimeters) of the scale drawing of a beetle if the beetle is actually 9.0 centimeters long?

   A.   3.6 centimeters
   B.   4.0 centimeters
   C.   4.5 centimeters
   D.   18.0 centimeters

28. A spinner for a board game has 4 red sections, 3 yellow sections, 2 blue sections, and 1 green section. The sections are all of equal size. What is the probability of spinning red on the first spin and green on the second spin?

   A. $\dfrac{1}{50}$

   B. $\dfrac{1}{25}$

   C. $\dfrac{1}{4}$

   D.   4

29. Gabri and Dora are conducting a survey of the opinions of the 400 seventh graders in their middle school on whether students should be required to wear uniforms. Which method of surveying the students will allow Gabri and Dora to make valid conclusions about the seventh-grade students' opinions about wearing uniforms?

   A.   Ask 100 seventh-grade students at the next after-school spirit rally.
   B.   Ask 100 students in the middle school whose names are chosen at random.
   C.   Ask 100 seventh-grade students in the middle school whose names are chosen at random.
   D.   Ask 100 students randomly selected from those who ride a bus home from school.

30. Liu has quiz grades of 75, 89, 67, 56, and 92 in her social studies class and quiz grades of 75, 78, 83, 84, 80, and 77 in her mathematics class. Which statement correctly describes Liu's quiz grades in the two classes?

   A.   The quiz grades in the social studies class have greater variability.
   B.   The quiz grades in the mathematics class have greater variability.
   C.   The mean of the quiz grades in the social studies class is higher than the mean in the mathematics class.
   D.   The means of the quiz grades in the two classes are equal.

Directions: For questions 31–40, enter your answer in the answer box below the question. Enter the exact answer unless you are told to round your answer.

31. What is the approximate diameter of a circle with a circumference of 48 inches? Use $\pi \approx 3.14$. Round your answer to the nearest one-hundredth.

    [_____] inches

32. Forty-two percent of the students in attendance at the game are girls. There are 210 girls in attendance. How many students are in attendance at the game?

    [_____]

33. Three hundred dollars is what percent of $500?

    [_____] %

34. A home stereo system is on sale for 20% off its list price of $640. What is the sale price of the stereo system after the 20% discount?

    $ [_____]

35. Trisha bought a pair of shoes for $40 and a blouse for $35. Trisha's purchases are subject to a sales tax rate of 8.75%. Including tax, what did Trisha pay for the shoes and blouse? Give your answer to the nearest cent.

    $ [_____]

36. Payton works at a department store that pays a commission rate of 6% to employees for sales. Yesterday, Payton's total sales were $754. What commission did he earn for yesterday's sales?

$$ \$\boxed{} $$

37. A smart phone is marked down from $198.00 to $174.24. What is the percent decrease in the price of the phone?

$$ \boxed{}\% $$

38. Solve for x: $5x + 14 = -26$

$$ \boxed{} $$

39. Solve for x: $\dfrac{2}{5}(x+30)=-48$

$$ \boxed{} $$

40. The original price of a shirt is increased by $15. Patrick buys two of the shirts. The total price before sales tax is added is $86. What was the original price of the shirt?

$$ \$\boxed{} $$

Answer Key

1. C	11. B	21. D	31. 15.29 inches
2. B	12. A	22. B	32. 500
3. C	13. C	23. C	33. 60%
4. A	14. B	24. B	34. $512
5. B	15. D	25. A	35. $81.56
6. D	16. D	26. C	36. $45.24
7. B	17. A	27. A	37. 12%
8. C	18. C	28. B	38. −8
9. C	19. B	29. C	39. −150
10. B	20. C	30. A	40. $28

Answer Explanations

1. **C.** Choice C is the correct response.

Method 1: $\dfrac{\frac{9}{16}}{\frac{1}{4}} = \dfrac{9}{16} \div \dfrac{1}{4} = \dfrac{9}{16} \times \dfrac{4}{1} = \dfrac{9}{{}_4\cancel{16}} \times \dfrac{\cancel{4}^{1}}{1} = \dfrac{9}{4}$

Method 2: $\dfrac{\frac{9}{16}}{\frac{1}{4}} = \dfrac{\left(\frac{9}{16}\right) \cdot \frac{16}{1}}{\left(\frac{1}{4}\right) \cdot \frac{16}{1}} = \dfrac{\left(\frac{9}{{}_1\cancel{16}}\right) \cdot \frac{\cancel{16}^{1}}{1}}{\left(\frac{1}{{}_1\cancel{4}}\right) \cdot \frac{\cancel{16}^{4}}{1}} = \dfrac{9}{4}$

2. **B.** Choice B is the correct response.

$\dfrac{1\frac{1}{8} \text{ miles}}{\frac{1}{4} \text{ hour}} = \dfrac{\left(\frac{9}{8}\right) \cdot \frac{8}{1} \text{ miles}}{\left(\frac{1}{4}\right) \cdot \frac{8}{1} \text{ hours}} = \dfrac{\left(\frac{9}{{}_1\cancel{8}}\right) \cdot \frac{\cancel{8}^{1}}{1} \text{ miles}}{\left(\frac{1}{{}_1\cancel{4}}\right) \cdot \frac{\cancel{8}^{2}}{1} \text{ hours}} = \dfrac{\frac{9}{1} \text{ miles}}{\frac{2}{1} \text{ hours}} = \dfrac{9 \text{ miles}}{2 \text{ hours}} = \dfrac{4.5 \text{ miles}}{1 \text{ hour}} = 4.5 \text{ miles per hour}$

Connor's rate is 4.5 miles per hour.

3. **C.** Choice C is the correct response.

$$1 \text{ second (s)} = \frac{1}{60} \text{ minutes (min)}$$

$$\text{So, 20 seconds} = \frac{20 \text{ s}}{1} \times \frac{1 \text{ min}}{60 \text{ s}} = \frac{\cancel{20}^{120} \text{ s}}{1} \times \frac{1 \text{ min}}{\cancel{60}_3 \text{ s}} = \frac{1}{3} \text{ min}$$

$$\frac{140 \text{ words}}{2\frac{1}{3} \text{ minutes}} = \frac{140}{\frac{7}{3}} \frac{\text{words}}{\text{minute}}$$

$$= \left(140 \div \frac{7}{3}\right) \frac{\text{words}}{\text{minute}}$$

$$= \left(\frac{140}{1} \times \frac{3}{7}\right) \frac{\text{words}}{\text{minute}}$$

$$= \left(\frac{\cancel{140}^{20}}{1} \times \frac{3}{\cancel{7}_1}\right) \frac{\text{words}}{\text{minute}}$$

$$= \frac{60}{1} \frac{\text{words}}{\text{minute}}$$

$$= 60 \text{ words per minute}$$

$$\frac{60 \text{ words}}{1 \text{ minute}} \times 10 \text{ minutes} = \frac{60 \text{ words}}{1 \text{ minute}} \times \frac{10 \text{ minutes}}{1} = 600 \text{ words}$$

Olivia can type 600 words in 10 minutes.

4. **A.** Choice A is the correct response. Check whether $\frac{y}{x}$ is a constant for each pair of points.

The points in Choice A represent a proportional relationship. The points (2, 2) and (5, 5) represent a proportional relationship because $\frac{2}{2} = 1$ and $\frac{5}{5} = 1$. Each ratio has a value of 1.

The points in Choice B do not represent a proportional relationship because $\frac{3}{1} = 3$ and $\frac{6}{3} = 2$ do not have the same value.

The points in Choice C do not represent a proportional relationship because $\frac{0}{2} = 0$ and $\frac{8}{4} = 2$ do not have the same value.

The points in Choice D do not represent a proportional relationship because $\frac{1}{6}$ and $\frac{6}{1} = 6$ do not have the same value.

5. **B.** Choice B is the correct response. The four points lie on a straight line that passes through the origin. The graphs in choices A and D do not pass through the origin. The graph in Choice C is not a straight line; one point is not aligned with the other points.

6. **D.** Choice D is the correct response. The equation is $c = kn$. The constant of proportionality is $k = \frac{c}{n}$.

$$\frac{24}{4} = 6; \quad \frac{42}{7} = 6; \quad \frac{48}{8} = 6; \quad \frac{66}{11} = 6$$

So, $k = 6$. The equation $c = 6n$ represents the proportional relationship between n and c.

7. **B.** Choice B is the correct response. Let g = the number of girls in the band. Then $18 + g$ = the number of students in the band. First, determine g.

The ratios 3 to 5 and 18 to g are equivalent. Write a proportion and solve for g.

$$\frac{3}{5} = \frac{18}{g}$$

Find the cross products.

$$3 \cdot g = 5 \cdot 18$$

Then solve for g.

$$3g = 90$$

$$\frac{3g}{3} = \frac{90}{3}$$

$$\frac{\cancel{3}g}{\cancel{3}} = 90 \div 3$$

$$1g = 30$$

$$g = 30$$

$$18 + g = 18 + 30 = 48$$

There are 48 students in the band.

Tip: Be sure to answer the question asked. After you find the number of girls in the band, you must compute the number of students in the band to answer the question.

8. **C.** Choice C is the correct response.

Let x = the number of spectators who are students. Write a percent statement for the question.

$$x \text{ is } 40\% \text{ of } 200$$

The part is x, the percent is 40%, and the whole is 200.

List the elements for the percent proportion.

$$r = 40$$

$$\text{part} = ? = x$$

$$\text{whole} = 200$$

Plug into the percent proportion.

$$\frac{r}{100} = \frac{\text{part}}{\text{whole}}$$

$$\frac{40}{100} = \frac{x}{200}$$

$$\frac{40 \div 10}{100 \div 10} = \frac{x}{200}$$

$$\frac{4}{10} = \frac{x}{200}$$

Solve the proportion.

$$\frac{4}{10} = \frac{x}{200}$$

Find the cross products.

$$4 \cdot 200 = 10 \cdot x$$

Then solve for x.

$$800 = 10x$$
$$10x = 800$$
$$\frac{10x}{10} = \frac{800}{10}$$
$$\frac{\cancel{10}x}{\cancel{10}} = 800 \div 10$$
$$1x = 80$$
$$x = 80$$

Eighty students are spectators.

9. **C.** Choice C is the correct response.

$$\frac{5}{8} = 8\overline{)\begin{array}{l} 0.625 \\ 5.000 \end{array}}$$
$$\underline{-48}$$
$$20$$
$$\underline{-16}$$
$$40$$
$$\underline{-40}$$
$$0$$

$$-\frac{5}{8} = -0.625$$

10. **B.** Choice B is the correct response.

$$37\frac{1}{2}\% = \frac{37\frac{1}{2}}{100} = \frac{\frac{75}{2}}{100} = \frac{\left(\frac{75}{\cancel{2}_1}\right) \cdot \cancel{2}^1}{100 \cdot 2} = \frac{75}{200} = \frac{75 \div 25}{200 \div 25} = \frac{3}{8}$$

11. **B.** Choice B is the correct response.

$$108\% = 108(0.01) = 1.08$$

12. **A.** Choice A is the correct response.

$$-\frac{4}{5}+-\frac{3}{5}=-\frac{7}{5}$$

13. **C.** Choice C is the correct response.

$$25+-17=8$$

14. **B.** Choice B is the correct response.

$$6.135-9.4=6.135+-9.4=-3.265$$

15. **D.** Choice D is the correct response.

$$7.95--19.34=7.95+19.34=27.29$$

16. **D.** Choice D is the correct response.

$$(-40)(-50)=2,000\ (\text{because}\ -\cdot-=+)$$

17. **A.** Choice A is the correct response.

$$\frac{-24}{8}=-3\ \left(\text{because}\ \frac{-}{+}=-\right)$$

18. **C.** Choice C is the correct response.

$$\text{Omitting units,}\ |-345--762|=|-345+762|=|417|=417$$

The vertical distance is 417 feet.

19. **B.** Choice B is the correct response.

$$7.4-15+2.6=7.4+-15+2.6$$
$$=(7.4+2.6)+-15$$
$$=(10.0)+-15$$
$$=-5$$

20. **C.** Choice C is the correct response. Both the magnitude (60) and the sign (–) are correct in Choice C. Choice A is incorrect because division by zero is undefined. The signs are incorrect in choices B and D.

21. **D.** Choice D is the correct response.

$$2(5x+3)=2\cdot5x+2\cdot3$$
$$=(2\cdot5)x+2\cdot3$$
$$=10x+6$$

22. **B.** Choice B is the correct response.

$$(3x+5)+(2x-5)=(3x+5)+(2x+-5)$$
$$=3x+5+2x+-5$$
$$=3x+2x+5+-5$$
$$=(3x+2x)+(5+-5)$$
$$=5x+0$$
$$=5x$$

23. **C.** Choice C is the correct response.

$$(15x-20)-(-3x+25)=(15x+-20)-(-3x+25)$$
$$=15x+-20+3x+-25$$
$$=15x+3x+-20+-25$$
$$=(15x+3x)+(-20+-25)$$
$$=18x+-45$$
$$=18x-45$$

24. **B.** Choice B is the correct response. The sum of the measures of the interior angles of a triangle is 180°. Thus, the measure of $\angle B$ is 180° − 25° − 60° = 95°. An obtuse angle measures more than 90° but less than 180°. Angle B is greater than 90° but less than 180°. It is obtuse, Choice B.

An acute angle (Choice A) measures more than 0° but less than 90°. A right angle (Choice C) measures exactly 90°. A straight angle (Choice D) measures exactly 180°.

25. **A.** Choice A is the correct response. In a triangle, the sum of the lengths of any two sides must be greater than the length of the third side. The lengths given in Choice A satisfy this criterion. That is, 8 + 14 > 18, 8 + 18 > 14, and 14 + 18 > 8. The lengths given in the other answer choices do not satisfy this criterion.

26. **C.** Choice C is the correct response.

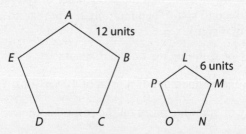

Given $ABCDE$ and $LMNOP$ are regular pentagons, they are similar figures. In similar figures, corresponding sides are proportional. The ratio of proportionality of the sides of $ABCDE$ to $LMNOP$ is $\dfrac{12\text{ units}}{6\text{ units}}=\dfrac{2}{1}$. In other words, the length of each side of $ABCDE$ is twice the length of its corresponding side in $LMNOP$. The scale factor is 2. Therefore, the ratio of the area of $ABCDE$ to $LMNOP$ is $\dfrac{(2)^2}{(1)^2}=\dfrac{4}{1}$ or 4:1, Choice C.

27. **A.** Choice A is the correct response.

Let $x =$ the length (in centimeters) of the beetle scale drawing.

Set up a proportion to represent the facts of the problem.

$$\frac{x}{9 \text{ cm}} = \frac{1 \text{ cm}}{2.5 \text{ cm}}$$

Solve the proportion, omitting units for convenience.

$$\frac{x}{9} = \frac{1}{2.5}$$

Find the cross products.

$$x \cdot 2.5 = 9 \cdot 1$$

Then solve for x.

$$2.5x = 9$$
$$\frac{2.5x}{2.5} = \frac{9}{2.5}$$
$$\frac{2.5x}{2.5} = 9 \div 2.5$$
$$1x = 3.6$$
$$x = 3.6$$

The length of the scale drawing is 3.6 centimeters.

28. **B.** Choice B is the correct response. You should eliminate Choice D immediately because probabilities cannot be greater than 1. Probabilities are always greater than or equal to 0 and less than or equal to 1. This is an independent events probability problem because the outcome of the first spin has no effect on the outcome of the second spin. To find the probability of spinning red on the first spin and green on the second spin, do three steps. First, find the probability of red on the first spin. Next, find the probability of green on the second spin. Then multiply the probabilities of these two events: P(red on first spin) $\times$ P(green on second spin).

Step 1. Find the probability of spinning red on the first spin.

There are 4 red sections on the spinner, out of a total of 10 sections: P(red on first spin) $= \dfrac{4}{10} = \dfrac{2}{5}$.

Step 2. Find the probability of spinning green on the second spin.

There is 1 green section on the spinner, out of a total of 10 sections: P(green on second spin) $= \dfrac{1}{10}$.

Step 3. Multiply the probabilities from steps 1 and 2.

$$P(\text{red on first spin}) \times P(\text{green on second spin}) = \frac{2}{5} \times \frac{1}{10} = \frac{\overset{1}{2}}{5} \times \frac{1}{\underset{5}{10}} = \frac{1}{25}$$

The probability of spinning red on the first spin and green on the second spin is $\dfrac{1}{25}$, Choice B.

29. **C.** Choice C is the correct response. Asking 100 randomly selected seventh graders will allow Gabri and Dora to make valid conclusions about seventh-grade students' opinions about wearing uniforms. The sample is random and of sufficient size. Eliminate Choice A because the opinions of students at the spirit rally might be different from those of seventh-grade students in general. Gabri and Dora are interested in the opinions of seventh graders only, so eliminate choices B and D because some of the students selected might not be seventh graders.

30. **A.** Choice A is the correct response. Check each answer choice to determine which statement is true.

    Check A: To decide which set of grades has greater variability, you can look at the range of the two sets. The range of a set of data equals the greatest value minus the least value in the set. The range in the social studies class is 92 – 56 = 36. The range in the mathematics class is 84 – 75 = 9. Because 36 > 9, Choice A is a correct statement.

    You would not have to continue checking because you know Choice A is true.

    Check B: This choice is incorrect because 9 is not greater than 36.

    Check C: You have to calculate the means in the two classes.

    The mean in the social studies class is

    $$\frac{75+89+67+56+92}{5} = \frac{379}{5} = 75.8$$

    The mean in the mathematics class is

    $$\frac{75+78+83+84+80+77}{6} = \frac{477}{6} = 79.5$$

    Choice C is incorrect because the mean in the social studies class is not higher than the mean in the mathematics class.

    Check D: This choice is incorrect because the means in the two classes are not equal.

31. **15.29 inches**

    The circumference of a circle is equal to the product of π and the diameter of the circle: $C = \pi d$. To find the diameter, plug in 48 inches (in) for C and 3.14 for π and solve for d:

    $$C = \pi d$$
    $$48 \text{ in} = 3.14d$$
    $$3.14d = 48 \text{ in}$$
    $$\frac{\cancel{3.14}d}{\cancel{3.14}} = \frac{48 \text{ in}}{3.14}$$
    $$1d = 48 \div 3.14$$
    $$d \approx 15.29 \text{ in}$$

32. **500**

    Let s = the number of students in attendance at the game. Write a percent statement for the question.

    $$210 \text{ is } 42\% \text{ of } s$$

    The part is 210, the percent is 42%, and the whole is s.

    List the elements for the percent proportion.

    $$r = 42$$
    $$\text{part} = 210$$
    $$\text{whole} = ? = s$$

Plug into the percent proportion.

$$\frac{r}{100} = \frac{part}{whole}$$

$$\frac{42}{100} = \frac{210}{s}$$

$$\frac{42 \div 2}{100 \div 2} = \frac{210}{s}$$

$$\frac{21}{50} = \frac{210}{s}$$

Solve the proportion.

$$\frac{21}{50} = \frac{210}{s}$$

Find the cross products.

$$21 \cdot s = 50 \cdot 210$$

Then solve for *s*.

$$21s = 10,500$$

$$\frac{21s}{21} = \frac{10,500}{21}$$

$$\frac{\cancel{21}s}{\cancel{21}} = 10,500 \div 21$$

$$1s = 500$$

$$s = 500$$

There are 500 students in attendance at the game.

33. **60%**

Let $r\%$ = the percent. Write a percent statement for the question (omitting units for convenience).

$$300 \text{ is } r\% \text{ of } 500$$

The part is 300, the percent is $r\%$, and the whole is 500.

List the elements for the percent proportion.

$$r = ?$$
$$part = 300$$
$$whole = 500$$

Plug into the percent proportion.

$$\frac{r}{100} = \frac{300}{500}$$

$$\frac{r}{100} = \frac{300 \div 100}{500 \div 100}$$

$$\frac{r}{100} = \frac{3}{5}$$

Solve the proportion.

$$\frac{r}{100} = \frac{3}{5}$$

Find the cross products.

$$r \cdot 5 = 100 \cdot 3$$

Then solve for r.

$$5r = 300$$
$$\frac{5r}{5} = \frac{300}{5}$$
$$\frac{\cancel{5}r}{\cancel{5}} = 300 \div 5$$
$$1r = 60$$
$$r\% = 60\%$$

Three hundred dollars is 60% of $500.

34. **$512**

The sale price of the stereo system is the list price minus 20% of the list price. The sale price = $640 – (20% of $640).

Method 1: To determine the sale price, find 20% of $640, and then subtract the amount from $640.
Step 1. Find 20% of $640.
Let x = 20% of $640.
List the elements for the percent proportion (omitting units for convenience).

$$r = 20$$
$$\text{part} = ? = x$$
$$\text{whole} = 640$$

Plug into the percent proportion.

$$\frac{r}{100} = \frac{\text{part}}{\text{whole}}$$
$$\frac{20}{100} = \frac{x}{640}$$
$$\frac{20 \div 20}{100 \div 20} = \frac{x}{640}$$
$$\frac{1}{5} = \frac{x}{640}$$

Solve the proportion.

$$\frac{1}{5} = \frac{x}{640}$$

Find the cross products.

$$1 \cdot 640 = 5 \cdot x$$

Then solve for x.

$$640 = 5x$$
$$5x = 640$$
$$\frac{5x}{5} = \frac{640}{5}$$
$$\frac{\cancel{5}x}{\cancel{5}} = 640 \div 5$$
$$1x = 128$$
$$x = 128$$

$128 is 20% of $640.

Step 2. Subtract the amount from $640.

$$\$640 - \$128 = \$512$$

The sale price of the stereo system is $512.

Method 2: The sale price = $640 – (20% of $640).

Step 1. Determine the percent of the list price to be paid.

$$\$640 - (20\% \text{ of } \$640) =$$

$$\begin{array}{l} 100\% \text{ of } \$640 \\ -20\% \text{ of } \$640 \\ \hline 80\% \text{ of } \$640 \end{array}$$ ***Tip:*** A whole is always 100% of itself.

Tip: Do Step 1 mentally. Think: *"If you save 20% of the list price, then the percent you pay of the list price is 100% – 20% = 80%."*

Step 2. Determine the sale price by finding 80% of $640.

Identify the elements (omitting units for convenience).

$$r = 80$$
$$\text{part} = ? = x$$
$$\text{whole} = 640$$

Plug into the percent proportion.

$$\frac{r}{100} = \frac{\text{part}}{\text{whole}}$$

$$\frac{80}{100} = \frac{x}{640}$$

$$\frac{80 \div 20}{100 \div 20} = \frac{x}{640}$$

$$\frac{4}{5} = \frac{x}{640}$$

Solve the proportion.

$$\frac{4}{5} = \frac{x}{640}$$

Find the cross products.

$$4 \cdot 640 = 5 \cdot x$$

Then solve for x.

$$2,560 = 5x$$

$$5x = 2,560$$

$$\frac{5x}{5} = \frac{2,560}{5}$$

$$\frac{\cancel{5}x}{\cancel{5}} = 2,560 \div 5$$

$$1x = 512$$

$$x = 512$$

Eighty percent of $640 is $512, the sale price.

35. **$81.56**

Method 1:

Step 1. Find the total amount of Trisha's purchases.

$$\$40 + \$35 = \$75$$

Step 2. Determine the sales tax on Trisha's purchases.

$$\text{sales tax} = 8.75\% \text{ of } \$75$$

Let $x = 8.75\%$ of $75.

List the elements for the percent proportion (omitting units for convenience).

$$r = 8.75$$

$$\text{part} = ? = x$$

$$\text{whole} = 75$$

Plug into the percent proportion.

$$\frac{r}{100} = \frac{\text{part}}{\text{whole}}$$

$$\frac{8.75}{100} = \frac{x}{75}$$

Solve the proportion.

$$\frac{8.75}{100} = \frac{x}{75}$$

Find the cross products.

$$8.75 \cdot 75 = 100 \cdot x$$

Then solve for x.

$$656.25 = 100x$$
$$100x = 656.25$$
$$\frac{100x}{100} = \frac{656.25}{100}$$
$$\frac{\cancel{100}x}{\cancel{100}} = 656.25 \div 100$$
$$1x = 6.5625$$
$$x = 6.5625$$

To the nearest cent, the sales tax is $6.56.

Step 3. Add the sales tax to the purchases.

$$\$75.00 + \$6.56 = \$81.56$$

Including tax, Trisha paid $81.56 for the shoes and blouse.

Method 2:

Step 1. Find the total amount of Trisha's purchases.

$$\$40 + \$35 = \$75$$

Step 2. Determine the total percentage Trisha paid.

Trisha paid $75 plus (8.75% of $75).

$$\$75 + (8.75\% \text{ of } \$75) =$$

$$\begin{aligned} 100\% \quad &\text{of } \$75 \\ + \quad 8.75\% &\text{ of } \$75 \\ \hline 108.75\% &\text{ of } \$75 \end{aligned}$$

Trisha paid 108.75% of $75.

Let x = 108.75% of $75.

List the elements for the percent proportion (omitting units for convenience).

$$r = 108.75$$
$$\text{part} = ? = x$$
$$\text{whole} = 75$$

Plug into the percent proportion.

$$\frac{r}{100} = \frac{\text{part}}{\text{whole}}$$
$$\frac{108.75}{100} = \frac{x}{75}$$

Solve the proportion.

$$\frac{108.75}{100} = \frac{x}{75}$$

Find the cross products.

$$108.75 \cdot 75 = 100 \cdot x$$

Then solve for x.

$$8{,}156.25 = 100x$$
$$100x = 8{,}156.25$$
$$\frac{100x}{100} = \frac{8{,}156.25}{100}$$
$$\frac{\cancel{100}x}{\cancel{100}} = 8{,}156.25 \div 100$$
$$x = 81.5625$$

To the nearest cent, Trisha paid \$81.56 for the shoes and blouse, including tax.

36. **\$45.24**

The commission is 6% of \$754.

Let $x = 6\%$ of \$754.

List the elements for the percent proportion (omitting units for convenience).

$$r = 6$$
$$\text{part} = ? = x$$
$$\text{whole} = 754$$

Plug into the percent proportion.

$$\frac{r}{100} = \frac{\text{part}}{\text{whole}}$$
$$\frac{6}{100} = \frac{x}{754}$$
$$\frac{6 \div 2}{100 \div 2} = \frac{x}{754}$$
$$\frac{3}{50} = \frac{x}{754}$$

Solve the proportion.

$$\frac{3}{50} = \frac{x}{754}$$

Find the cross products.

$$3 \cdot 754 = 50 \cdot x$$

Then solve for x.

$$2{,}262 = 50x$$
$$50x = 2{,}262$$
$$\frac{50x}{50} = \frac{2{,}262}{50}$$
$$\frac{\cancel{50}x}{\cancel{50}} = 2{,}262 \div 50$$
$$1x = 45.24$$
$$x = 45.24$$

Payton's commission was $45.24.

37. **12%**

The old price is $198.00. The new price is $174.24. Plug into the formula (omitting units for convenience).

$$\text{Percent Decrease} = \frac{|\text{New Value} - \text{Old Value}|}{\text{Old Value}} \times 100\%$$

$$= \frac{|174.24 - 198.00|}{198.00} \times 100\% = \frac{|-23.76|}{198.00} \times 100\% = \frac{23.76}{198.00} \times 100\% = 0.12 \times 100\% = 12\%$$

The price of the phone decreased by 12%.

38. **–8**

$$5x + 14 = -26$$
$$5x + 14 - 14 = -26 - 14$$
$$5x + 14 - 14 = -26 + -14$$
$$5x + 0 = -40$$
$$5x = -40$$
$$\frac{5x}{5} = \frac{-40}{5}$$
$$\frac{\cancel{5}x}{\cancel{5}} = -40 \div 5$$
$$1x = -8$$
$$x = -8$$

39. **−150**

$$\frac{2}{5}(x+30) = -48$$

$$\frac{2}{5} \cdot x + \frac{2}{5}(30) = -48$$

$$\frac{2}{5}x + 12 = -48$$

$$\frac{2}{5}x + 12 - 12 = -48 - 12$$

$$\frac{2}{5}x + 0 = -48 + -12$$

$$\frac{2}{5}x = -60$$

$$\frac{\cancel{5}}{\cancel{2}} \cdot \frac{\cancel{2}}{\cancel{5}}x = \frac{5}{2} \cdot -60$$

$$1x = -150$$

$$x = -150$$

40. **$28**

Let s = the original price of the shirt.

Write an equation to represent the facts of the problem.

$$2(s + \$15) = \$86$$

Solve the equation, omitting units for convenience.

$$2(s+15) = 86$$

$$2 \cdot s + 2(15) = 86$$

$$2s + 30 = 86$$

$$2s + 30 - 30 = 86 - 30$$

$$2s = 56$$

$$\frac{2s}{2} = \frac{56}{2}$$

$$\frac{\cancel{2}s}{\cancel{2}} = 56 \div 2$$

$$1x = 28$$

$$x = 28$$

The shirt's original price was $28.

7. Practice Test 2

Directions: For questions 1–30, select the best answer choice.

1. Simplify the complex fraction: $\dfrac{1\frac{2}{3}}{\frac{5}{6}}$

   A. $\dfrac{1}{5}$

   B. $\dfrac{1}{2}$

   C. 2

   D. 5

2. A motor uses $1\frac{1}{4}$ gallons of gasoline every $\frac{1}{2}$ hour. What is the rate of gallons per hour?

   A. 0.4 gallons per hour
   B. 0.8 gallons per hour
   C. 2.5 gallons per hour
   D. 5.0 gallons per hour

3. A recipe requires $\frac{2}{3}$ cup of milk for $1\frac{1}{2}$ cups of flour. How many cups of milk are needed for 4 cups of flour?

   A. $\dfrac{9}{16}$ cup

   B. $\dfrac{3}{4}$ cup

   C. $1\dfrac{1}{3}$ cups

   D. $1\dfrac{7}{9}$ cups

4. Which pair of points represents a proportional relationship?

   A. (2, 6) and (5, 15)
   B. (1, 4) and (4, 6)
   C. (3, 0) and (3, 6)
   D. (1, 2) and (2, 1)

5. Which graph represents a proportional relationship containing the plotted points?

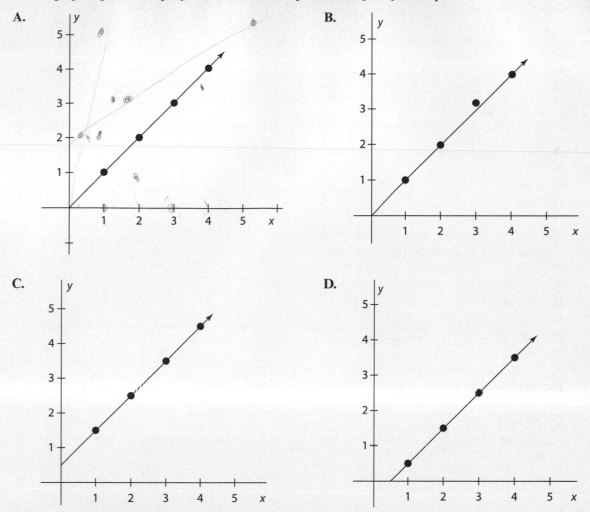

6. The table shows a proportional relationship between the cost, c (in dollars), and the number, n, of streaming videos rented.

Number, n, of Videos Rented	Cost, c (in Dollars)
4	15.96
7	27.93
8	31.92
11	43.89

Write an equation that represents the proportional relationship between n and c.

A. $n = c + 3.99$
B. $n = 3.99c$
C. $c = n + 3.99$
D. $c = 3.99n$

7. The ratio of girls in the club to the number of members in the club is 3 to 5. There are 35 members in the club. How many boys are in the club?

    A. 8
    B. 14
    C. 21
    D. 30

8. Forty percent of 400 students are seventh graders. How many of the students are seventh graders?

    A. 80
    B. 120
    C. 160
    D. 200

9. Express $-\dfrac{7}{8}$ as an equivalent decimal.

    A. −0.0875
    B. −0.780
    C. −0.875
    D. −8.750

10. Express $16\dfrac{2}{3}\%$ as an equivalent fraction in reduced form.

    A. 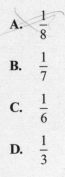 $\dfrac{1}{8}$

    B. $\dfrac{1}{7}$

    C. $\dfrac{1}{6}$

    D. $\dfrac{1}{3}$

11. Express 275% as an equivalent decimal.

    A. 0.275
    B. 2.75
    C. 27.5
    D. 275

12. Compute: $-\dfrac{5}{9} + \dfrac{2}{9}$

    A. $\quad -\dfrac{7}{9}$

    B. $\quad -\dfrac{1}{3}$

    C. $\quad \dfrac{1}{3}$

    D. $\quad \dfrac{7}{9}$

13. Compute: $-25 + -17$

    A. -42
    B. -8
    C. 8
    D. 42

14. Compute: $7.26 - 8.3$

    A. -15.56
    B. -1.04
    C. 1.04
    D. 15.56

15. Compute: $-6.85 - -13.25$

    A. -20.1
    B. -6.4
    C. 6.4
    D. 20.1

16. Which statement is TRUE?

    A. $(-25)(-8) = -200$
    B. $(-25)(8) = -200$
    C. $(25)(-8) = 200$
    D. $(-25)(8) = 200$

17. Which statement is TRUE?

    A. $\dfrac{-63}{-7} = -9$

    B. $\dfrac{-63}{7} = 9$

    C. $\dfrac{63}{-7} = 9$

    D. $\dfrac{-63}{-7} = 9$

18. Find the vertical distance between an elevation of –258 feet and an elevation of 620 feet.

    A. –878 feet
    B. –362 feet
    C. 362 feet
    D. 878 feet

19. Evaluate: 18.2 – 35 + 1.8

    A. –55
    B. –15
    C. 15
    D. 55

20. Which statement is TRUE?

    A. $\dfrac{100}{0} = 0$

    B. $\left(\dfrac{1}{5}\right)(-30)(-2)(-1) = 12$

    C. $(-1)(-1)(-40)(-1)(-1) = -40$

    D. $\dfrac{-200}{-200} = -1$

21. Expand: $-2(7x + 1)$

    A. $-16x$
    B. $-13x$
    C. $-14x + 2$
    D. $-14x - 2$

22. Find the sum of $5x + 3$ and $3x - 4$.

    A. $8x - 1$
    B. $8x - 7$
    C. $15x - 1$
    D. $15x - 7$

23. Find the difference of $4x - 25$ and $-3x + 40$.

    A. $x - 65$
    B. $x - 15$
    C. $7x - 65$
    D. $7x - 15$

24. In triangle ABC, if $\angle A$ measures 35° and $\angle C$ measures 60°, what type of angle is angle B?

    A. acute
    B. obtuse
    C. right
    D. straight

25. Which set of numbers could be the lengths of the sides of a triangle?

    A. 5, 6, 7
    B. 3, 3, 6
    C. 4, 11, 7
    D. 1, 3, 5

26. Use the diagram below to answer the question that follows.

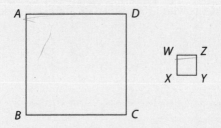

    $ABCD$ and $WXYZ$ are squares. If $AB = 15$ units and $WX = 3$ units, what is the ratio of the area of $ABCD$ to the area of $WXYZ$?

    A. 1:5
    B. 5:1
    C. 1:25
    D. 25:1

27. A picture book has scale drawings of various animals. The scale shows that 0.25 inches in the drawing represents 5 inches of actual length. What is the length (in inches) of the scale drawing of a cheetah if the cheetah is actually 60 inches long?

    A. 3.0
    B. 3.5
    C. 4.0
    D. 4.5

28. A spinner for a board game has 6 red sections, 4 yellow sections, 2 blue sections, and 3 green sections. The sections are all of equal size. What is the probability of spinning red on the first spin and green on the second spin?

    A. $\dfrac{2}{25}$

    B. $\dfrac{3}{25}$

    C. $\dfrac{3}{10}$

    D. $\dfrac{3}{5}$

29. Letizia and Caleb are conducting a survey of the opinions of the 900 students in their middle school on whether the school should offer after-school tutorials. Which method of surveying the students will allow Letizia and Caleb to make valid conclusions about the students' opinions?

    A. Stand at the school entrance and ask the first 100 students who walk in.
    B. Randomly select 100 students in the cafeteria at lunch to survey.
    C. Obtain a list of the students in the school and randomly select 100 to survey.
    D. Randomly select 100 students who are waiting for buses after school to survey.

30. The scores of 20 seventh graders on the mathematics end-of-year (EOY) assessment have a greater mean and less variability than the scores on the mathematics beginning-of-year (BOY) assessment. Which set of dot plots best depicts this outcome?

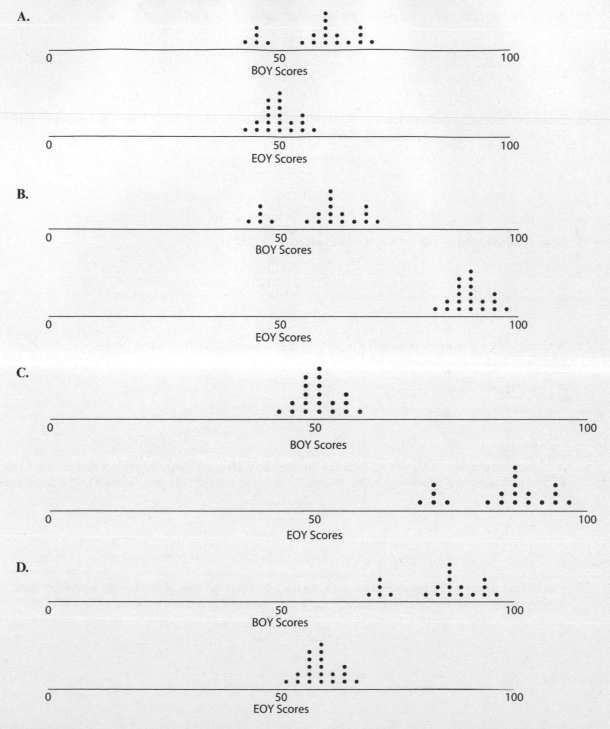

Directions: For questions 31–40, enter your answer in the answer box below the question. Enter the exact answer unless you are told to round your answer.

31. What is the approximate area of a circle with a diameter of 40 centimeters? Use $\pi \approx 3.14$.

    [ ] cm²

32. Forty-five percent of the students in the auditorium are boys. There are 261 boys in the auditorium. How many students are in the auditorium?

    [ ]

33. Nine hundred seventy-five dollars is what percent of $7,800?

    [ ] %

34. A touch-screen computer is on sale for 25% off its list price of $499. What is the sale price of the computer after the 25% discount?

    $[ ]

35. Abram bought a pair of shoes for $85 and a shirt for $55. His purchases are subject to a sales tax rate of 8.25%. Including tax, what did Abram pay for the shoes and shirt? Give your answer to the nearest cent.

    $[ ]

36. Charmaine works at a department store that pays a commission rate of 3% to employees for sales. Yesterday Charmaine's total sales were $572. What commission did she earn for yesterday's sales?

    $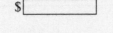

37. An Internet cable TV subscription is marked up from $59.00 per month to $61.95. What is the percent increase in the price of the subscription?

 %

38. Solve for x: $2.5x + 30 = 92.5$

39. Solve for x: $-\dfrac{3}{4}(x+28)=42$

40. The original price of a set of carving knives increased by $10. A customer buys three sets of the carving knives. The total price before sales tax is added is $149.85. What was the original price of one set of the carving knives?

$

Answer Key

1. C	11. B	21. D	31. $1,256 \text{ cm}^2$
2. C	12. B	22. A	32. 580
3. D	13. A	23. C	33. 12.5%
4. A	14. B	24. A	34. $374.25
5. A	15. C	25. A	35. $151.55
6. D	16. B	26. D	36. $17.16
7. B	17. D	27. A	37. 5%
8. C	18. D	28. A	38. 25
9. C	19. B	29. C	39. −84
10. C	20. C	30. B	40. $39.95

Answer Explanations

1. **C.** Choice C is the correct response.

$$\text{Method 1: } \frac{1\frac{2}{3}}{\frac{5}{6}} = 1\frac{2}{3} \div \frac{5}{6} = \frac{5}{3} \times \frac{6}{5} = \frac{\cancel{5}^{1}}{\cancel{3}_{1}} \times \frac{\cancel{6}^{2}}{\cancel{5}_{1}} = \frac{2}{1} = 2$$

$$\text{Method 2: } \frac{1\frac{2}{3}}{\frac{5}{6}} = \frac{\left(\frac{5}{3}\right) \cdot \frac{6}{1}}{\left(\frac{5}{6}\right) \cdot \frac{6}{1}} = \frac{\left(\frac{5}{_{1}\cancel{3}}\right) \cdot \frac{\cancel{6}^{2}}{1}}{\left(\frac{5}{_{1}\cancel{6}}\right) \cdot \frac{\cancel{6}^{1}}{1}} = \frac{\frac{10}{1}}{\frac{5}{1}} = \frac{10}{5} = 2$$

2. **C.** Choice C is the correct response.

The rate of gallons (gal) per hour (hr) is $\dfrac{1\frac{1}{4} \text{ gal}}{\frac{1}{2} \text{ hr}} = \dfrac{\frac{5}{4}}{\frac{1}{2}} \cdot \dfrac{\text{gal}}{\text{hr}} = \dfrac{\left(\frac{5}{_{1}\cancel{4}}\right) \cdot \frac{\cancel{4}^{1}}{1}}{\left(\frac{1}{_{1}\cancel{2}}\right) \cdot \frac{\cancel{4}^{2}}{1}} = \dfrac{5}{2} = 2.5$ gallons per hour.

The motor's rate is 2.5 gallons per hour.

3. **D.** Choice D is the correct response.

$$\frac{\frac{2}{3} \text{ cup}}{1\frac{1}{2} \text{ cup}} = \frac{\left(\frac{2}{3}\right) \cdot \frac{6}{1} \text{ cup}}{\left(\frac{3}{2}\right) \cdot \frac{6}{1} \text{ cup}} = \frac{\left(\frac{2}{1\cancel{3}}\right) \cdot \frac{\cancel{6}^2}{1}}{\left(\frac{3}{1\cancel{2}}\right) \cdot \frac{\cancel{6}^3}{1}} = \frac{\frac{4}{1}}{\frac{9}{1}} = \frac{4}{9}$$

For every 1 cup of flour, the recipe requires $\frac{4}{9}$ cup of milk.

$$\text{Omitting units, } \frac{4}{9} \times 4 = \frac{16}{9} = 1\frac{7}{9} \text{ cups of milk}$$

$1\frac{7}{9}$ cups of milk are needed for 4 cups of flour.

4. **A.** Choice A is the correct response. Check whether $\frac{y}{x}$ is a constant for each pair of points.

The points in Choice A represent a proportional relationship. The points (2, 6) and (5, 15) represent a proportional relationship because $\frac{6}{2} = 3$ and $\frac{15}{5} = 3$. Each ratio has a value of 3.

The points in Choice B do not represent a proportional relationship because $\frac{4}{1} = 4$ and $\frac{6}{4} = 1.5$ do not have the same value.

The points in Choice C do not represent a proportional relationship because $\frac{0}{3} = 0$ and $\frac{6}{3} = 2$ do not have the same value.

The points in Choice D do not represent a proportional relationship because $\frac{2}{1} = 2$ and $\frac{1}{2}$ do not have the same value.

5. **A.** Choice A is the correct response. The four points lie on a straight line that passes through the origin. The graph in Choice B is not a straight line; one point is not aligned with the other points. The graphs in choices C and D do not pass through the origin.

6. **D.** Choice D is the correct response. The equation is $c = kn$. The constant of proportionality is $k = \frac{c}{n}$.

$$\frac{15.96}{4} = 3.99; \quad \frac{27.93}{7} = 3.99; \quad \frac{31.92}{8} = 3.99; \quad \frac{43.89}{11} = 3.99$$

So, $k = 3.99$. The equation $c = 3.99n$ represents the proportional relationship between n and c.

7. **B.** Choice B is the correct response. Let g = the number of girls in the club. Then $35 - g$ = the number of boys in the club. First, determine g.

The ratios 3 to 5 and g to 35 are equivalent. Write a proportion and solve for g.

$$\frac{3}{5} = \frac{g}{35}$$

Find the cross products.

$$3 \cdot 35 = 5 \cdot g$$

Then solve for g.

$$105 = 5g$$
$$5g = 105$$
$$\frac{5g}{5} = \frac{105}{5}$$
$$\frac{\cancel{5}g}{\cancel{5}} = 105 \div 5$$
$$1g = 21$$
$$g = 21$$

$35 - g = 35 - 21 = 14$

There are 14 boys in the club.

Tip: Be sure to answer the question asked. After you find the number of girls in the club, you must compute the number of boys in the club to answer the question.

8. **C.** Choice C is the correct response.

Let x = the number of students who are seventh graders. Write a percent statement for the question.

x is 40% of 400

The part is x, the percent is 40%, and the whole is 400.

List the elements for the percent proportion.

$$r = 40$$
$$\text{part} = ? = x$$
$$\text{whole} = 400$$

Plug into the percent proportion.

$$\frac{r}{100} = \frac{\text{part}}{\text{whole}}$$
$$\frac{40}{100} = \frac{x}{400}$$
$$\frac{40 \div 20}{100 \div 20} = \frac{x}{400}$$
$$\frac{2}{5} = \frac{x}{400}$$

Solve the proportion.

$$\frac{2}{5} = \frac{x}{400}$$

Find the cross products.

$$2 \cdot 400 = 5 \cdot x$$

Then solve for x.

$$800 = 5x$$
$$5x = 800$$
$$\frac{5x}{5} = \frac{800}{5}$$
$$\frac{\cancel{5}x}{\cancel{5}} = 800 \div 5$$
$$1x = 160$$
$$x = 160$$

One hundred sixty students are seventh graders.

9. **C.** Choice C is the correct response.

$$\frac{7}{8} = 8 \overline{)\,7.000}^{\,0.875}$$
$$\frac{-64}{\quad 60}$$
$$\frac{-56}{\quad 40}$$
$$\frac{-40}{\quad 0}$$

$$-\frac{7}{8} = -0.875$$

10. **C.** Choice C is the correct response.

$$16\frac{2}{3}\% = \frac{16\frac{2}{3}}{100} = \frac{\frac{50}{3}}{100} = \frac{\left(\frac{50}{\cancel{3}_1}\right) \cdot \cancel{3}^1}{100 \cdot 3} = \frac{\frac{50}{1}}{300} = \frac{50 \div 50}{300 \div 50} = \frac{1}{6}$$

11. **B.** Choice B is the correct response.

$$275\% = 275(0.01) = 2.75$$

12. **B.** Choice B is the correct response.

$$-\frac{5}{9}+\frac{2}{9}=-\frac{3}{9}=-\frac{1}{3}$$

13. **A.** Choice A is the correct response.

$$-25 + -17 = -42$$

14. **B.** Choice B is the correct response.

$$7.26 - 8.3 = 7.26 + -8.3 = -1.04$$

15. **C.** Choice C is the correct response.

$$-6.85 - -13.25 = -6.85 + 13.25 = 6.4$$

16. **B.** Choice B is the correct response.

$$(-25)(8) = -200 \text{ (because } - \cdot + = -)$$

17. **D.** Choice D is the correct response.

$$\frac{-63}{-7} = 9 \text{ (because } \frac{-}{-} = +)$$

18. **D.** Choice D is the correct response.

$$\text{Omitting units, } |620 - -258| = |620 + 258| = |878| = 878$$

The vertical distance is 878 feet.

19. **B.** Choice B is the correct response.

$$18.2 - 35 + 1.8 = 18.2 + -35 + 1.8$$
$$= (18.2 + 1.8) + -35$$
$$= (20.0) + -35$$
$$= -15$$

20. **C.** Choice C is the correct response. Both the magnitude (40) and the sign (–) are correct in Choice C. Choice A is incorrect because division by zero is undefined. The signs are incorrect in choices B and D.

21. **D.** Choice D is the correct response.

$$-2(7x+1) = -2 \cdot 7x + -2 \cdot 1$$
$$= (-2 \cdot 7)x + -2 \cdot 1$$
$$= -14x + -2$$
$$= -14x - 2$$

22. **A.** Choice A is the correct response.

$$(5x+3)+(3x-4) = (5x+3)+(3x+-4)$$
$$= 5x+3+3x+-4$$
$$= 5x+3x+3+-4$$
$$= (5x+3x)+(3+-4)$$
$$= 8x+-1$$
$$= 8x-1$$

23. **C.** Choice C is the correct response.

$$(4x - 25) - (-3x + 40) = (4x + -25) - (-3x + 40)$$
$$= 4x + -25 + 3x + -40$$
$$= 4x + 3x + -25 + -40$$
$$= (4x + 3x) + (-25 + -40)$$
$$= 7x + -65$$
$$= 7x - 65$$

24. **A.** Choice A is the correct response. The sum of the measures of the interior angles of a triangle is 180°. So, the measure of $\angle B$ is $180° - 35° - 60° = 85°$. An acute angle (Choice A) measures more than 0° but less than 90°. Angle B is more than 0° but less than 90°. It is acute, Choice A.

An obtuse angle (Choice B) measures more than 90° but less than 180°. A right angle (Choice C) measures exactly 90°. A straight angle (Choice D) measures exactly 180°.

25. **A.** Choice A is the correct response. In a triangle, the sum of the lengths of any two sides must be greater than the length of the third side. The lengths given in Choice A satisfy this criterion. That is, $5 + 6 > 7$, $5 + 7 > 6$, and $6 + 7 > 5$. The lengths given in the other answer choices do not satisfy this criterion.

26. **D.** Choice D is the correct response.

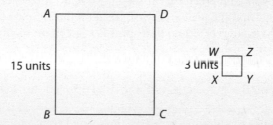

Given $ABCD$ and $WXYZ$ are squares, they are similar figures. In similar figures, corresponding sides are proportional. The ratio of proportionality of the sides of $ABCD$ to $WXYZ$ is $\dfrac{15 \text{ units}}{3 \text{ units}} = \dfrac{5}{1}$. In other words, the length of each side of $ABCD$ is five times the length of its corresponding side in $WXYZ$. The scale factor is 5. Therefore, the ratio of the area of $ABCD$ to $WXYZ$ is $\dfrac{(5)^2}{(1)^2} = \dfrac{25}{1}$ or 25:1, Choice D.

27. **A.** Choice A is the correct response.

Let $x =$ the length (in inches) of the cheetah scale drawing.

Set up a proportion to represent the facts of the problem.

$$\frac{x}{60 \text{ in}} = \frac{0.25 \text{ in}}{5 \text{ in}}$$

Solve the proportion, omitting units for convenience.

$$\frac{x}{60} = \frac{0.25}{5}$$

Find the cross products.

$$x \cdot 5 = 60 \cdot 0.25$$

Then solve for x.

$$5x = 15$$
$$\frac{5x}{5} = \frac{15}{5}$$
$$\frac{\cancel{5}x}{\cancel{5}} = 15 \div 5$$
$$1x = 3$$
$$x = 3$$

The length of the scale drawing is 3 inches.

28. **A.** Choice A is the correct response. This is an independent events probability problem because the outcome of the first spin has no effect on the outcome of the second spin. To find the probability of spinning red on the first spin and green on the second spin, do three steps. First, find the probability of red on the first spin. Next, find the probability of green on the second spin. Then multiply the probabilities of these two events: $P(\text{red on first spin}) \times P(\text{green on second spin})$.

Step 1. Find the probability of spinning red on the first spin.

There are 6 red sections on the spinner, out of a total of 15 sections: $P(\text{red on first spin}) = \frac{6}{15} = \frac{2}{5}$.

Step 2. Find the probability of spinning green on the second spin.

There are 3 green sections on the spinner, out of a total of 15 sections: $P(\text{green on second spin}) = \frac{3}{15} = \frac{1}{5}$.

Step 3. Multiply the probabilities from steps 1 and 2.

$P(\text{red on first spin}) \times P(\text{green on second spin}) = \frac{2}{5} \times \frac{1}{5} = \frac{2}{25}$. The probability of spinning red on the

first spin and green on the second spin is $\frac{2}{25}$, Choice A.

29. **C.** Choice C is the correct response. Asking 100 randomly selected students will allow Letizia and Caleb to make valid conclusions about the students' opinions. This is a representative sample because it is random and has an acceptable size. The opinions of the students in this sample will likely be representative of the opinions of the 900 students in the school. The opinions of the students in the samples obtained using the methods in the other answer choices might not be representative of the opinions of the entire student body.

30. **B.** Choice B is the correct response. The BOY scores lie to the left of the EOY scores and are more spread out than the EOY scores, indicating the mean of the BOY scores is lower than the mean of the EOY scores and the BOY scores have greater variability. In Choice A, the BOY scores have greater variability, but the means of the two sets of scores are close to the same value. In Choice C, the mean of the EOY scores is greater than the mean of the BOY scores, but the EOY scores have greater variability. In Choice D, the BOY scores have greater variability, but the mean of the BOY scores is greater than the mean of the EOY scores.

31. **1,256 cm²**

    The area of a circle is equal to the product of π and the square of the circle's radius: $A = \pi r^2$. The radius is half the diameter. So, the radius is $\frac{1}{2}(40 \text{ cm}) = 20$ cm. To find the area, plug the values into the formula.

$$A = \pi r^2$$
$$A = (3.14)(20 \text{ cm})^2$$
$$A = (3.14)(400 \text{ cm}^2)$$
$$A = 1,256 \text{ cm}^2$$

32. **580**

    Let s = the number of students in the auditorium. Write a percent statement for the question.

$$261 \text{ is } 45\% \text{ of } s$$

The part is 261, the percent is 45%, and the whole is s.
List the elements for the percent proportion.

$$r = 45$$
$$\text{part} = 261$$
$$\text{whole} = ? = s$$

Plug into the percent proportion.

$$\frac{r}{100} = \frac{\text{part}}{\text{whole}}$$
$$\frac{45}{100} = \frac{261}{s}$$
$$\frac{45 \div 5}{100 \div 5} = \frac{261}{s}$$
$$\frac{9}{20} = \frac{261}{s}$$

Solve the proportion.

$$\frac{9}{20} = \frac{261}{s}$$

Find the cross products.

$$9 \cdot s = 20 \cdot 261$$

Then solve for s.

$$9s = 5,220$$

$$\frac{9s}{9} = \frac{5,220}{9}$$

$$\frac{\cancel{9}s}{\cancel{9}} = 5,220 \div 9$$

$$1s = 580$$

$$s = 580$$

There are 580 students in the auditorium.

33. **12.5%**

Let $r\%$ = the percent. Write a percent statement for the question (omitting units for convenience).

975 is $r\%$ of 7,800

The part is 975, the percent is $r\%$, and the whole is 7,800.
List the elements for the percent proportion.

$$r = ?$$
$$\text{part} = 975$$
$$\text{whole} = 7,800$$

Plug into the percent proportion.

$$\frac{r}{100} = \frac{975}{7,800}$$

$$\frac{r}{100} = \frac{975 \div 975}{7,800 \div 975}$$

$$\frac{r}{100} = \frac{1}{8}$$

Solve the proportion.

$$\frac{r}{100} = \frac{1}{8}$$

Find the cross products.

$$r \cdot 8 = 100 \cdot 1$$

Then solve for r.

$$8r = 100$$

$$\frac{8r}{8} = \frac{100}{8}$$

$$\frac{\cancel{8}r}{\cancel{8}} = 100 \div 8$$

$$1r = 12.5$$

$$r\% = 12.5\%$$

Nine hundred seventy-five dollars is 12.5% of \$7,800.

Tip: Once you determine that 975 is $\frac{1}{8}$ of 7,800, you should recall that $\frac{1}{8} = 12\frac{1}{2}\% = 12.5\%$, without having to work out the answer.

34. **\$374.25**

The sale price of the computer is the list price minus 25% of the list price. The sale price = \$499 – (25% of \$499).

Method 1: To determine the sale price, find 25% of \$499, and then subtract the discount amount from \$499.

Step 1. Find 25% of \$499.

Let $x = 25\%$ of \$499.

List the elements for the percent proportion (omitting units for convenience).

$$r = 25$$
$$\text{part} = ? = x$$
$$\text{whole} = 499$$

Plug into the percent proportion.

$$\frac{r}{100} = \frac{\text{part}}{\text{whole}}$$

$$\frac{25}{100} = \frac{x}{499}$$

$$\frac{25 \div 25}{100 \div 25} = \frac{x}{499}$$

$$\frac{1}{4} = \frac{x}{499}$$

Solve the proportion.

$$\frac{1}{4} = \frac{x}{499}$$

Find the cross products.

$$1 \cdot 499 = 4 \cdot x$$

Then solve for x.

$$499 = 4x$$

$$4x = 499$$

$$\frac{4x}{4} = \frac{499}{4}$$

$$\frac{\cancel{4}x}{\cancel{4}} = 499 \div 4$$

$1x = 124.75$ Carry the division to 2 places because the question is dealing with money.

$x = 124.75$

$124.75 is 25% of $499.

Step 2. Subtract the discount amount from $499.

$$\$499.00 - \$124.75 = \$374.25$$

The sale price of the computer is $374.25.

Method 2: The sale price = $499 – (25% of $499).

Step 1. Determine the percent of the list price to be paid.

$$\$499 - (25\% \text{ of } \$499) =$$

100% of $499 ***Tip:*** A whole is always 100% of itself.

−25% of $499

75% of $499

Tip: Do Step 1 mentally. Think: *"If you save 25% of the list price, then the percent you pay of the list price is 100% − 25% = 75%."*

Step 2. Determine the sale price by finding 75% of $499.

Identify the elements (omitting units for convenience).

$$r = 75$$

$$\text{part} = ? = x$$

$$\text{whole} = 499$$

Plug into the percent proportion.

$$\frac{r}{100} = \frac{\text{part}}{\text{whole}}$$

$$\frac{75}{100} = \frac{x}{499}$$

$$\frac{75 \div 25}{100 \div 25} = \frac{x}{499}$$

$$\frac{3}{4} = \frac{x}{499}$$

Solve the proportion.

$$\frac{3}{4} = \frac{x}{499}$$

Find the cross products.

$$3 \cdot 499 = 4 \cdot x$$

Then solve for x.

$$1,497 = 4x$$
$$4x = 1,497$$
$$\frac{4x}{4} = \frac{1,497}{4}$$
$$\frac{\cancel{4}x}{\cancel{4}} = 1,497 \div 4$$
$$1x = 374.25$$
$$x = 374.25$$

Seventy-five percent of $499 is $374.25, the sale price.

35. **$151.55**

   Method 1:

   Step 1. Find the total amount of Abram's purchases.

   $$\$85 + \$55 = \$140$$

   Step 2. Determine the sales tax on the purchases.

   $$\text{sales tax} = 8.25\% \text{ of } \$140$$

   Let $x = 8.25\%$ of $140.

   List the elements for the percent proportion (omitting units for convenience).

   $$r = 8.25$$
   $$\text{part} = ? = x$$
   $$\text{whole} = 140$$

   Plug into the percent proportion.

   $$\frac{r}{100} = \frac{\text{part}}{\text{whole}}$$
   $$\frac{8.25}{100} = \frac{x}{140}$$

   Solve the proportion.

   $$\frac{8.25}{100} = \frac{x}{140}$$

   Find the cross products.

   $$8.25 \cdot 140 = 100 \cdot x$$

Then solve for x.

$$1,155 = 100x$$
$$100x = 1,155$$
$$\frac{100x}{100} = \frac{1,155}{100}$$
$$\frac{\cancel{100}x}{\cancel{100}} = 1,155 \div 100$$
$$1x = 11.55$$
$$x = 11.55$$

The sales tax is $11.55.

Step 3. Add the sales tax to the purchases.

$$\$140.00 + \$11.55 = \$151.55$$

Including tax, Abram paid $151.55 for the shoes and shirt.

Method 2:

Step 1. Find the total amount of Abram's purchases.

$$\$85 + \$55 = \$140$$

Step 2. Determine the total percentage Abram paid.

Abram paid $140 plus (8.25% of $140).

$$\$140 + (8.25\% \text{ of } \$140) =$$

$$\begin{array}{r} 100.00\% \text{ of } \$140 \\ + \quad 8.25\% \text{ of } \$140 \\ \hline 108.25\% \text{ of } \$140 \end{array}$$

Tip: Do this step mentally.

Abram paid 108.25% of $140.

Let x = 108.25% of $140.

List the elements for the percent proportion (omitting units for convenience).

$$r = 108.25$$
$$\text{part} = ? = x$$
$$\text{whole} = 140$$

Plug into the percent proportion.

$$\frac{r}{100} = \frac{\text{part}}{\text{whole}}$$
$$\frac{108.25}{100} = \frac{x}{140}$$

Solve the proportion.

$$\frac{108.25}{100} = \frac{x}{140}$$

Find the cross products.

$$108.25 \cdot 140 = 100 \cdot x$$

Then solve for x.

$$15,155 = 100x$$
$$100x = 15,155$$
$$\frac{100x}{100} = \frac{15,155}{100}$$
$$\frac{\cancel{100}x}{\cancel{100}} = 15,155 \div 100$$
$$1x = 151.55$$
$$x = 151.55$$

Abram paid $151.55 for the shoes and shirt, including tax.

36. **$17.16**

The commission is 3% of $572.

Let x = 3% of $572.

List the elements for the percent proportion (omitting units for convenience).

$$r = 3$$
$$\text{part} = ? = x$$
$$\text{whole} = 572$$

Plug into the percent proportion.

$$\frac{r}{100} = \frac{\text{part}}{\text{whole}}$$
$$\frac{3}{100} = \frac{x}{572}$$

Solve the proportion.

$$\frac{3}{100} = \frac{x}{572}$$

Find the cross products.

$$3 \cdot 572 = 100 \cdot x$$

Then solve for x.

$$1,716 = 100x$$
$$100x = 1,716$$
$$\frac{100x}{100} = \frac{1,716}{100}$$
$$\frac{\cancel{100}x}{\cancel{100}} = 1,716 \div 100$$
$$1x = 17.16$$
$$x = 17.16$$

Charmaine's commission was $17.16.

37. **5%**

The old price is $59.00. The new price is $61.95. Plug into the formula (omitting units for convenience).

$$\text{Percent Increase} = \frac{|\text{New Value} - \text{Old Value}|}{\text{Old Value}} \times 100\%$$
$$= \frac{|61.95 - 59.00|}{59.00} \times 100\%$$
$$= \frac{|2.95|}{59.00} \times 100\%$$
$$= \frac{2.95}{59.00} \times 100\%$$
$$= 0.05 \times 100\%$$
$$= 5\%$$

The price of the subscription increased by 5%.

38. **25**

$$2.5x + 30 = 92.5$$
$$2.5x + 30 - 30 = 92.5 - 30$$
$$2.5x + 0 = 62.5$$
$$2.5x = 62.5$$
$$\frac{2.5x}{2.5} = \frac{62.5}{2.5}$$
$$\frac{\cancel{2.5}x}{\cancel{2.5}} = 62.5 \div 2.5$$
$$1x = 25$$
$$x = 25$$

39. –84

$$-\frac{3}{4}(x+28)=42$$

$$-\frac{3}{4}\cdot x+-\frac{3}{4}\cdot 28=42$$

$$-\frac{3}{4}x+-21=42$$

$$-\frac{3}{4}x-21+21=42+21$$

$$-\frac{3}{4}x+0=63$$

$$-\frac{3}{4}x=63$$

$$-\frac{4}{3}\cdot-\frac{3}{4}x=-\frac{4}{3}(63)$$

$$-\frac{\cancel{4}}{\cancel{3}}\cdot-\frac{\cancel{3}}{\cancel{4}}x=-\frac{4}{3}(63)$$

$$1x=-84$$

$$x=-84$$

40. $39.95

Let s = the original price of one set of the carving knives.
Write an equation to represent the facts of the problem.

$$3(s + \$10) = \$149.85$$

Solve the equation, omitting units for convenience.

$$3(s+10)=149.85$$

$$3\cdot s+3(10)=149.85$$

$$3s+30=149.85$$

$$3s+30-30=149.85-30$$

$$3s=119.85$$

$$\frac{3s}{3}=\frac{119.85}{3}$$

$$\frac{\cancel{3}s}{\cancel{3}}=119.85\div 3$$

$$1s=39.95$$

$$s=39.95$$

The original price of one set of the carving knives was $39.95.

Appendix A: Measurement Conversions

U.S. Customary Units	Conversion
Length	
Inch (in)	$1 \text{ in} = \dfrac{1}{12} \text{ ft}$
Foot (ft)	$1 \text{ ft} = 12 \text{ in}$ $1 \text{ ft} = \dfrac{1}{3} \text{ yd}$
Yard (yd)	$1 \text{ yd} = 36 \text{ in}$ $1 \text{ yd} = 3 \text{ ft}$
Mile (mi)	$1 \text{ mi} = 5{,}280 \text{ ft}$ $1 \text{ mi} = 1{,}760 \text{ yd}$
Weight	
Pound (lb)	$1 \text{ lb} = 16 \text{ oz}$
Ton (T)	$1 \text{ T} = 2{,}000 \text{ lb}$
Capacity	
Fluid ounce (fl oz)	$1 \text{ fl oz} = \dfrac{1}{8} \text{ c}$
Cup (c)	$1 \text{ c} = 8 \text{ fl oz}$
Pint (pt)	$1 \text{ pt} = 2 \text{ c}$
Quart (qt)	$1 \text{ qt} = 32 \text{ fl oz}$ $1 \text{ qt} = 4 \text{ c}$ $1 \text{ qt} = 2 \text{ pt}$ $1 \text{ qt} = \dfrac{1}{4} \text{ gal}$
Gallon (gal)	$1 \text{ gal} = 128 \text{ fl oz}$ $1 \text{ gal} = 16 \text{ c}$ $1 \text{ gal} = 8 \text{ pt}$ $1 \text{ gal} = 4 \text{ qt}$

Metric Units	Conversion
Length	
Millimeter (mm)	$1\text{ mm} = \dfrac{1}{10}\text{ cm}$ $1\text{ mm} = \dfrac{1}{1000}\text{ m}$
Centimeter (cm)	$1\text{ cm} = 10\text{ mm}$ $1\text{ cm} = \dfrac{1}{100}\text{ m}$
Meter (m)	$1\text{ m} = 1000\text{ mm}$ $1\text{ m} = 100\text{ cm}$ $1\text{ m} = \dfrac{1}{1000}\text{ km}$
Kilometer (km)	$1\text{ km} = 1000\text{ m}$
Mass	
Milligram (mg)	$1\text{ mg} = \dfrac{1}{1000}\text{ g}$
Gram (g)	$1\text{ g} = 1000\text{ mg}$ $1\text{ g} = \dfrac{1}{1000}\text{ kg}$
Kilogram (kg)	$1\text{ kg} = 1000\text{ g}$
Capacity	
Milliliter (mL)	$1\text{ mL} = \dfrac{1}{1000}\text{ L}$
Liter (L)	$1\text{ L} = 1000\text{ mL}$

Time	Conversion
Second (s)	$1\text{ s} = \dfrac{1}{60}\text{ min}$ $1\text{ s} = \dfrac{1}{3{,}600}\text{ hr}$
Minute (min)	$1\text{ min} = 60\text{ s}$ $1\text{ min} = \dfrac{1}{60}\text{ hr}$
Hour (hr)	$1\text{ hr} = 3{,}600\text{ s}$ $1\text{ hr} = 60\text{ min}$ $1\text{ hr} = \dfrac{1}{24}\text{ d}$
Day (d)	$1\text{ d} = 24\text{ hr}$
Week (wk)	$1\text{ wk} = 7\text{ d}$
Year (yr)	$1\text{ yr} = 365\text{ d}$ $1\text{ yr} = 52\text{ wk}$

Appendix B: Table of Random Digits

06902	33797	30026	07243	90700	18295	81471	45296	66417	46047
92543	98296	76461	65566	15163	90376	36058	04942	34178	29469
09390	66246	60588	51890	27937	43978	34739	78542	53092	22718
06064	77426	22940	30309	39167	64104	40303	23666	08155	23600
69202	62496	77261	31794	89989	56280	76040	95364	57450	42126
01783	12202	16234	84535	36161	52932	76294	37133	02482	99160
47413	43747	88371	24814	98830	16399	91564	17606	22253	36468
86164	01581	36001	15892	57621	85239	96470	65144	53360	07616
74520	02972	56177	87580	66794	48123	48898	29724	88303	18150
01430	97022	65380	91304	32853	99729	43154	33740	11092	30661
05814	67583	01277	77815	60558	75920	94316	98015	06006	51357
80498	26935	56306	38710	77239	47139	50419	17091	78228	17665
40614	21201	75983	35695	60517	14579	70657	17096	00691	54658
70789	02628	26124	68322	01436	85994	18682	14949	15547	06416
27702	93635	69404	76323	33459	70041	63542	23946	01083	20994
09224	08984	81320	03226	60959	78246	03919	08318	19804	13837
12069	04415	78662	28295	46513	92889	25933	63964	73951	11939
46169	13070	18401	14382	48262	53177	45617	73521	12086	99420
80156	53531	36891	29620	72532	47368	32112	05166	24175	22722
18068	87733	74995	61843	88472	15736	37360	26919	95668	42417
60040	47619	57452	92819	34401	48782	60565	00452	85458	63697
92461	94060	67951	28895	79309	91897	78121	22103	57231	66277

Source: http://hcoop.net/~ntk/random/

This table shows a list of random digits. The digits appear in groups of five to make the table easier to read. You can read the digits in any order, across a row or down a column. Each digit in the table is equally likely to be any of the 10 digits, 0, 1, 2, 3, 4, 5, 6, 7, 8, 9. Similarly, each two-digit group is equally likely to be any of the 100 possible groups, 00, 01, 02, …, 99. Each three-digit group is equally likely to be any of the 1,000 possible groups, 000, 001, 002, …, 999.

To select a random sample, do the following:

Step 1. Give each member of the population a numerical label. Use the same number of digits for each one, but use the shortest possible label. Use one digit for a population up to 10 members, two digits for 11 to 99, three digits for 100 to 999 and so on. For example, labels for 100 people could be 001, 002, …, 099, 100.

Step 2. Start anywhere in the table. For convenience, count off and accept or reject groups of three successive digits at a time across a row, one group after the other. Move along the row and continue to the next row until you encounter one of the labels from Step 1. Reject all other three-digit groups. For instance, if you begin in the first row, the first label you encounter is 069, then 023, 026, 072, 070, and 018 (see below). The people labeled 069, 023, 026, 072, 070, and 018 go into the sample. Continue moving along the rows until 100 people are selected.

06902 3**3797** 30**026** **072**43 **90700** **18**295 81471 45296 66417 46047

$\frac{5}{8} \times \frac{6}{1} = \frac{30}{8} =$

$\begin{array}{r} 45 \\ 5\overline{)225} \\ 20 \\ \hline 025 \end{array}$